CHEAP REPOSITORY

TRACTS;

ENTERTAINING,

MORAL, AND RELIGIOUS.

———•••◉•◎•••———

LONDON:

SOLD BY F. AND C. RIVINGTON, NO. 62, ST. PAUL'S
CHURCH-YARD; J. EVANS, NO. 41, LONG LANE, WEST-
SMITHFIELD; J. HATCHARD, NO. 173, PICCADILLY;
AND S. HAZARD, BATH.

1798.

[𝔈ntered at 𝔖tationers-𝔥all.]

ADVERTISEMENT.

THESE Tracts were first published and sold in monthly numbers, under the patronage of a large and very respectable body of subscribers, and they are now collected into volumes. The present volume contains the longer Tales, and some Poetry, and is well suited to the use of Boarding Schools, as well as private families.

There is another volume, containing the shorter Stories and Ballads.

And there is also a volume of Sunday Readings.

Any of these volumes may be had separately.

The

ADVERTISEMENT.

The sale of the Cheap Repository Tracts has been exceedingly great, near two millions (bearing the price of about a halfpenny and a penny each) having been sold within the first year, besides great numbers in Ireland. The success of the plan has been much extended, both by the zeal of individuals, and also by the active co-operation of some very respectable Societies, which have been formed in various towns for this purpose. Many persons have exerted their influence, not only by circulating the Tracts in their own families, in schools, and among their dependants, but also by encouraging booksellers to supply themselves with them; by inspecting retailers and hawkers, giving them a few in the first instance, and directing them in the purchase; also by recommending the Tracts to the occupier of a stall at a fair, and by sending them to hospitals, workhouses, and prisons. The Tracts have also been liberally distributed among Soldiers and Sailors, through the influence of their commanders.

The

ADVERTISEMENT.

The great object had in view in publishing them, has been to supplant the multitude of vitious Tracts circulated by hawkers, and to supply, instead of them, some useful reading, which may be likely to prove entertaining also.

The profits which may arise from the sale of any of these volumes will be applied to the purpose of forwarding the more extensive circulation of the individual Tracts, which are sold by Mr. EVANS, No. 41 and 42, Long-lane, West-Smithfield; and also by Mr. HATCHARD, No. 173, Piccadilly, London.

CONTENTS.

	Page
THE Shepherd of Salisbury Plain	1
The Two Shoemakers	38
The Two Wealthy Farmers; or, the History of Mr. Bragwell	130
The History of Tom White, the Postilion	260
The Cottage Cook; or, Mrs. Jones's Cheap Dishes; shewing the Way to do much good with little Money	304
The Sunday School	320
The History of Hester Wilmot; or, the Second Part of the Sunday School	341
The Beggarly Boy. A Parable	374
The Pilgrims. An Allegory	389
The Servant Man turned Soldier; or, the Fair Weather Christian. A Parable	407
The Sorrows of Yamba; or, the Negro Woman's Lamentation	422
The Shopkeeper turned Sailor; or, the Folly of going out of our Element	430

CONTENTS.

	Page
The True Heroes; or, the Noble Army of Martyrs	451
A New Chriſtmas Hymn	454
A Hymn of Praiſe for the abundant Harveſt of 1796; after a Year of Scarcity	457

THE
SHEPHERD
OF
SALISBURY-PLAIN.

MR. JOHNSON, a very worthy charitable Gentleman, was travelling sometime ago across one of those vast Plains which are well known in Wiltshire. It was a fine summer's evening, and he rode slowly that he might have leisure to admire

B

God

God in the works of his creation. For this Gentleman was of opinion, that a walk or a ride, was as proper a time as any to think about good things; for which reason, on such occasions, he seldom thought so much about his money, or his trade, or public news, as at other times, that he might with more ease and satisfaction enjoy the pious thoughts which the visible works of the great Maker of heaven and earth are intended to raise in the mind.

His attention was all of a sudden called off by the barking of a Shepherd's dog, and looking up he spied one of those little huts, which are here and there to be seen on those great Downs; and near it was the Shepherd himself busily employed with his dog in collecting together his vast flock of sheep. As he drew nearer, he perceived him to be a clean, well looking, poor man, near fifty years of age. His coat, though at first it had probably been of one dark colour, had been in a long course of years so often patched with different sorts of cloth, that it was now become hard to say which had been the original colour. But this, while it gave a plain proof of the Shepherd's poverty, equally proved the exceeding neatness, industry, and good management of his wife. His stockings no less proved her good housewifery, for they were entirely covered with darns of different coloured worsted, but had not a hole in them; and his shirt, though nearly as coarse as the sails of a ship, was as white as the drifted snow, and was

neatly

neatly mended where time had either made a rent, or worn it thin. This furnishes a rule of judging, by which one shall seldom be deceived. If I meet with a labourer, hedging, ditching, or mending the highways with his stockings and shirt tight and whole, however mean and bad his other garments are, I have seldom failed, on visiting his cottage, to find that also clean and well ordered, and his wife notable, and worthy of encouragement. Whereas a poor woman, who will be lying a bed, or gossiping with her neighbours when she ought to be fitting out her husband in a cleanly manner, will seldom be found to be very good in other respects.

This was not the case with our Shepherd: and Mr. Johnson was not more struck with the decency of his mean and frugal dress, than with his open honest countenance, which bore strong marks of health, cheerfulness, and spirit.

Mr. Johnson, who was on a journey, and somewhat fearful from the appearance of the sky, that rain was at no great distance, accosted the Shepherd with asking what sort of weather he thought it would be on the morrow.—It will be such weather as pleases me, answered the Shepherd. Though the answer was delivered in the mildest and civilest tone that could be imagined, the Gentleman thought the words themselves rather rude and surly, and asked him how that could be. Because, replied the Shepherd, it will be such weather as shall please God, and whatever pleases him always pleases me.

Mr. Johnson, who delighted in good men and good things, was very well satisfied with his reply. For he justly thought that though an hypocrite may easily contrive to appear better than he really is to a stranger; and that no one should be too soon trusted, merely for having a few good words in his mouth; yet as he knew that " out of the abundance of the heart the mouth speaketh;" he always accustomed himself to judge favourably of those who had a serious deportment and solid manner of speaking. It looks as if it proceeded from a good habit, said he, and though I may now and then be deceived by it, yet it has not often happened to me to be so. Whereas if a man accosts me with an idle, dissolute, vulgar, indecent, or prophane expression, I have never been deceived in him, but have generally on inquiry found his character to be as bad as his language gave me room to expect.

He entered into conversation with the Shepherd in the following manner:—Your's is a troublesome life, honest friend, said he.—To be sure, Sir, replied the Shepherd, 'tis not a very lazy life; but 'tis not near so toilsome as that which my GREAT MASTER led for my sake; and he had every state and condition of life at his choice, and chose a hard one; while I only submit to the lot that is appointed me.—You are exposed to great cold and heat, said the Gentleman;—true, Sir, said the Shepherd; but then I am not exposed to great temptations; and so throwing one thing against another, GOD is pleased to contrive to make

make things more equal than we poor, ignorant, short-sighted creatures, are apt to think. David was happier when he kept his father's sheep on such a plain as this, and employed in singing some of his own Psalms perhaps, than ever he was when he became king of Israel and Judah. And I dare say we should never have had some of the most beautiful texts in all those fine Psalms, if he had not been a Shepherd, which enabled him to make so many fine comparisons and similitudes, as one may say, from country life, flocks of sheep, hills, and vallies, and fountains of water.

You think then, said the Gentleman, that a laborious life is a happy one. I do, Sir, and more so especially, as it exposes a man to fewer sins. If king Saul had continued a poor laborious man to the end of his days, he might have lived happy and honest, and died a natural death in his bed at last, which you know, Sir, was more than he did. But I speak with reverence, for it was divine Providence overruled all that, you know, Sir, and I do not presume to make comparisons. Besides, Sir, my employment has been particularly honoured—Moses was a Shepherd in the plains of Midian. It was to " Shepherds keeping their flocks by night," that the angels appeared in Bethlehem, to tell the best news, the gladdest tidings, that ever were revealed to poor sinful men: often and often has the thought warmed my poor heart in the coldest night, and filled me with more joy and thankfulness than the best supper could have done.

Here the Shepherd stopped, for he began to feel that he had made too free, and had talked too long. But Mr. JOHNSON was so well pleased with what he said, and with the cheerful contented manner in which he said it, that he desired him to go on freely, for that it was a pleasure to him to meet with a plain man, who, without any kind of learning but what he had got from the Bible, was able to talk so well on a subject in which all men, high and low, rich and poor, are equally concerned.

Indeed I am afraid I make too bold, Sir, for it better becomes me to listen to such a Gentleman as you seem to be, than to talk in my poor way; but as I was saying, Sir, I wonder all working men do not derive as great joy and delight as I do from thinking how GOD has honoured poverty! Oh! Sir, what great, or rich, or mighty men have had such honour put on them, or their condition, as Shepherds, Tent-makers, Fishermen, and Carpenters have had?

My honest friend, said the Gentleman, I perceive you are well acquainted with scripture. Yes, Sir, pretty well, blessed be God! through his mercy I learnt to read when I was a little boy; though reading was not so common when I was a child, as I am told, through the goodness of Providence and the generosity of the rich, it is likely to become now-a-days. I believe there is no day for the last thirty years, that I have not peeped at my Bible. If we can't find time to read a chapter, I defy any man to say he can't find

find time to read a verse; and a single text, Sir, well followed and put in practice every day, would make no bad figure at the year's end; three hundred and sixty-five texts, without the loss of a moment's time, would make a pretty stock, a little golden treasury, as one may say, from new-year's day to new-year's day; and if children were brought up to it, they would come to look for their text as naturally as they do for their breakfast. No labouring man, 'tis true, has so much leisure as a Shepherd, for while the flock is feeding, I am obliged to be still, and at such times I can now and then tap a shoe for my children or myself, which is a great saving to us, and while I am doing that I repeat a bit of a chapter, which makes the time pass pleasantly in this wild solitary place. I can say the best part of the Bible by heart; I believe I should not say the best part, for every part is good, but I mean the greatest part. I have led but a lonely life, and have often had but little to eat, but my Bible has been meat, drink, and company to me, as I may say, and when want and trouble have come upon me, I don't know what I should have done indeed, Sir, if I had not had the promises of this book for my stay and support.

You have had great difficulties then? said Mr. Johnson. Why, as to that, Sir, not more than neighbours' fare; I have but little cause to complain, and much to be thankful; but I have had some little struggles, as I will leave you to judge. I have a wife and eight children, whom I bred

I bred up in that little cottage which you see under the hill about half a mile off. What, that with the smoke coming out of the chimney? said the Gentleman. O no, Sir, replied the Shepherd smiling, we have seldom smoke in the evening, for we have little to cook, and firing is very dear in these parts. 'Tis that cottage which you see on the left hand of the Church, near that little tuft of hawthorns. What that hovel with only one room above and below, with scarcely any chimney? how is it possible you can live there with such a family! O! it is very possible and very certain too, cried the Shepherd. How many better men have been worse lodged! how many good christians have perished in prisons and dungeons, in comparison of which my cottage is a palace! The house is very well, Sir, and if the rain did not sometimes beat down upon us through the thatch when we are a-bed, I should not desire a better; for I have health, peace, and liberty, and no man maketh me afraid.

Well, I will certainly call on you before it be long; but how can you contrive to lodge so many children? We do the best we can, Sir. My poor wife is a very sickly woman, or we should always have done tolerably well. There are no gentry in the parish, so that she has not met with any great assistance in her sickness. The good curate of the parish who lives in that pretty parsonage in the valley, is very willing, but not very able to assist us on these trying occasions, for he has little enough for himself, and a
large

large family into the bargain. Yet he does what he can, and more than many richer men do, and more than he can well afford. Besides that, his prayers and good advice we are always sure of, and we are truly thankful for that, for a man must give, you know, Sir, according to what he hath, and not according to what he hath not.

Are you in any distress at present? said Mr. Johnson. No, Sir, thank God, replied the Shepherd. I get my shilling a day, and most of my children will soon be able to earn something; for we have only three under five years old. Only! said the Gentleman, that is a heavy burden. Not at all; God fits the back to it. Though my wife is not able to do any out-of-door work, yet she breeds up our children to such habits of industry that our little maids, before they are six years old can, first get a halfpenny, and then a penny a day by knitting. The boys who are too little to do hard work, get a trifle by keeping the birds off the corn; for this the farmers will give them a penny or two-pence, and now and then a bit of bread and cheese into the bargain. When the season of crow keeping is over, then they glean or pick stones; any thing is better than idleness, Sir, and if they did not get a farthing by it, I would make them do it just the same, for the sake of giving them early habits of labour.

So you see, Sir, I am not so badly off as many are; nay, if it were not that it costs me so much in 'Potecary's stuff for my poor wife, I should

should reckon myself well off; nay, I do reckon myself well off, for blessed be God, he has granted her life to my prayers, and I would work myself to a 'natomy, and live on one meal a day, to add any comfort to her valuable life; indeed I have often done the last, and thought it no great matter neither.

While they were in this part of the discourse, a fine plump cherry-cheek little girl ran up out of breath, with a smile on her young happy face, and without taking any notice of the Gentleman, cried out with great joy—Look here, father, only see how much I have got to! Mr. Johnson was much struck with her simplicity, but puzzled to know what was the occasion of this great joy. On looking at her he perceived a small quantity of coarse wool, some of which had found its way through the holes of her clean, but scanty and ragged woollen apron. The father said, this has been a successful day indeed, Molly, but don't you see the Gentleman? Molly now made a curtsey down to the very ground; while Mr. Johnson inquired into the cause of the mutual satisfaction which both father and daughter had expressed, at the unusual good fortune of the day.

Sir, said the Shepherd, poverty is a great sharpener of the wits.—My wife and I cannot endure to see our children (poor as they are) without shoes and stockings, not only on account of the pinching cold which cramps their poor little limbs, but because it degrades and debases them;

them; and poor people who have but little regard to appearances will seldom be found to have any great regard for honesty and goodness; I don't say this is always the case; but I am sure it is so too often. Now shoes and stockings being very dear, we could never afford to get them without a little contrivance. I must shew you how I manage about the shoes when you condescend to call at our cottage, Sir; as to stockings, this is one way we take to help to get them. My young ones who are too little to do much work, sometimes wander at odd hours over the hills for the chance of finding what little wool the sheep may drop when they rub themselves, as they are apt to do, against the bushes.* These scattered bits of wool the children pick out of the brambles, which I see have torn sad holes in Molly's apron to-day; they carry this wool home, and when they have got a pretty parcel together, their mother cards it; for she can sit and card in the chimney corner, when she is not able to wash, or work about house. The biggest girl then spins it; it does very well for us without dying, for poor people must not stand for the colour of their stockings. After this our little boys knit it for themselves, while they are employed in keeping cows in the fields, and after they get home at night. As for the knitting the girls and their mother do, that is chiefly for sale, which helps to pay our rent.

* This piece of frugal industry is not imaginary, but a real fact, as is the character of the Shepherd, and his uncommon knowledge of the scriptures.

Mr. Johnson lifted up his eyes in silent astonishment at the shifts which honest poverty can make rather than beg or steal; and was surprised to think how many ways of subsisting there are which those who live at their ease little suspect. He secretly resolved to be more attentive to his own petty expences than he had hitherto been; and to be more watchful that nothing was wasted in his family.

But to return to the Shepherd. Mr. Johnson told him that as he must needs be at his friend's house, who lived many miles off, that night, he could not, as he wished to do, make a visit to his cottage at present. But I will certainly do it, said he, on my return, for I long to see your wife and her nice little family, and to be an eye witness of her neatness and good management. The poor man's tears started into his eyes on hearing the commendation bestowed on his wife; and wiping them off with the sleeve of his coat, for he was not worth a handkerchief in the world, he said—Oh Sir, you just now, I am afraid, called me an humble man, but indeed I am a very proud one. Proud! exclaimed Mr. Johnson, I hope not—Pride is a great sin, and as the poor are liable to it as well as the rich, so good a man as you seem to be, ought to guard against it. Sir, said he, you are right, but I am not proud of myself, God knows, I have nothing to be proud of. I am a poor sinner, but indeed Sir, I am proud of my wife: she is not only the most tidy, notable woman on the Plain, but she is the kindest wife and mother, and the most contented, thankful christian that I know. Last year I thought I should have lost her in a violent fit of the rheumatism, caught by going to work too soon after her lying-in, I fear; for 'tis but a bleak coldish place, as you may see, Sir, in winter, and sometimes the snow lies so long under the hill, that I can hardly make myself a path to get out and buy a few necessaries in the next village; and we are afraid to send out the children, for fear they should be lost when the snow is deep. So, as I was saying, the poor soul was very bad indeed, and for several weeks lost the use of all her limbs except her hands; a merciful providence spared her the use of these, so that when she could not turn in her bed, she could contrive to patch a rag or two for her family. She was always saying, had it not been for the great goodness of God, she might have had her hands lame as well as her feet, or the palsy instead of the rheumatism, and then she could have done nothing—but, nobody had so many mercies as she had.

I will not tell you what we suffered during that bitter weather, Sir, but my wife's faith and patience during that trying time, were as good a lesson to me as any Sermon I could hear, and yet Mr. Jenkins gave us very comfortable ones too, that helped to keep up my spirits.

One Sunday afternoon when my wife was at the worst, as I was coming out of Church, for I went one part of the day, and my eldest daughter

the

the other, so my poor wife was never left alone; as I was coming out of church, I say, Mr. Jenkins, the minister, called out to me, and asked me how my wife did, saying he had been kept from coming to see her by the deep fall of snow, and indeed from the parsonage-house to my hovel it was quite impassable. I gave him all the particulars he asked, and I am afraid a good many more, for my heart was quite full. He kindly gave me a shilling, and said he would certainly try to pick out his way and come and see her in a day or two.

While he was talking to me, a plain farmer-looking Gentleman in boots, who stood by, listened to all I said, but seemed to take no notice. It was Mr. Jenkins's wife's father, who was come to pass the Christmas-holidays at the parsonage-house. I had always heard him spoken of as a plain frugal man, who lived close himself, but was remarked to give away more than any of his show-away neighbours.

Well! I went home with great spirits at this seasonable and unexpected supply; for we had tapped our last sixpence, and there was little work to be had on account of the weather. I told my wife I had not come back empty handed. No, I dare say not, says she, you have been serving a master "who filleth the hungry with good things, though he sendeth the rich empty away." True, Mary, says I; we seldom fail to get good spiritual food from Mr. Jenkins, but to day he has kindly supplied our bodily wants. She was more
thankful

thankful when I shewed her the shilling, than, I dare say, some of your great people are when they get a hundred pounds.

Mr. Johnson's heart smote him when he heard such a value set upon a shilling; surely, said he to himself, I will never waste another; but he said nothing to the Shepherd, who thus pursued his story.

Next morning before I went out, I sent part of the money to buy a little ale and brown sugar to put into her water gruel; which you know, Sir, made it nice and nourishing. I went out to cleave wood in a farm-yard, for there was no standing out on the plain, after such snow as had fallen in the night. I went with a lighter heart than usual, because I had left my poor wife a little better; and comfortably supplied for this day, and I now resolved more than ever to trust God for the supplies of the next. When I came back at night, my wife fell a crying as soon as she saw me. This, I own, I thought but a bad return for the blessings she had so lately received, and so I told her. O, said she, it is too much, we are too rich; I am now frightened, not lest we should have no portion in this world, but for fear we should have our whole portion in it. Look here, John! So saying, she uncovered the bed whereon she lay, and shewed me two warm, thick, new blankets. I could not believe my own eyes, Sir, because when I went out in the morning, I had left her with no other covering than our little old thin blue rug. I was still

more

more amazed when she put half a crown into my hand, telling me she had had a visit from Mr. Jenkins, and Mr. Jones, the latter of whom had bestowed all these good things upon us. Thus, Sir, have our lives been crowned with mercies. My wife got about again, and I do believe, under Providence, it was owing to these comforts; for the rheumatism, Sir, without blankets by night and flannel by day, is but a baddish job, especially to people who have little or no fire. She will always be a weakly body; but thank God her soul prospers and is in health. But I beg your pardon, Sir, for talking on at this rate.—Not at all, not at all, said Mr. Johnson; I am much pleased with your story, you shall certainly see me in a few days. Good night. So saying, he slipped a crown into his hand and rode off. Surely, said the Shepherd, " *goodness and mercy have followed me all the days of my life,*" as he gave the money to his wife when he got home at night.

As to Mr. Johnson, he found abundant matter for his thoughts during the rest of his journey. On the whole he was more disposed to envy than to pity the Shepherd. I have seldom seen, said he, so happy a man. It is a sort of happiness which the world could not give, and which I plainly see, it has not been able to take away. This must be the true spirit of Religion. I see more and more, that true goodness is not merely a thing of words and opinions, but a Living Principle brought into every common action of a man's a man's life. What else could have supported this poor couple under every bitter trial of want and sickness? No, my honest Shepherd, I do not pity, but I respect and even honour thee; and I will visit thy poor hovel on my return to Salisbury with as much pleasure as I am now going to the house of my friend.

If Mr. Johnson keeps his word in sending me the account of his visit to the Shepherd's cottage, I shall be very glad to entertain my readers with it.

PART II.

I AM willing to hope that my readers will not be sorry to hear some farther particulars of their old acquaintance *the Shepherd of Salisbury Plain.* They will call to mind that at the end of the first part, he was returning home full of gratitude for the favours he had received from Mr. Johnson, whom we left pursuing his journey, after having promised to make a visit to the Shepherd's cottage.

Mr. Johnson after having passed some time with his friend, sat out on his return to Salisbury, and on the Saturday evening reached a very small inn, a mile or two distant from the Shepherd's Village; for he never travelled on a Sunday. He went the next morning to the Church

nearest

nearest the house where he had passed the night; and after taking such refreshment as he could get at that house, he walked on to find out the Shepherd's cottage. His reason for visiting him on a Sunday was chiefly, because he supposed it to be the only day which the Shepherd's employment allowed him to pass at home with his family, and as Mr. Johnson had been struck with his talk, he thought it would be neither unpleasant nor unprofitable to observe how a man who carried such an appearance of piety spent his Sunday; for though he was so low in the world, this Gentleman was not above entering very closely into his character, of which he thought he should be able to form a better judgment, by seeing whether his practice at home kept pace with his professions abroad. For it is not so much by observing how people talk, as how they live, that we ought to judge of their characters.

After a pleasant walk Mr. Johnson got within sight of the cottage, to which he was directed by the clump of hawthorns and the broken chimney. He wished to take the family by surprise; and walking gently up to the house he stood awhile to listen. The door being half open, he saw the Shepherd, (who looked so respectable in his Sunday coat that he should hardly have known him) his Wife, and their numerous young family, drawing round their little table, which was covered with a clean though very coarse cloth. There stood on it a large dish of potatoes, a brown pitcher, and a piece of a coarse loaf. The
wife

wife and children stood in silent attention, while the Shepherd with up-lifted hands and eyes, devoutly begged the blessing of Heaven on their homely fare. Mr. Johnson could not help sighing to reflect, that he had sometimes seen better dinners eaten with less appearance of thankfulness.

The Shepherd and his wife then sat down with great seeming chearfulness, but the children stood; and while the mother was helping them, little fresh-coloured Molly who had picked the wool from the bushes with so much delight, cried out, Father, I wish I was big enough to say grace, I am sure I should say it very heartily to day, for I was thinking what must *poor* people do who have no salt to their potatoes, and do but look, our dish is quite full.—That is the true way of thinking, Molly, said the Father; in whatever concerns bodily wants and bodily comforts, it is our duty to compare our own lot with the lot of those who are worse off, and this will keep us thankful: on the other hand, whenever we are tempted to set up our own wisdom or goodness, we must compare ourselves with those who are wiser and better, and that will keep us humble. Molly was now so hungry, and found the potatoes so good, that she had no time to make any more remarks; but was devouring her dinner very heartily, when the barking of the great dog drew her attention from her trencher to the door, and spying the stranger, she cried out, Look father, see here, if yonder is
not

not the good Gentleman! Mr. Johnson finding himself discovered, immediately walked in, and was heartily welcomed by the honest Shepherd, who told his wife that this was the Gentleman to whom they were so much obliged.

The good Woman began, as some very neat people are rather too apt to do, with making many apologies that her house was not cleaner, and that things were not in fitter order to receive such a Gentleman. Mr. Johnson however, on looking round, could discover nothing but the most perfect neatness. The trenchers on which they were eating were almost as white as their linen; and notwithstanding the number and smallness of the children, there was not the least appearance of dirt or litter. The furniture was very simple and poor, hardly indeed amounting to bare necessaries. It consisted of four brown wooden chairs, which, by constant rubbing, were become as bright as a looking glass; an iron pot and kettle; a poor old grate which scarcely held a handful of coal, and out of which the little fire that had been in it appeared to have been taken, as soon as it had answered the end for which it had been lighted, that of boiling their potatoes. Over the chimney stood an old-fashioned broad bright candlestick, and a still brighter spit; it was pretty clear that this last was kept rather for ornament than use. An old carved elbow chair, and a chest of the same date which stood in the corner, were considered as the most valuable part of the Shepherd's goods,
having

having been in his family for three generations. But all these were lightly esteemed by him, in comparison of another possession, which, added to the above, made up the whole of what he had inherited from his father; and which last he would not have parted with, if no other could have been had, for a king's ransom: this was a large old Bible, which lay on the window seat, neatly covered with brown cloth, variously patched. This sacred book was most reverendly preserved from dog's ears, dirt, and every other injury, but such as time and much use had made it suffer in spite of care. On the clean white walls was pasted, a hymn on the Crucifixion of our Saviour, a print of the Prodigal Son, the Shepherd's Hymn, a *New History of a True Book*, and Patient Joe, or the Newcastle Collier.*

After the first salutations were over, Mr. Johnson said, that if they would go on quietly with their dinner he would sit down. Though a good deal ashamed, they thought it more respectful to obey the Gentleman, who having cast his eye on their slender provisions, gently rebuked the Shepherd for not having indulged himself, as it was Sunday, with a morsel of bacon to relish his potatoes. The Shepherd said nothing, but poor Mary coloured and hung down her head, saying, Indeed, Sir, it is not my fault, I did beg my husband to allow himself a

---

* Printed for the Cheap Repository, price 2d. each.

bit of meat to-day out of your honour's bounty; but he was too good to do it, and it is all for my sake. The Shepherd seemed unwilling to come to an explanation, but Mr. Johnson desired Mary to go on. So she continued, you must know, Sir, that both of us, next to a sin, dread a debt, and indeed in some cases a debt is a sin; but with all our care and pains we have never been able quite to pay off the Doctor's bill for that bad fit of rheumatism which I had last winter. Now when you were pleased to give my husband that kind present the other day, I heartily desired him to buy a bit of meat for Sunday, as I said before, that he might have a little refreshment for himself out of your kindness. But, answered he, Mary, it is never out of my mind long together that we still owe a few shillings to the Doctor, (and thank God it is all we did owe in the world). Now if I carry him this money directly it will not only shew him our honesty and our good-will; but it will be an encouragement to him to come to you another time in case you should be taken once more in such a bad fit; for I must own, added my poor husband, that the thought of your being so terribly ill without any help, is the only misfortune that I want courage to face.

Here the grateful woman's tears ran down so fast that she could not go on. She wiped them with the corner of her apron, and humbly begged pardon for making so free. Indeed, Sir, said the Shepherd, though my wife is full as
unwilling

unwilling to be in debt as myself, yet I could hardly prevail on her to consent to my paying this money just then, because she said it was hard I should not have a taste of the Gentleman's bounty myself. But for once, Sir, I would have my own way. For you must know, as I pass best part of my time alone, tending my sheep, 'tis a great point with me, Sir, to get comfortable matter for my own thoughts; so that 'tis rather self interest in me to allow myself in no pleasures and no practices that won't bear thinking on over and over. For when one is a good deal alone you know, Sir, all one's bad deeds do so rush in upon one, as I may say, and so torment one, that there is no true comfort to be had but in keeping clear of wrong doings, and false pleasures; and that I suppose may be one reason why so many folks hate to stay a bit by themselves.—But as I was saying—when I came to think the matter over on the hill yonder, said I to myself, a good dinner is a good thing I grant, and yet it will be but cold comfort to me a week after, to be able to say—to be sure I had a nice shoulder of mutton last Sunday for dinner, thanks to the good Gentleman, but then I am in debt.—I *had* a rare dinner, that's certain, but the pleasure of that has long been over, and the debt still remains. I have spent the crown, and now if my poor wife should be taken in one of those fits again, die she must, unless God work a miracle to prevent it, for I can get no help for her. This thought settled all; and I set off directly and paid
the

the crown to the Doctor with as much chearfulness as I should have felt on sitting down to the fattest shoulder of mutton that ever was roasted. And if I was contented at the time, think how much more happy I have been at the remembrance! O Sir, there are no pleasures worth the name but such as bring no plague or penitence after them.

Mr. Johnson was satisfied with the Shepherd's reasons; and agreed that though a good dinner was not to be despised, yet it was not worthy to be compared with *a contented Mind which* (as the Bible truly says) *is a continual Feast.* " But come, said the good Gentleman, what have we got in this brown mug? As good water, said the Shepherd, as any in the King's dominions. I have heard of countries beyond sea in which there is no wholesome water; nay, I have been myself in a great town not far off where they are obliged to buy all the water which they get, while a good Providence sends to my very door a spring as clear and fine as Jacob's well. When I am tempted to repine that I have often no other drink, I call to mind, that it was nothing better than a cup of cold water which the woman of Samaria drew for the greatest guest that ever visited this world.

Very well, replied Mr. Johnson; but as your honesty has made you prefer a poor meal to being in debt, I will at least send and get something for you to drink. I saw a little public house just by the church, as I came along.

Let

Let that little rosy-faced fellow fetch a mug of beer. So saying, he looked full at the boy who did not offer to stir; but cast an eye at his father to know what he was to do. Sir, said the Shepherd, I hope we shall not appear ungrateful, if we seem to refuse your favour; my little boy would, I am sure, fly to serve you on any other occasion. But, good Sir, it is Sunday, and should any of my family be seen at a Public-house on a Sabbath-day, it would be a much greater grief to me than to drink water all my life. I am often talking against these doings to others, and if I should say one thing and do another, you can't think what an advantage it would give many of my neighbours over me, who would be glad enough to report that they had caught the Shepherd's son at the Ale-house, without explaining how it happened. Christians you know, Sir, must be doubly watchful, or they will not only bring disgrace on themselves, but what is much worse, on that holy name by which they are called.

Are you not a little too cautious, my honest friend? said Mr. Johnson. I humbly ask your pardon, Sir, replied the Shepherd, if I think that is impossible. In my poor notion I no more understand how a man can be too cautious, than how he can be too strong, or too healthy.

You are right indeed, said Mr. Johnson, as a general principle; but this struck me as a very small thing.—Sir, said the Shepherd,

I am afraid you will think me very bold, but you encourage me to speak out.—'Tis what I wish, said the Gentleman. Then, Sir, resumed the Shepherd, I doubt, if where there is a temptation to do wrong any thing can be called small; that is, in short, if there is any such thing as a small wilful sin. A poor man like me is seldom called out to do great things, so that it is not by a few striking deeds his character can be judged by his neighbours, but by the little round of daily customs he allows himself in.—While they were thus talking, the children who had stood very quietly behind, and had not stirred a foot, now began to scamper about all at once, and in a moment ran to the window-seat to pick up their little old hats. Mr. Johnson looked surprised at this disturbance; the Shepherd asked his pardon, telling him it was the sound of the Church Bell which had been the cause of their rudeness; for their mother had brought them up with such a fear of being too late for Church, that it was but who could catch the first stroke of the bell, and be first ready. He had always taught them to think that nothing was more indecent than to get into Church after it was begun; for as the service opened with an exhortation to repentance, and a confession of sin, it looked very presumptuous not to be ready to join in it; it looked as if people did not feel themselves to be sinners. And though such as lived at a great distance might plead difference of clocks as an excuse, yet those who lived with-

in

in the sound of the bell, could pretend neither ignorance nor mistake.

Mary and her children set forward. Mr. Johnson and the shepherd followed, taking care to talk the whole way on such subjects as might fit them for the solemn duties of the place to which they were going. I have often been sorry to observe, said Mr. Johnson, that many who are reckoned decent, good kind of people, and who would on no account neglect going to church, yet seem to care but little in what frame or temper of mind they go thither. They will talk of their worldly concerns till they get within the door, and then take them up again the very minute the sermon is over, which makes me ready to fear they lay too much stress on the mere form of going to a place of worship. Now for my part, I always find that it requires a little time to bring my mind into a state fit to do any *common* business well, much more this great and most necessary business of all.— Yes, Sir, said the Shepherd, and then I think too how busy I should be in preparing my mind, if I was going into the presence of a great Gentleman, or a Lord, or the King; and shall the King of kings be treated with less respect? Besides one likes to see people feel as if going to church was a thing of choice and pleasure, as well as a duty, and that they were as desirous not to be the last there, as they would be if they were going to a feast, or a fair.

After service, Mr. Jenkins the Clergyman, who was well acquainted with the character of Mr. Johnson, and had a great respect for him, accosted him with much civility; expressing his concern that he could not enjoy just now so much of his conversation as he wished, as he was obliged to visit a sick person at a distance, but hoped to have a little talk with him before he left the Village. As they walked along together, Mr. Johnson made such inquiries about the Shepherd, as served to confirm him in the high opinion he entertained of his piety, good sense, industry, and self-denial. They parted, the Clergyman promising to call in at the cottage in his way home.

The Shepherd, who took it for granted that Mr. Johnson was gone to the Parsonage, walked home with his wife and children, and was beginning in his usual way to catechise and instruct his family, when Mr. Johnson came in, and insisted that the Shepherd should go on with his instructions, just as if he were not there. This gentleman who was very desirous of being useful to his own servants and workmen in the way of religious instruction, was sometimes sorry to find that though he took a good deal of pains, they did not now and then quite understand him, for though his meaning was very good, his language was not always very plain; and though the *things* he said were not hard to be understood, yet the *words* were, especially to such as were very ignorant. And he now began to find out

out that if people were ever so wise and good, yet if they had not a simple, agreeable and familiar way of expressing themselves, some of their plain hearers would not be much the better for them. For this reason he was not above listening to the plain, humble way in which this honest man taught his family, for though he knew that he himself had many advantages over the Shepherd, had more learning, and could teach him many things, yet he was not too proud to learn even of so poor a man, in any point where he thought the Shepherd might have the advantage of him.

This gentleman was much pleased with the knowledge and piety which he discovered in the answers of the children; and desired the Shepherd to tell him how he contrived to keep up a sense of divine things in his own mind, and in that of his family with so little leisure, and so little reading. O as to that, Sir, said the Shepherd, we do not read much except in one book to be sure; but my hearty prayer for God's blessing on the use of that book, what little knowledge is needful seems to come of course, as it were. And my chief study has been to bring the fruits of the Sunday reading into the week's business, and to keep up the same sense of God in the heart, when the Bible is in the cupboard as when it is in the hand. In short, to apply what I read in the book, to what I meet with in the field.

I don't quite understand you, said Mr. Johnson. Sir, replied the Shepherd, I have but a poor gift at conveying these things to others, though I have much comfort from them in my own mind; but I am sure that the most ignorant and hard-working people, who are in earnest about their salvation, may help to keep up devout thoughts and good affections during the week, though they have hardly any time to look at a book; and it will help them to keep out bad thoughts too which is no small matter. But then they must know the Bible; they must have read the word of God diligently; that is a kind of stock in trade for a Christian to set up with; and it is this which makes me so careful in teaching it to my children; and even in storing their memories with Psalms and Chapters. This is a great help to a poor hard-working man, who will scarcely meet with any thing but what he may turn to some good account. If one lives in the fear and the love of God, almost every thing one sees abroad will teach one to adore his power and goodness, and bring to mind some texts of Scripture, which shall fill the heart with thankfulness, and the mouth with praise. When I look upwards *the Heavens declare the glory of God*; and shall I be silent and ungrateful? If I look round and see the valleys standing thick with corn, how can I help blessing that Power who *giveth me all things richly to enjoy?* I may learn gratitude from the beasts of the field, for the *Ox knoweth his owner, and the Ass his Master's*

Master's Crib, and shall a Christian not know, shall a Christian not consider what great things God has done for him? I, who am a Shepherd, endeavour to fill my soul with a constant remembrance of that good Shepherd, who *feedeth me in green pastures, and maketh me to lie down beside the still waters, and whose rod and staff comfort me.*

You are happy, said Mr. Johnson, in this retired life by which you escape the corruptions of the world.—Sir, said the Shepherd, I do not escape the corruptions of my own evil nature. Even there on that wild solitary hill, I can find out that my heart is prone to evil thoughts. I suppose, Sir, that different states have different temptations. You great folks that live in the world, perhaps are exposed to some, of which such a poor man as I am, know nothing. But to one who leads a lonely life like me, evil thoughts are a chief besetting sin; and I can no more withstand these without the grace of God, than a rich gentleman can withstand the snares of evil company, without the same grace. And I feel that I stand in need of God's help continually, and if he should give me up to my own evil heart I should be lost.

Mr. Johnson approved of the Shepherd's sincerity, for he had always observed that where there was no humility, and no watchfulness against sin; there was no religion, and he said that the man who did not feel himself to be a sinner, in his opinion, could not be a christian.

Just as they were in this part of their discourse, Mr. Jenkins, the clergyman, came in. After the usual salutations, he said, Well, Shepherd, I wish you joy; I know you will be sorry to gain any advantage by the death of a neighbour; but old Wilson, my clerk, was so infirm, and I trust so well prepared, that there is no reason to be sorry for his death. I have been to pray by him, but he died while I staid. I have always intended you should succeed to his place; 'tis no great matter of profit, but every little is something.

No great matter, Sir, cried the Shepherd, indeed it is a great thing to me; it will more than pay my rent. Blessed be God for all his goodness. Mary said nothing, but lifted up her eyes full of tears in silent gratitude.

I am glad of this little circumstance, said Mr. Jenkins, not only for your sake, but for the sake of the office itself. I so heartily reverence every religious institution, that I would never have even the *Amen* added to the excellent prayers of our church, by vain or profane lips, and if it depended on me, there should be no such thing in the land as an idle, drunken, or irreligious Parish-Clerk. Sorry I am to say that this matter is not always sufficiently attended to, and that I know some of a very indifferent character.

Mr. Johnson now inquired of the Clergyman whether there were many children in the parish. More than you would expect, replied he, from

from the seeming smallness of it, but there are some little Hamlets which you do not see.—I think, returned Mr. Johnson, I recollect that in the conversation I had with the Shepherd on the hill yonder, he told me you had no Sunday School.—I am sorry to say we have none, said the Minister; I do what I can to remedy this misfortune by public catechising; but having two or three Churches to serve, I cannot give so much time as I wish to private instruction; and having a large family of my own, and no assistance from others, I have never been able to establish a school.

There is an excellent institution in London, said Mr. Johnson, called the Sunday-School Society, which kindly gives books and other helps, on the application of such pious Ministers as stand in need of their aid, and which I am sure would have assisted you; but I think we shall be able to do something ourselves.—Shepherd, continued he, if I were a King, and had it in my power to make you a rich and a great man, with a word speaking, I would not do it. Those who are raised by some sudden stroke, much above the station in which Divine Providence had placed them, seldom turn out very good, or very happy. I have never had any great things in my power, but as far as I have been able, I have been always glad to assist the worthy. I have, however, never attempted or desired to set any poor man much above his natural condition, but it is a pleasure to me to lend him such assistance, as may make that condition more easy to himself, and to put him in a way which shall call him to the performance of more duties than perhaps he could have performed without my help, and of performing them in a better manner.—What rent do you pay for this cottage?

Fifty shillings a year, Sir.

It is in a sad tattered condition, is there not a better to be had in the village?

That in which the poor Clerk lived, said the Clergyman, is not only more tight and whole, but has two decent chambers, and a very large light kitchen.—That will be very convenient, replied Mr. Johnson, pray what is the rent? I think, said the Shepherd, poor neighbour Wilson gave somewhat about four pounds a year, or it might be guineas.—Very well, said Mr. Johnson, and what will the Clerk's place be worth, think you? About three pounds, was the answer.

Now, continued Mr. Johnson, my plan is, that the Shepherd should take that house immediately; for as the poor man is dead, there will be no need of waiting till quarter day, if I make up the difference. True, Sir, said Mr. Jenkins, and I am sure my wife's father, whom I expect to-morrow, will willingly assist a little towards buying some of the Clerk's old goods. And the sooner they remove the better, for poor Mary caught that bad rheumatism by sleeping under a leeky thatch. The Shepherd was too much

much moved to speak, and Mary could hardly sob out, Oh Sir, you are too good, indeed this house will do very well. It may do very well for you and your children Mary, said Mr. Johnson, gravely, but it will not do for a school; the kitchen is neither large nor light enough. Shepherd, continued he, with your good Minister's leave, and kind assistance, I propose to set up in this parish a Sunday School, and to make you the master. It will not at all interfere with your weekly calling, and it is the only lawful way in which you could turn the Sabbath into a day of some little profit to your family, by doing, as I hope, a great deal of good to the souls of others. The rest of the week you will work as usual. The difference of rent between this house and the Clerk's I shall pay myself, for to put you into a better house at your own expence would be no great act of kindness.—As for honest Mary, who is not fit for hard labour, or any out-of-door work, I propose to endow a small weekly school, of which she shall be the mistress, and employ her notable turn to good account, by teaching ten or a dozen girls to knit, sew, spin, card, or any other useful way of getting their bread; for all this I shall only pay her the usual price, for I am not going to make you rich but useful.

Not rich, Sir? cried the Shepherd. How can I ever be thankful enough for such blessings? And will my poor Mary have a dry thatch over her head? and shall I be able to send for the doctor

doctor when I am like to lose her? Indeed my cup runs over with blessings, I hope God will give me humility.—Here he and Mary looked at each other and burst into tears. The Gentlemen saw their distress, and kindly walked out upon the little green before the door, that these honest people might give vent to their feelings. As soon as they were alone they crept into one corner of the room, where they thought they could not be seen, and fell on their knees, devoutly blessing and praising God for his mercies. Never were heartier prayers presented, than this grateful couple offered up for their benefactors. The warmth of their gratitude could only be equalled by the earnestness with which they besought the blessing of God on the work in which they were going to engage.

The two Gentlemen now left this happy family, and walked to the Parsonage, where the evening was spent in a manner very edifying to Mr. Johnson, who the next day took all proper measures for putting the Shepherd in immediate possession of his now comfortable habitation. Mr. Jenkins's father-in-law, the worthy Gentleman who gave the Shepherd's wife the blankets, in the first part of this history, arrived at the Parsonage before Mr. Johnson left it, and assisted in fitting up the Clerk's cottage.

Mr. Johnson took his leave, promising to call on the worthy Minister and his new Clerk once a year, in his summer's journey over the Plain,

Plain, as long as it should please GOD to spare his life.—We hope he will never fail to give us an account of these visits, which we shall be glad to lay before our readers, if they should contain instruction or amusement. Z.

THE
TWO SHOEMAKERS.

JACK BROWN and JAMES STOCK, were two lads apprenticed at nearly the same time, to Mr. Williams, a Shoemaker, in a small town in Oxfordshire: they were pretty near the same age, but of very different characters and dispositions.

Brown was eldest son to a farmer in good circumstances, who gave the usual apprentice fee
with

with him. Being a wild giddy boy, whom his father could not well manage or inſtruct in farming, he thought it better to ſend him out to learn a trade at a diſtance, than to let him idle about at home; for Jack always preferred bird's-neſting and marbles to any other employment; and would trifle away half the day, when his father thought he was at ſchool, with any boys he could meet with, who were as idle as himſelf; and never could be prevailed upon to do, or to learn any thing, while a game at taw could be had for love or money. All this time his little brothers, much younger than himſelf, were beginning to follow the plough, or to carry the corn to mill as ſoon as they were able to mount a cart-horſe.

Jack, however, who was a lively boy, and did not naturally want either ſenſe or good-nature, might have turned out well enough, if he had not had the misfortune to be his mother's favourite. She concealed and forgave all his faults. —To be ſure he was a little wild, ſhe would ſay, but he would not make the worſe man for that, for Jack had a good ſpirit of his own, and ſhe would not have it broke, and ſo make a mope of the boy. The farmer, for a quiet life, as it is called, gave up all theſe points to his wife; and, with them, gave up the future virtue and happineſs of his child. He was a laborious and induſtrious man, but he had no religion; he thought only of the gains and advantages of the preſent day, and never took the future into the account.

account. His wife managed him entirely, and as she was really notable, he did not trouble his head about any thing farther. If she had been careless in her dairy, he would have stormed and sworn; but as she only ruined one child by indulgence, and almost broke the hearts of the rest by unkindness, he gave himself little concern about the matter. The cheese, certainly, was good, and that indeed is a great point; but she was neglectful of her children, and a tyrant to her servants. Her husband's substance, indeed, was not wasted, but his happiness was not consulted. His house, it is true, was not dirty, but it was the abode of fury, ill-temper, and covetousness. And the farmer, though he did not care for drink, was too often driven to the publick-house in an evening, because his own was neither quiet nor comfortable. The mother was always scolding, and the children were always crying.

Jack, however, notwithstanding his idleness, picked up a little reading and writing, but never would learn to cast an account: that was too much labour. His mother was desirous he should continue at school, not so much for the sake of his learning, which she had not sense enough to value, but to save her darling from the fatigue of labour; for if he had not gone to school, she knew he must have gone to work, and she thought the former was the least tiresome of the two. Indeed this foolish woman had such an opinion of his genius, that she used, from a child,

child, to think he was too wife for any thing but a parson, and hoped she should live to see him one. She did not wish to see her son a minister because she loved either learning or goodness, but because she thought it would make Jack a gentleman, and set him above his brothers.

Farmer Brown still hoped, that though Jack was likely to make but an idle and ignorant farmer, yet he might make no bad tradesman, when he should be removed from the indulgences of a father's house, and from a silly mother, whose fondness kept him back in every thing. This woman was enraged when she found that so fine a scholar, as she took Jack to be, was to be put apprentice to a shoemaker. The farmer, however, for the first time in his life, would have his own way. But being a worldly man, and too apt to mind only what is falsely called *the main chance*; instead of being careful to look out for a sober, prudent, and religious master for his son, he left all that to accident, as if it had been a thing of little or no consequence. This is a very common fault; and fathers who are guilty of it, are in a great measure answerable for the future sins and errors of their children, when they grow up in the world, and set up for themselves. If a man gives his son a good education, a good example, and a good master, it is indeed *possible* that the son may not turn out well, but it does not often happen; and when it does, the father has no blame resting on him; and it is a great point towards a man's comfort to have his conscience

science quiet in that respect, however God may think fit to over-rule events.

The farmer, however, took care to desire his friends to inquire for a shoemaker who had good business, and was a good workman; and the mother did not forget to put in her word, and "desired that it might be one who was not *too strict*; for Jack had been brought up tenderly, was a meek boy, and could not bear to be contradicted in any thing." And this is the common notion of meekness among people who know no better.

Mr. Williams was recommended to the farmer as being the best shoemaker in the town in which he lived, and far from a strict master; and, without farther inquiries, to Mr. Williams he went.

James Stock, who was the son of an honest labourer in the next village, was bound out by the parish in consideration of his father having so numerous a family, that he was not able to put him out himself. James was in every thing the very reverse of his new companion. He was a modest, industrious, pious youth; and though so poor, and the child of a labourer, was a much better scholar than Jack, who was a wealthy farmer's son. His father had, it is true, been able to give him but very little schooling, for he was obliged to be put to work when quite a child. When very young he used to run of errands for Mr. Thomas, the curate of the parish; a very kind-hearted young gentleman, who boarded

next

next door to his father's cottage. He used also to rub down and saddle his horse, and do any other little job for him, in the most civil obliging manner. All this so recommended him to the clergyman, that he would often send for him in of an evening, after he had done his day's work in the field, and condescended to teach him himself to write and cast accounts, as well as to instruct him in the principles of his religion. It was not merely out of kindness for the little good-natured services James did him, that he shewed him this favour, but also for his readiness in the catechism, and his devout behaviour at church.

The first thing that drew the minister's attention to this boy, was the following:—He had frequently given him halfpence and pence for holding his horse and carrying him to water, before he was big enough to be further useful to him. On Christmas-Day he was surprised to see James at church, reading out of a handsome new prayer-book; he wondered how he came by it, for he knew there was nobody in the parish likely to have given it to him, for at that time there were no Sunday schools; and the father could not afford it, he was sure.

Well James, said he, as he saw him when they came out, you made a good figure at church to-day; it made you look like a man and a christian, not only to have so handsome a book, but to be so ready in all parts of the service. How came you by that book? James owned modestly, that he had been a whole year saving up the money
by

by single halfpence, all of which had been of the minister's own giving, and that in all that time he had not spent a single farthing on his own diversions. My dear boy, said good Mr. Thomas, I am much mistaken if thou dost not turn out well in the world, for two reasons:—first, from thy saving turn and self-denying temper; and next, because thou didst devote the first eighteen-pence thou wast ever worth in the world to so good a purpose.

James bowed and blushed, and from that time Mr. Thomas began to take more notice of him, and to instruct him as I said above. As James soon grew able to do him more considerable service, he would now and then give him sixpence. This he constantly saved till it became a little sum, with which he bought shoes and stockings; well knowing that his poor father, with a hard family and low wages, could not buy them for him. As to what little money he earned himself by his daily labour in the field, he constantly carried it to his mother every Saturday night, to buy bread for the family, which was a pretty help to them.

As James was not over stout in his make, his father thankfully accepted the offer of the parish officers to bind out his son to a trade. This good man, however, had not, like Farmer Brown, the liberty of chusing a master for his son, or he would carefully have enquired if he was a proper man to have the care of youth; but Williams the shoemaker was already fixed on, by those

who

who were to put the boy out, and if he wanted a master it must be him or none; for the overseers had a better opinion of Williams than he deserved, and thought it would be the making of the boy to go to him. The father knew that beggars must not be choosers, so he fitted out James for his new place, having indeed little to give him besides his blessing.

The worthy Mr. Thomas, however, kindly gave him an old coat and waistcoat, which his mother, who was a neat and notable woman, contrived to make up for him herself without a farthing expence, and when it was turned and made fit for his size, it made him a very handsome suit for Sundays, and lasted him a couple of years.

And here let me stop to remark what a pity it is, that poor women so seldom are able or willing to do these sort of little handy jobs themselves; and that they do not oftener bring up their daughters to be more useful in family work. They are great losers by it every way; not only as they are disqualifying their girls from making good wives hereafter, but they are losers in point of present advantage; for gentlefolks could much oftener afford to give a poor boy a jacket or a waistcoat, if it was not for the expence of making it, which adds very much to the cost. To my certain knowledge, many poor women would often get an old coat, or a bit of coarse new cloth given them to fit out a boy, if the mothers or sisters were known to be able to cut it out to advantage,

advantage, and to make it decently themselves. But half-a-crown for the making a bit of kersey, which costs but a few shillings, is more than many very charitable gentry can afford to give—so they often give nothing at all, when they see the mothers so little able to turn it to advantage. It is hoped they will take this hint kindly, as it is meant for their good.

But to return to our two young shoemakers. They were both now settled at Mr. Williams's, who, as he was known to be a good workman, had plenty of business. He had sometimes two or three journeymen, but no apprentices but Jack and James.

Jack, who, with all his faults, was a keen, smart boy, took to learn the trade quick enough, but the difficulty was to make him stick two hours together to his work. At every noise he heard in the street, down went the work—the last one way, the upper leather another; the sole dropped on the ground, and the thread he dragged after him, all the way up the street. If a blind fiddler, a ballad singer, a mountebank, a dancing bear, or a drum, were heard at a distance—out ran Jack—nothing could stop him, and not a stitch more could he be prevailed on to do that day. Every duty, every promise was forgot, for the present pleasure—he could not resist the smallest temptation—he never stopped for a moment to consider whether a thing was right or wrong, but whether he liked it or disliked it. And as his ill-judging mother took

care

care to send him privately a good supply of pocket-money, that deadly bane to all youthful virtue, he had generally a few pence ready to spend, and to indulge in the present diversion whatever it was. And what was still worse even than spending his money, he spent his time too, or rather his master's time. Of this he was continually reminded by James, to whom he always answered, What have you to complain about? It is nothing to you or any one else; I spend nobody's money but my own. That may be, replied the other, but you cannot say it is your own *time* that you spend. He insisted upon it that it was; but James fetched down their *indentures*, and there shewed him that he had solemnly bound himself by that instrument, not to waste his master's property. Now, quoth James, *thy own time is a very valuable part of thy master's property*. To this he replied, Every one's time was his own, and he should not sit moping all day over his last—for his part, he thanked God, *he* was no *parish 'prentice*.

James did not resent this piece of foolish impertinence, as some silly lads would have done; nor fly out into a violent passion: for even at this early age, he had begun to learn of him *who was meek and lowly of heart*; and therefore *when he was reviled, he reviled not again*. On the contrary he was so very kind and gentle, that even Jack, vain and idle as he was, could not help loving him, though he took care never to follow his advice.

Jack's

Jack's fondness for his boyish and silly diversions in the street, soon produced the effects which might naturally be expected; and the same idleness which led him to fly out into the town at the sound of a fiddle, or the sight of a puppet-show, soon led him to those places where all these fiddles and shows naturally lead, I mean the ALE-HOUSE. The acquaintance picked up in the street was carried on at the Greyhound; and the idle pastimes of the boy soon led to the destructive vices of the man.

As he was not an ill-tempered youth, nor naturally much given to drink; a sober and prudent master, who had been steady in his management, and regular in his own conduct; who had recommended good advice by a good example, might have made something of Jack. But I am sorry to say, that Mr. Williams, though a good workman, and not a very hard or severe master, was neither a sober nor a steady man—so far from it, that he spent much more time at the Greyhound, than at home. There was no order either in his shop or family. He left the chief care of the business to his two young apprentices; and being but a worldly man, he was at first disposed to shew favour to Jack much more than to James, because he had more money, and his father was better in the world than the father of poor James.

At first, therefore, he was disposed to consider James as a sort of drudge, who was to do all the menial work of the family, and he did not

care

care how little he taught him of his trade. With Mrs. Williams the matter was still worse; she constantly called him away from the business of his trade to wash the house, nurse the child, turn the spit, or run of errands. And here I must remark, that though parish apprentices are bound in duty to be submissive to both master and mistress, and always to make themselves as useful as they can in a family, and to be civil and humble; yet on the other hand, it is the duty of masters always to remember, that if they are paid for instructing them in their trade, they ought conscientiously to instruct them in it, and not to employ them the greater part of their time in such household or other drudgery, as to deprive them of the opportunity of acquiring their trade.

Mr. Williams soon found out that his favourite Jack would be of little use to him in the shop; for though he worked well enough, he did not care how little he did. Nor could he be of the least use to his master in keeping an account, or writing out a bill upon occasion, for, as he never could be made to learn to cypher, he did not know addition from multiplication.

One day one of the customers called at the shop in a great hurry, and desired his bill might be made out that minute; Mr. Williams, having taken a cup too much, made several attempts to put down a clear account, but the more he tried, the less he found himself able to do it. James, who was sitting at his last, rose up, and with

D great

great modesty, asked his master if he would please to give him leave to make out the bill, saying that though but a poor scholar, he would do his best, rather than keep the gentleman waiting. Williams gladly accepted his offer, and confused as his head was with liquor, he yet was able to observe with what neatness, dispatch, and exactness, the account was drawn out. From that time he no longer considered James as a drudge, but as one fitted for the higher employments of the trade, and he was now regularly employed to manage the accounts, with which all the customers were so well pleased, that it contributed greatly to raise him in his master's esteem; for there were now never any of those blunders or false charges, for which the shop had before been so famous.

James went on in a regular course of industry, and soon became the best workman Mr. Williams had, but there were many things in the family which he greatly disapproved. Some of the journeymen used to swear, drink, and sing very licentious songs. All these things were a great grief to his sober mind; he complained to his master, who only laughed at him; and indeed, as Williams did the same himself, he put it out of his own power to correct his servants, if he had been so disposed. James, however, used always to reprove them with great mildness indeed, but with great seriousness also. This, but still more his own excellent example, produced at length very good effects on such of the men as were not quite hardened in sin,

What grieved him most, was the manner in which the Sunday was spent. The master lay in bed all the morning, nor did the mother or her children ever go to church, except there was some new finery to be shewn, or a christening to be attended. The town's people were coming to the shop all the morning, for work which should have been sent home the night before, had not the master been at the ale-house. And what wounded James to the very soul was, that the master expected the two apprentices to carry home shoes to the country customers on the Sunday morning; which he wickedly thought was a saving of time, as it prevented their hindering their work on the Saturday. These shameful practices greatly afflicted poor James; he begged his master, with tears in his eyes, to excuse him, but he only laughed at his squeamish conscience, as he called it.

Jack did not dislike this part of the business, and generally after he had delivered his parcel, wasted good part of the day in nutting, playing at fives, or dropping in at the public-house: any thing was better than going to church.

James, on the other hand, when he was compelled, sorely against his conscience, to carry home any goods of a Sunday morning, always got up as soon as it was light, knelt down, and prayed heartily to God to forgive him a sin which it was not in his power to avoid; he took care not to lose a moment by the way, but as he was taking his walk with the utmost speed, to leave his shoes with the customers, he spent his time in endeavouring to keep up good thoughts in his mind, and praying that the day might come when his conscience might be delivered from this grievous burthen. He was now particularly thankful, that Mr. Thomas had formerly taught him so many psalms and chapters, which he used to repeat in these walks with great devotion.

He always got home before the rest of the family was up, dressed himself very clean, and went twice to church; and as he greatly disliked the company and practices of his master's house, particularly on the Sabbath-day, he preferred spending his evening alone, reading his Bible, which I forgot to say the worthy clergyman had given him when he left his native village. Sunday evening, which is to some people such a burthen, was to James the highest holiday. He had formerly learnt a little how to sing a psalm of the clerk of his own parish, and this was now become a very delightful part of his evening exercise. And as Will Simpson, one of the journeymen, by James's advice and example, was now beginning to be of a more serious way of thinking, he often asked him to sit an hour with him, when they read the Bible, and talked it over together in a manner very pleasant and improving; and as Will was a famous singer, a psalm or two sung together, was a very innocent pleasure.

James's good manners and civility to the customers drew much business to the shop; and his skill as a workman was so great, that every one desired his shoes might be made by James. Williams grew so very idle and negligent, that he now totally neglected his affairs, and to hard drinking added deep gaming. All James's care, both of the shop and the accounts, could not keep things in any tolerable order: he represented to his master that they were growing worse and worse; and exhorted him, if he valued his credit as a tradesman, his comfort as a husband and father, his character as a master, and his soul as a christian, to turn over a new leaf. Williams swore a great oath, that he would not be restrained in his pleasures to please a canting parish 'prentice, nor to humour a parcel of squalling brats—that let people say what they would of him, they should never say he was a *hypocrite*, and as long as they could not call him that, he did not care what else they called him.

In a violent passion he immediately went to the Greyhound, where he now spent, not only every evening, which he had long done, but good part of the day and night also. His wife was very dressy, extravagant, and fond of company, and spent at home as fast as her husband did abroad; so that all the neighbours said, if it had not been for James his master must have broke long ago, but they were sure he could not hold it much longer.

As Jack Brown sung a good song, and played many diverting tricks, Williams liked his company, and often allowed him to make one at the Greyhound, where he would laugh heartily at his stories; so that every one thought Jack was much the greater favourite—so he was as a companion in frolick, and foolery, and *pleasure*, as it is called; but he would not trust him with an inch of leather or sixpence in money: No, no—when business was to be done, or trust was to be reposed, James was the man: the idle and the drunken never trust one another, if they have common sense. They like to laugh, and sing, and riot, and drink together: but when they want a friend, a counsellor, a help in business or in trouble, they go farther a-field; and Williams, while he would drink with Jack, would trust James with untold gold; and even was foolishly tempted to neglect his business the more from knowing that he had one at home who was taking care of it.

In spite of all James's care and diligence, however, things were growing worse and worse: the more James saved, the more his master and mistress spent. One morning, just as the shop was opened, and James had set every body to their respective work, and he himself was settling the business for the day, he found that his master was not yet come from the Greyhound. As this was now become a common case, he only grieved but did not wonder at it. While he was indulging sad thoughts on what would be the end of all this, in ran the tapster from the Greyhound out of breath, and with a look of terror and dismay, desired James would step over to the publick-house with him that moment, for that his master wanted him.

James went immediately, surprised at this unusual message. When he got into the kitchen of the publick-house, which he now entered for the first time in his life, though it was just opposite the house in which he lived, he was shocked at the beastly disgusting appearance of every thing he beheld. There was a table covered with tankards, punch-bowls, broken glasses, pipes, and dirty greasy packs of cards, and all over wet with liquor; the floor was strewed with broken earthen cups, odd cards, and an EO table shivered to pieces in a quarrel; behind the table stood a crowd of dirty fellows with matted locks, hollow eyes, and faces smeared with tobacco; James made his way after the tapster, through this wretched looking crew, to a settle which stood in the chimney corner. Not a word was uttered, but the silent horror seemed to denote something more than a mere common drunken bout.

What was the dismay of James, when he saw his miserable master stretched out on the settle, in all the agonies of death! He had fallen into a fit, after having drank hard best part of the night, and seemed to have but a few minutes to live. In his frightful countenance was displayed the dreadful picture of sin and death; for he
struggled

struggled at once under the guilt of intoxication, and the pangs of a dying man. He recovered his senses for a few moments, and called out to ask if his faithful servant was come: James went up to him, took him by his cold hand, but was too much moved to speak. Oh! James, James, cried he in a broken voice, pray for me, comfort me. James spoke kindly to him, but was too honest to give him false comfort, as is too often done by mistaken friends in these dreadful moments.

James, said he, I have been a bad master to you—you would have saved me soul and body, but I would not let you—I have ruined my wife, my children, and my own soul. Take warning, oh, take warning by my miserable end, said he to his stupified companions; but none were able to attend to him but James, who bid him lift up his heart to GOD, and prayed heartily for him himself. Oh! said the dying man, it is too late, too late for me—but you have still time, said he to the half-drunken terrified crew around him. Where is Jack? Jack Brown came forward, but was too much frightened to speak. O wretched boy, said he, I fear I shall have the ruin of thy soul, as well as my own, to answer for. Stop short!—Take warning—now, in the days of thy youth. O James, James, thou dost not pray for me. Death is dreadful to the wicked—O the sting of death to a guilty conscience! Here he lifted up his ghastly eyes in speechless horror, grasped hard the hand of James,

James, gave a deep hollow groan, and closed his eyes never to open them but in an awful eternity.

This was death in all its horrors! The gay companions of his sinful pleasures could not stand the sight; all slunk away like guilty thieves from their late favourite friend—no one was left to assist him, but his two apprentices. Brown was not so hardened but that he shed many tears for his unhappy master; and even made some hasty resolutions of amendment, which were too soon forgotten.

While Brown stepped home to call the workmen to come and assist in removing their poor master, James staid alone with the corpse, and employed those awful moments in indulging the most serious thoughts, and praying heartily to God, that so terrible a lesson might not be thrown away upon him; but that he might be enabled to live in a constant state of preparation for death. The resolutions he made at this moment, as they were not made in his own strength, but in an humble reliance on God's gracious help, were of use to him as long as he lived; and if ever he was for a moment tempted to say, or do a wrong thing, the remembrance of his poor dying master's last agonies, and the dreadful words he uttered, always instantly checked him.

When Williams was buried, and his affairs came to be inquired into, they were found to be in a sad condition. His wife, indeed, was the less to be pitied, as she had contributed her full share to the common ruin. James, however, did pity her, and by his skill in accounts, his known honesty, and the trust the creditors put in his word, things came to be settled rather better than Mrs. Williams expected.

Both Brown and James were now within a month or two of being out of their time. The creditors, as was said before, employed James to settle his late master's accounts, which he did in a manner so creditable to his abilities, and his honesty, that they proposed to him to take the shop himself. He assured them it was utterly out of his power for want of money. As the creditors had not the least fear of being repaid, if it should please God to spare his life, they generously agreed among themselves, to advance him a small sum of money without any security but his bond; for this he was to pay a very reasonable interest, and to return the whole in a given number of years. James shed tears of gratitude at this testimony to his character, and could hardly be prevailed on to accept their kindness, so great was his dread of being in debt.

He took the remainder of the lease from his mistress, and in settling affairs with her, took care to make every thing as advantageous to her as possible. He never once allowed himself to think how unkind she had been to him, he only saw in her the needy widow of his deceased master, and the distressed mother of an infant family; and was heartily sorry it was not in his power to contribute

contribute to their support; it was not only his duty, but his delight to return good for evil— for he was a CHRISTIAN.

James Stock was now, by the blessing of GOD, on his own earnest endeavours, master of a considerable shop, and was respected by the whole town for his prudence, honesty, and piety. How he behaved in his new station, and also what befel his comrade Brown, must be the subject of another book; and I hope my readers will look forward with some impatience for some further account of this worthy young man. In the mean time, other apprentices will do well to follow so praise-worthy an example, and to remember, that the respectable master of a large shop, and a profitable business, was raised to that creditable situation, without money, friends, or connections, from the low beginning of a *parish 'prentice*, by sobriety, industry, *the fear of God*, and an obedience to the divine principles of the CHRISTIAN RELIGION.

Z.

PART II.

THE APPRENTICE TURNED MASTER.

THE first part of this History left off with the dreadful sudden death of Williams the idle Shoemaker, who died in a drunken fit at the Greyhound.

hound. It also shewed how James Stock, his faithful apprentice, by his honest and upright behaviour, so gained the love and respect of his late master's creditors, that they set him up in business, though he was not worth a shilling of his own, such is the power of a good character! And when we last parted from him he had just got possession of his master's shop.

This sudden prosperity was a time of trial for James; who, as he was now become a creditable tradesman, I shall hereafter think proper to call Mr. James Stock. I say, this sudden rise in life was a time of trial; for we hardly know what we are ourselves till we become our own masters. There is indeed always a reasonable hope that a good servant will not make a bad master, and that a faithful apprentice will prove an honest tradesman. But the heart of man is deceitful; and some folks who seem to behave very well while they are under subjection, no sooner get a little power than their heads are turned, and they grow prouder than those who are gentlemen born. They forget at once that they were lately poor and dependent themselves, so that one would think that with their poverty they had lost their memory too. I have known some who had suffered most hardships in their early days, become the most hard and oppressive in their turn; so that they seem to forget that fine considerate reason which God gives to the children of Israel why they should be merciful to their servants,

servants, "remembering" saith he, "that thou thyself wast a bondman."

Young Mr. Stock did not so forget himself. He had indeed the only sure guard from falling into this error. It was not from any easiness in his natural disposition: for that only just serves to make folks good-natured when they are pleased, and patient when they have nothing to vex them. James went upon higher ground. He brought his religion into all his actions; he did not give way to abusive language, because he knew it was a sin. He did not use his apprentices ill, because he knew he had himself a Master in heaven.

He knew he owed his present happy situation to the kindness of the creditors. But did he grow easy and careless because he knew he had such friends? No indeed. He worked with double diligence in order to get out of debt, and to let these friends see he did not abuse their kindness. Such behaviour as this is the greatest encouragement in the world to rich people to lend a little money. It creates friends, and it keeps them.

His shoes and boots were made in the best manner; this *got* him business; he set out with a rule to tell no lies and deceive no customers; this *secured* his business. He had two reasons for not promising to send home goods when he knew he should not be able to keep his word. The first, because he knew a lie was a sin, the next, because it was a folly. There is no credit
sooner

sooner worn out than that which is got by false pretences. After a little while no one is deceived by them. Falsehood is so soon found out that I believe most tradesmen are the poorer for it in the long run. Deceit is the worst part of a shopkeeper's stock in trade.

James was now at the head of a family. This is a serious situation, (said he to himself, one fine summer's evening, as stood leaning over the half door of his shop to enjoy a little fresh air) I am now master of a family. My cares are doubled, and so are my duties. I see the higher one gets in life the more one has to answer for. Let me now call to mind the sorrow I used to feel when I was made to carry work home on a Sunday by an ungodly master; and let me now *keep* the resolutions I then formed.

So what his heart found right to do he resolved to do quickly; and he set out at first as he meant to go on. The Sunday was truly a day of rest at Mr. Stock's. He would not allow a pair of shoes to be given out on that day to oblige the best customer he had. And what did he lose by it? Why nothing. For when the people were once used to it, they liked Saturday night just as well. But had it been otherwise he would have given up his gains to his conscience.

Shewing how Mr. Stock behaved to his Apprentices.

When he got up in the world so far as to have apprentices, he thought himself as accountable for

for their behaviour as if they had been his children. He was very kind to them, and had a chearful merry way of talking to them, so that the lads who had seen too much of swearing, reprobate masters, were very fond of him. They were never afraid of speaking to him, they told him all their little troubles, and considered their master as their best friend, for they said they would do any thing for a good word and a kind look. As he did not swear at them when they had been guilty of a fault, they did not lie to him to conceal it, and thereby make one fault two. But though he was very kind, he was very watchful also, for he did not think neglect any part of kindness. He brought them to one very pretty method, which was, on a Sunday evening to divert themselves with writing out half a dozen texts of Scripture in a pretty copy-book with gilt covers. You may have the same at any of the Stationer's; they do not cost above four pence, and will last nearly a year.

When the boys carried him their books, he justly commended him whose texts were written in the fairest hand. And now my boys, said he, let us see which of you will learn your texts best in the course of the week; he who does shall chuse for next Sunday. Thus the boys soon got many psalms and chapters by heart, almost without knowing how they came by them. He taught them how to make a practical use of what they learnt; for, said he, it will answer little purpose to learn texts if we do not try to live

up

up to them. One of the boys being apt to play in his abfence, and to run back again to his work when he heard his mafter's ftep, he brought him to a fenfe of his fault by the laft Sunday's texts, which happened to be the 6th of Ephefians. He fhewed him what was meant by being obedient to his mafter in finglenefs of heart as unto Chrift, and explained to him with fo much kindnefs what it was, not to work with eye-fervice as men pleafers, but doing the will of God from the heart, that the lad faid he fhould never forget it, and it did more towards curing him of idlenefs than the foundeft horfe-whipping would have done.

How Mr. Stock got out of Debt.

Stock's behaviour was very regular, and he was much beloved for his kind and peaceable temper. He had alfo a good reputation for fkill in his trade, and his induftry was talked of through the whole town, fo that he had foon more work than he could poffibly do. He paid all his dealers to the very day, and took care to carry his intereft money to the creditors the moment it became due. In two or three years he was able to begin to pay off a fmall part of the principal. His reafon for being fo eager to pay money as foon as it became due was this:—He had obferved tradefmen, and efpecially his old mafter, put off the day of payment as long as they could, even though they had

had the means in their power. This deceived them: for having money in their pockets they forgot it belonged to the creditor, and not to themselves, and so got to fancy they were rich when they were really poor. This false notion led them to indulge in idle expences, whereas, if they had paid regularly, they would have had this one temptation the less. A young tradesman, when he is going to spend money, should at least ask himself whether this money is his own or his creditors'. This little question might help to prevent many a bankruptcy.

A true Christian always goes heartily to work to find out what is his besetting sin; and when he has found it, (which he easily may if he looks sharp) against this sin he watches narrowly. Now I know it is the fashion among some folks (and a bad fashion it is) to fancy that good people have no sin; but this only shews their ignorance. It is not true. That good man St. Paul knew better*. And when men do not own their sins, it is not because there is no sin in their hearts, but because they are not anxious to search for it, nor humble to confess it, nor penitent to mourn over it. But this was not the case with James Stock. Examine yourselves truly, said he, is no bad part of the catechism. He began to be afraid that his desire of living creditably, and without being a burthen to any one, might, under the mask of honesty and in-

* See Romans vii.

dependence,

dependence, lead him into pride and covetousness. He feared that the bias of his heart lay that way. So instead of being proud of his sobriety; instead of bragging that he never spent his money idly, nor went to the ale-house; instead of boasting how hard he worked, and how he denied himself, he strove in secret that even these good qualities might not grow out of a wrong root. The following event was of use to him in the way of indulging any disposition to covetousness:

One evening as he was standing at the door of his shop, a poor dirty boy without stockings and shoes came up and asked him for a bit of broken victuals, for he had eaten nothing all day. In spite of his dirt and rags he was a very pretty, lively, civil spoken boy, and Mr. Stock could not help thinking he knew something of his face. He fetched him out a good piece of bread and cheese, and while the boy was devouring it, asked him if he had no parents, and why he went about in that vagabond manner? Daddy has been dead some years, said the boy, he died in a fit over at the Grey-hound. Mammy says he used to live at this shop, and then we did not want for cloaths nor victuals neither. Stock was melted almost to tears on finding that this dirty beggar-boy was Tommy Williams, the son of his old master. He blessed God on comparing his own happy condition with that of this poor destitute child, but he was not proud at the comparison, and while he was thankful for his own prosperity,

prosperity, he pitied the helpless boy.—Where have you been living of late? said he to him, for I understand you all went home to your mother's friends. So we did Sir, said the boy, but they are grown tired of maintaining us, because they said that Mammy spent all the money which should have gone to buy victuals for us, on snuff and drams. And so they have sent us back to this place, which is Daddy's parish.

And where do you live here? said Mr. Stock. O Sir, we are all put into the parish poor-house. —And does your mother do any thing to help to maintain you? No, Sir, for Mammy says she was not brought up to work like poor folks, and she would rather starve than spin or knit; so she lies a-bed all the morning, and sends us about to pick up what we can, a bit of victuals or a few halfpence. And have you any money in your pocket now? Yes, Sir, I have got three halfpence which I have begged to-day. Then, as you were so very hungry, how came you not to buy a roll at that baker's over the way? Because, Sir, I was going to lay it out in tea for Mammy, for I never lay out a farthing for myself. Indeed Mammy says she *will* have her tea twice a-day if we beg or starve for it. Can you read, my boy? said Mr. Stock: a little, Sir, and say my prayers too. And can you say your catechism? I have almost forgot it all, Sir, though I remember about honouring my father and mother, and that makes me still carry the halfpence home to Mammy instead of buying cakes.

cakes. Who taught you thefe good things? One Jemmy Stock, Sir, who was a parifh 'prentice to my Daddy. He taught me one queftion out of the catechifm every night, and always made me fay my prayers to him before I went to bed. He told me I fhould go to the wicked place if I did not fear God, fo I am ftill afraid to tell lies like the other boys. Poor Jemmy gave me a piece of gingerbread every time I learnt well; but I have no friend now; Jemmy was very good to me, though Mammy did nothing but beat him.

Mr. Stock was too much moved to carry on the difcourfe; he did not make himfelf known to the boy, but took him over to the baker's fhop; as they walked along he could not help repeating aloud, a verfe or two of that beautiful hymn, fo defervedly the favourite of all children:

"Not more than others I deferve,
"Yet God hath given me more;
"For I have food while others ftave,
"Or beg from door to door."

The little boy looked up in his face, faying, Why, Sir, that's the very hymn which Jemmy Stock gave me a penny for learning. Stock made no anfwer, but put a couple of three-penny loaves into his hand to carry home, and told him to call on him again at fuch a time in the following week.

How

How Mr. Stock continued to be charitable without any Expence.

Stock had abundant subject for meditation that night. He was puzzled what to do with the boy. While he was carrying on his trade upon borrowed money, he did not think it right to give any part of that money to assist the idle, or even to help the distressed. I must be just, said he, before I am generous. Still he could not bear to see this fine boy given up to certain ruin. He did not think it safe to take him into his shop in his present ignorant unprincipled state. At last he hit upon this thought: I work for myself twelve hours in the day. Why shall I not work one hour or two for this boy in the evening? It will be but for a year, and I shall then have more right to do what I please. My money will then be my own, I shall have paid my debts.

So he began to put his resolution in practice that very night, sticking to his old notion of not putting off till to-morrow what should be done to-day; and it was thought he owed much of his success in life, as well as his growth in goodness, to this little saying. I am young and healthy, said he, one hour's work more will do me no harm; I will set aside all I get by these over-hours, and put the boy to school. I have not only no right to punish this child for the sins of his father, but I consider that though God hated

hated those sins, he has made them be instruments for my advancement.

Tommy Williams called at the time appointed. In the mean time Mr. Stock's maid had made him a tidy little suit of cloaths out of an old coat of her master's. She had also knit him a pair of stockings, and Mr. Stock made him sit down in the shop, while he himself fitted him with a pair of new shoes. The maid having washed and dressed him, Mr. Stock took him by the hand and walked along with him to the parish poor-house to find his mother. They found her dressed in ragged filthy finery, standing at the door, where she passed most of her time, quarrelling with half a dozen women as idle and dirty as herself; when she saw Tommy so neat and well-dressed, she fell a-crying for joy. She said it put her in mind of old times, for Tommy always used to be dressed like a gentleman. So much the worse, said Mr. Stock, if you had not begun by making him look like a gentleman, you needed not have ended by making him look like a beggar. Oh Jem, said she, (for though it was four years since she had seen him, she soon recollected him) fine times for you! set a beggar on horseback—you know the proverb. I shall beat Tommy well for finding you out, and exposing me to you.

Instead of entering into any dispute with this bad woman, or praising himself at her expence; or putting her in mind of her past ill behaviour to him, or reproaching her with the bad use she had made of her prosperity, he mildly said to her,—Mrs. Williams, I am sorry for your misfortunes; I am come to relieve you of part of your burthen. I will take Tommy off your hands. I will give him a year's board and schooling, and by that time I shall see what he is fit for. I will promise nothing, but if the boy turns out well I will never forsake him. I shall make but one bargain with you, which is, that he must not come to this place to hear all this railing and swearing, nor shall he keep company with these pilfering idle children. You are welcome to go and see him when you please, but here he must not come.

The foolish woman burst out a-crying, saying, she should lose her poor dear Tommy for ever. Mr. Stock might give *her* the money he intended to pay at the school, for nobody could do so well by him as his own mother. The truth was, she wanted to get these new cloaths into her clutches, which would all have been pawned at the dram shop before the week was out. This Mr. Stock well knew. From crying she fell to scolding and swearing. She told him he was an unnatural wretch, that wanted to make a child despise his own mother because she was poor. She even went so far as to say she would not part from him; she said she hated your godly people, they had no bowels of compassion, but tried to set men, women, and children against their own flesh and blood.

Mr.

Mr. Stock now almost lost his patience, and for one moment a thought came across him to strip the boy, carry back the cloaths, and leave him to his unnatural mother. Why, said he, should I work over-hours, and wear out my strength for this wicked woman? But he soon checked this thought, by reflecting on the patience and long-suffering of God with rebellious sinners. This cured his anger in a moment, and he mildly reasoned with her on her folly and blindness in opposing the good of her child.

One of the neighbours who stood by, said, what a fine thing it was for the boy, but some people were born to be lucky! She wished Mr. Stock would take a fancy to *her* child, he should have him soon enough. Mrs. Williams now began to be frightened left Mr. Stock should take the woman at her word, and sullenly consented to let the boy go, from envy and malice, not from prudence and gratitude; and Tommy was sent to school that very night, his mother crying and roaring, instead of thanking God for such a blessing.

And here I cannot forbear telling a very good-natured thing of Will Simpson, one of the workmen. By-the-bye it was that very young fellow who was reformed by Stock's good example when he was an apprentice, and who used to sing psalms with him on a Sunday evening when they got out of the way of Williams's junketing. Will coming home early one evening, was surprised to find his master at work by himself, long

long after the usual time. He begged so heartily to know the reason, that Stock owned the truth. Will was so struck with this piece of kindness, that he snatched up a last, crying out, Well master, you shall not work by yourself however; we will go snacks in maintaining Tommy: it shall never be said that Will Simpson was idling about, when his master was working for charity. This made the hour pass chearfully, and doubled the profits.

In a year or two Mr. Stock, by God's blessing on his labours, became quite clear of the world. He now paid off his creditors; but he never forgot his obligation to them, and found many opportunities of shewing kindness to them, and to their children after them. He now cast about for a proper wife, and as he was thought a prosperous man, and very well-looking besides, most of the smart girls of the place, with their tawdry finery, used to be often parading before the shop, and would even go to church in order to put themselves in his way. But Mr. Stock when he went to church had other things in his head, and if ever he thought about these gay damsels at all, it was with concern in seeing them so improperly tricked out, so that the very means they took to please him, made him dislike them.

There was one Betsy West, a young woman of excellent character and very modest appearance. He had seldom seen her out, as she was employed night and day in waiting on an aged widowed mother who was both lame and blind.

This good girl was indeed almost truly eyes and feet to her helpless parent, and Mr. Stock used to see her, through the little casement window, lifting her up and feeding her with a tenderness which greatly raised his esteem for her. He used to tell Will Simpson, as they sat at work, that such a dutiful daughter could hardly fail to make a faithful wife. He had not, however, the heart to try to draw her off from her care of her sick mother. The poor woman declined very fast. Betsy was much employed in reading or praying by her while she was awake, and passed good part of the night while she slept, in doing some fine works to sell in order to supply her sick mother with little niceties which their poor pittance could not afford, while she herself lived on a crust.

Mr. Stock knew that Betsy would have little or nothing after her mother's death, as she had only a life income. On the other hand Mr. Thompson, the tanner, had offered him two hundred pounds with his daughter Nancy: but he was almost sorry that he had not in this case an opportunity of resisting his natural bias, which rather lay on the side of loving money: For, said he, putting principle and putting affection out of the question, I shall do a more *prudent* thing by marrying Betsy West, who will conform to her station, and is a religious, humble, industrious girl, without a shilling, than by having an idle dressy lass, who will neglect my family and fill my house with company, though she

she should have twice the fortune which Nancy Thompson would bring.

At length poor old Mrs. West was released from all her sufferings. At a proper time Mr. Stock proposed marriage to Betsy, and was accepted. All the disappointed girls in the town wondered what any body could like in such a dowdy as that. Had the man no eyes? They thought Mr. Stock had had more taste. Oh! how it did provoke all the vain idle things to find, that staying at home, dressing plainly, serving God, and nursing a blind Mother, should do that for Betsy West, which all their contrivances, flaunting, and dancing, could not do for them.

He was not disappointed of meeting with a good wife in Betsy, as indeed those who mary on right grounds seldom are. But if religious persons will, for the sake of money, chuse partners for life who have no religion, do not let them complain that they are unhappy; they might have known that beforehand.

Tommy Williams was now taken home to Stock's house and bound apprentice. He was always kind and attentive to his mother; and every penny which Will Simpson or his master gave him for learning a chapter, he would save to buy a bit of tea and sugar for her. When the other boys laughed at him for being so foolish as to deny himself cakes and apples, to give his money to her who was so bad a woman, he would answer, It may be so, but she is my mother for all that.

Mr. Stock was much moved at the change in this boy, who turned out a very good youth. He resolved, as God should prosper him, that he would try to snatch other helpless creatures from sin and ruin. For, said he, it is owing to God's blessing on the instructions of my good minister when I was a child, that I have been saved from the broad way of destruction. He still gave God the glory of every thing he did aright, and when Will Simpson one day said to him, Master, I wish I were half as good as you are. Hold William, answered he gravely, I once read in a book, that the Devil is willing enough we should appear to do good actions, if he can but make us proud of them.

But we must not forget our other old acquaintance, Mr. Stock's fellow-prentice. So next month you may expect a full account of the many tricks and frolicks of idle Jack Brown, being the third part of the History of the Two Shoemakers.

Z.

PART III.

YOU have not, I hope, forgotten your old acquaintance idle Jack Brown, the fellow-apprentice of James Stock. I gave a little account of him

him and his wild tricks in the firſt part of this hiſtory, from which I dare ſay you expect to hear no great good of him. The ſecond part ſhewed how James Stock, from a pariſh apprentice, became a top Shoemaker. You ſhall now hear what befel idle Jack, who, being a farmer's ſon, had many advantages to begin life with. But he who wants prudence may be ſaid to want every thing, becauſe he turns all his advantages to no account.

Jack Brown was juſt out of his time when his maſter Williams died in that terrible drunken fit at the Greyhound. You know already how Stock ſucceeded to his maſter's buſineſs, and proſpered in it. Jack wiſhed very much to enter into partnerſhip with him. His father and mother too were deſirous of it, and offered to advance a hundred pounds with him. Here is a freſh proof of the power of a good character! The old farmer, with all his covetouſneſs, was eager to get his ſon into partnerſhip with Stock, though the latter was not worth a ſhilling, and even Jack's mother, with all her pride, was eager for it, for they had both ſenſe enough to ſee it would be the making of Jack. The father knew that Stock would look to the main chance; and the mother that he would take the labouring oar, and ſo her darling would have little to do.

Stock, however, young as he was, was too old a bird to be caught with chaff. His wiſdom was an overmatch for their cunning. He had a kindneſs for Brown, but would on no account enter into business with him. One of these three things, said he, I am sure will happen if I do; he will either hurt my principles, my character, or my trade; perhaps all. And here, by-the-bye, let me drop a hint to other young men who are about to enter into partnership. Let them not do that in haste which they may repent at leisure. Next to marriage it is a tie the hardest to break; and next to that it is an engagement which ought to be entered into with the most caution. Many things go to the making such a connection suitable, safe, and pleasant. There is many a rich man need not be above taking a hint in this respect from James Stock the Shoemaker.

Brown was still unwilling to part from him, indeed he was too idle to look out for business, so he offered Stock to work with him as a journeyman; but this he also mildly refused. It hurt his good-nature to do so; but he reflected that a young man who has his way to make in the world must not only be good-natured, he must be prudent also. I am resolved, said he, to employ none but the most sober, regular young men I can get. Evil communications corrupt good manners, and I should be answerable for all the disorders of my own house if I knowingly took a wild drinking young fellow into it. That which might be kindness to one, would be injustice to many, and therefore a sin in myself.

Brown's

Brown's mother was in a great rage when she heard that her son had stooped so low as to make this offer. She thought pride was a grand thing. Poor woman! She did not know that it is the meanest thing in the world. It was her ignorance which made her proud, as is apt to be the case. You mean-spirited rascal, said she to Jack, I had rather follow you to your grave, as well as I love you, than see you disgrace your family by working under Jem Stock, the parish apprentice. She forgot already what pains she had taken about the partnership, but pride and passion have a bad memory.

It is hard to say which was now uppermost in her mind, her desire to be revenged on Stock, or to see her son make a figure. She raised every shilling she could get from her husband, and all she could crib from the dairy to set up Jack in a showy way. So the very next market day she came herself, and took for him the new white house, with the two little sash windows painted blue, and blue posts before the door. It is that house which has the old cross just before it, as you turn down between the Church and the Greyhound. It's being so near the church to be sure was no recommendation to Jack, but it's being so near the Greyhound was, and so taking one thing with the other it was to be sure no bad situation; but what weighed most with the mother was, that it was a much more showy shop than Stock's, and the house, though not half so convenient, was far more smart.

In order to draw custom, his foolish mother advised him to undersell his neighbours just at first; to buy ordinary but showy goods, and employ cheap workmen. In short, she charged him to leave no stone unturned to ruin his old comrade Stock. Indeed she always thought with double satisfaction of Jack's prosperity, because she always joined to it the hope that his success would be the ruin of Stock, for she owned it would be the joy of her heart to bring that proud upstart to a morsel of bread. She did not understand, for her part, why such beggars must become tradesmen, it was making a velvet purse of a sow's ear.

Stock however set out on quite another set of principles. He did not allow himself always to square his own behaviour to others by theirs to him. He seldom asked himself what he should *like* to do: but he had a mighty way of saying I wonder now what is my duty to do? And when he was once clear in that matter he generally did it, always begging God's blessing and direction. So instead of setting Brown at defiance; instead of all that vulgar selfishness, of catch he that catch can—and two of a trade can never agree—he resolved to be friendly towards him. Instead of joining in the laugh against Brown for making his house so fine, he was sorry for him, because he feared he would never be able to pay such a rent. So he very kindly called upon him, told him there was business enough for them both, and gave him many useful

ful hints for his going on. He warned him to go oftener to church and seldomer to the Greyhound: put him in mind how following the one and forsaking the other had been the ruin of their poor master, and added the following

Advice to young Tradesmen.

Buy the best goods; cut the work out yourself; let the eye of the master be every where; employ the soberest men; avoid all the low deceits of trade; never lower the credit of another to raise your own; make short payments; keep exact accounts; avoid idle company, and be very strict to your word.

For a short time things went on swimmingly. Brown was merry and civil. The shop was well situated for gossip; and every one who had something to say, and nothing to do, was welcome. Every idle story was first spread, and every idle song first sung in Brown's shop. Every customer who came to be measured was promised that his shoes should be done first. But the misfortune was, if twenty came in a day the same promise was made to all; so that nineteen were disappointed and of course affronted. He never said *No* to any one. It is indeed a word which it requires some honesty to pronounce. By all these false promises he was thought the most obliging fellow that ever made a shoe. And as he set out on the principle of underselling, people took a mighty fancy to the Cheap Shop. And it was agreed among all the young and giddy, that he would beat Stock hollow, and that the old shop would be soon knocked up.

All is not Gold that glistens.

After a few months, however, folks began to be not quite so fond of the Cheap Shop; one found out that the leather was bad, another that the work was slight. Those who liked substantial goods went all of them to Stock's, for they said Brown's heel taps did not last a week; his new boots let in water; and they believed he made his soles of brown paper. Besides it was thought by most, that his promising all, and keeping his word with none, hurt his business as much as any thing. Indeed I question, putting religion out of the question, if lying ever answers in the long run.

Brown had what is commonly called *a good heart*; that is he had a thoughtless good nature, and a sort of feeling for the moment which made him seem sorry when others were in trouble. But he was not apt to put himself to any inconvenience, nor go a step out of his way, nor give up any pleasure to serve the best friend he had. He loved *fun*; and those who do should always see that it be harmless, and that they do not give up more for it than it is worth. I am not going to say a word against innocent merriment. I like it myself. But what the proverb says of gold, may be said of mirth, it may be bought too dear. If a young man finds that what he
fancies

fancies is a good joke may possibly offend God, hurt his neighbour, afflict his parent, or make a modest girl blush, let him then be assured it is not fun but wickedness, and he had better let it alone.

Jack Brown then, as *good a heart* as he had, did not know what it was to deny himself any thing. He was so *good-natured* indeed that he never in his life refused to make one of a jolly set; but he was not good-natured enough to consider that those men whom he kept up all night roaring and laughing, had wives and children at home, who had little to eat, and less to wear, because *they* were keeping up the character of merry fellows at the public house.

The Mountebank.

One day he saw his father's plough-boy come galloping up to his door in great haste. This boy brought Brown word that his mother was dangerously ill, and that his father had sent his own best bay mare Smiler, that his son might lose no time, but set out directly to see his mother before she died. Jack burst into tears, lamented the danger of so fond a mother, and all the people in the shop extolled his *good heart*.

He sent back the boy directly, with a message that he would follow him in half an hour, as soon as the mare had baited; for he well knew that his father would not thank him for any haste he might make if Smiler was hurt.

Jack accordingly set off, and rode with such speed to the next town, that both himself and Smiler had a mind to another bait. They stopped at the Star, unluckily it was Fair-day, and as he was walking about while Smiler was eating her oats, a bill was put into his hand setting forth, that on a stage opposite the Globe a Mountebank was showing away, and his Andrew performing the finest tricks that ever were seen. He read—he stood still—he went on—It will not hinder me, says he; Smiler must rest; and I shall see my poor dear mother quite as soon if I just take a peep, as if I sit moping at the Star.

The tricks were so merry that the time seemed short, and when they were over he could not forbear going into the Globe and treating these choice spirits with a bowl of punch. Just as they were taking the last glass Jack happened to say that he was the best fives player in the country. That is lucky, said the Andrew, for there is a famous match now playing in the court, and you may never again have such an opportunity to show your skill. Brown declared he could not stay, for that he had left his horse at the Star, and must set off on urgent business. They now all pretended to call his skill in question. This roused his pride, and he thought another half hour could break no squares. Smiler had now had a good feed of corn, and he would only have to push her on a little more; so to it he went.

He

He won the first game. This spurred him on; and he played till it was so dark they could not see a ball. Another bowl was called for from the winner. Wagers and betts now drained Brown not only of all the money he had won, but of all he had in his pocket, so that he was obliged to ask leave to go to the house where his horse was, to borrow enough to discharge his reckoning at the Globe.

All these losses brought his poor dear mother to his mind, and he marched off with rather a heavy heart to borrow the money, and to order Smiler out of the stable. The landlord expressed much surprise at seeing him, and the ostler declared there was no Smiler there; that he had been rode off above two hours ago by the Merry Andrew, who said he came by order of the owner, Mr. Brown, to fetch him to the Globe, and to pay for his feed. It was indeed one of the neatest tricks the Andrew ever performed, for he made such a clean conveyance of Smiler, that neither Jack nor his father ever heard of her again.

It was night: no one could tell what road the Andrew took, and it was another hour or two before an advertisement could be drawn up for apprehending the horse-stealer. Jack had some doubts whether he should go on or return back. He knew that though his father might fear his wife most, yet he loved Smiler best. At length he took that courage from a glass of brandy which he ought to have taken from a hearty repentance, and he resolved to pursue his journey.

He

He was obliged to leave his watch and silver buckles in pawn for a little old hack which was nothing but skin and bone, and would hardly trot three miles an hour.

He knocked at his father's door about five in the morning. The family were all up. He asked the boy who opened the door how his mother was? She is dead, said the boy, she died yesterday afternoon. Here Jack's heart smote him, and he cried aloud, partly from grief, but more from the reproaches of his own conscience, for he found by computing the hours, that had he come strait on, he should have been in time to receive his mother's blessing.

The Farmer now calling from within, I hear Smiler's step. Is Jack come? Yes father, said Jack, in a low voice. Then, cried the Farmer, run every man and boy of you and take care of the mare. Tom, do thou go and rub her down; Jem, run and get her a good feed of corn. Be sure walk her about that she may not catch cold. Young Brown came in. Are you not an undutiful dog? said the father; you might have been here twelve hours ago. Your mother could not die in peace without seeing you. She said it was a cruel return for all her fondness that you could not make a little haste to see her; but it was always so, for she had wronged her other children to help you, and this was her reward. Brown sobbed out a few words, but his father replied, Never cry Jack, for the boy told me that it was out of regard for Smiler that you were not
here

here as soon as he was; and if 'twas your over care of her, why there's no great harm done. You could not have saved your poor mother, and you might have hurt the mare. Here Jack's double guilt flew into his face. He knew that his father was very covetous, and had lived on bad terms with his wife; and also that his own unkindness to her had been forgiven by him out of love to the horse; but to break to him how he had lost that horse through his own folly and want of feeling, was more than Jack had courage to do. The old man, however, soon got at the truth, and no words can describe his fury. Forgetting that his wife lay dead above stairs, he abused his son in a way not fit to be repeated; and though his covetousness had just before found an excuse for a favourite son neglecting to visit a dying parent, yet he now vented his rage against Jack as an unnatural brute, whom he would cut of with a shilling, and bade him never see his face again.

Jack was not allowed to attend his mother's funeral, which was a real grief to him; nor would his father advance even the little money which was needful to redeem his things at the Star. He had now no fond mother to assist him, and he set out on his return home on his borrowed hack, full of grief. He had the added mortification of knowing, that he had also lost by his folly a little hoard of money which his mother had saved up for him.

When Brown got back to his own town he found that the story of Smiler and the Andrew had

had got thither before him, and it was thought a very good joke at the Greyhound. He soon recovered his spirits as far as related to the horse, but as to his behaviour to his dying mother it troubled him at times to the last day of his life, though he did all he could to forget it. He did not however go on at all better, nor did he engage in one frolick the less for what had passed at the Globe; his *good heart* continually betraying him into acts of levity and vanity.

Jack began at length to feel the reverse of that proverb, Keep your shop and your shop will keep you. He had neglected his customers, and they forsook him. Quarter-day came round; there was much to pay and little to receive. He owed two years rent. He was in arrears to his men for wages. He had a long account with his Currier. It was in vain to apply to his father. He had now no mother. Stock was the only true friend he had in the world, and had helped him out of many petty scrapes, but he knew Stock would advance no money in so hopeless a case. Duns came fast about him. He named a speedy day for payment, but as soon as they were out of the house, and the danger put off to a little distance, he forgot every promise, was as merry as ever, and run the same round of thoughtless gaiety. Whenever he was in trouble Stock did not shun him, because that was the moment he thought to throw in a little good advice. He one day asked him if he always intended to go on in this course? No, said

said he, I am resolved by-and-bye to reform, grow sober, and go to church. Why I am but five and twenty, man, I am stout and healthy, and likely to live long; I can repent, and grow melancholy and good at any time.

Oh Jack, said Stock, don't cheat thyself with that false hope. What thou dost intend to do, do quickly. Did thou never read about the heart growing hardened by long indulgence in sin? Some folk, who pretend to mean well, show that they mean nothing at all, by never beginning to put their good resolutions into practice; which made a wise man once say, that hell is paved with good intentions. We cannot repent when we please. It is the goodness of God which leadeth us to repentance.

Michaelmas-day was at hand. The Landlord declared he would be put off no longer, but would seize for rent if it was not paid him on that day, as well as for a considerable sum due to him for leather. Brown now began to be frightened. He applied to Stock to be bound for him. This Stock flatly refused. Brown now began to dread the horrors of a jail, and really seemed so very contrite, and made so many vows and promises of amendment, that at length Stock was prevailed on, together with two or three of Brown's other friends, to advance each a small sum of money to quiet the Landlord, Brown promising to make over to them every part of his stock, and to be guided in future by their advice, declaring that he would turn over a new leaf,

leaf, and follow Mr. Stock's example, as well as his direction in every thing.

Stock's good-nature was at last wrought upon, and he raised the money. The truth is, he did not know the worst, nor how deeply Brown was involved; Brown joyfully set out on the very quarter-day to a town at some distance to carry his Landlord the money, raised by the imprudent kindness of his friend. At his departure Stock put him in mind of the old story of *Smiler* and the *Merry Andrew*, and he promised of his own head that he would not even call at a public house till he had paid the money.

He was as good as his word. He very triumphantly passed by several. He stopped a little under the window of one where the sounds of merriment and loud laughter caught his ear. At another he heard the enticing notes of a fiddle and the light heels of the merry dancers. Here his heart had well-nigh failed him, but the dread of a jail on the one hand, and what he feared almost as much, Mr. Stock's anger on the other, spurred him on; and he valued himself not a little at having got the better of this temptation. He felt quite happy when he found he had reached the door of his landlord without having yielded to one idle inclination.

He knocked at the door. The maid who opened it said her master was not at home. I am sorry for it, said he, strutting about, and with a boasting air he took out his money. I want to pay him my rent: he need not have been afraid of of me. The servant, who knew her master was very much afraid of him, desired him to walk in, for her master would be at home in half an hour. I will call again, said he; but no, let him call on me, and the sooner the better: I shall be at the Blue Posts. While he had been talking he took care to open his black leather case, and to display the Bank Bills to the servant, and then, in a swaggering way, he put up his money and marched off to the Blue Posts.

He was by this time quite proud of his own resolution, and having tendered the money, and being clear in his own mind that it was the landlord's own fault and not his, that it was not paid, he went to refresh himself at the Blue Posts. In a barn belonging to this public house some strollers were just going to perform some of that sing-song ribaldry by which our villages are corrupted, the laws broken, and that money is drawn from the poor for pleasure, which is wanted by their families for bread. The name of the last new song which made part of the entertainment, made him think himself in high luck, that he should have just that half hour to spare. He went into the barn, but was too much delighted with the actor, who sung his favourite song, to remain a quiet hearer. He leaped out of the pit, and got behind the two ragged blankets which served for a curtain. He sung so much better than the actors themselves, that they praised and admired him to a degree which awakened all his vanity. He was so intoxicated with their flattery,

flattery, that he could do no less than invite them all to supper, an invitation which they were too hungry not to accept.

He did not however quite forget his appointment with his landlord; but the half hour was long since past by. And so, says he, as I know he is a mean curmudgeon, who goes to bed I suppose by day light to save candle, it will be too late to speak with him to-night; besides, let him call upon me; it is his business and not mine. I left word where I was to be found, the money is ready, and if I don't pay him to-night, I can do it before breakfast.

By the time these firm resolutions were made, supper was ready. There never was a more jolly evening. Ale and punch were as plenty as water. The actors saw what a vain fellow was feasting them; and as they wanted victuals, and he wanted flattery, the business was soon settled. They ate, and Brown sung. They pretended to be in raptures. Singing promoted drinking, and every fresh glass produced a song, or a story still more merry than the former. Before morning those who were engaged to act in another barn a dozen miles off, stole away quietly. Brown having dropt asleep they left him to finish his nap by himself: as to him his dreams were gay and pleasant, and the house being quite still, he slept comfortably till morning.

As soon as he had breakfasted, the business of the night before popped into his head. He set off once more to his landlord's in high spirits,

gaily

gaily singing by the way scraps of all the tunes he had picked up the night before from his new friends. The landlord opened the door himself, and reproached him with no small surliness for not having kept his word with him the evening before, adding, that he supposed he was come now with some more of his shallow excuses. Brown put on all that haughtiness which is common to people who are generally apt to be in the wrong, when they catch themselves doing a right action; and he looked big, as some sort of people do, when they have money to pay. You need not have been so anxious about your money, said he, I was not going to break or run away. The landlord knew this was the common language of those who are ready to do both. Brown haughtily added, You shall see I am a man of my word; give me a receipt. The landlord had it ready and gave it him.

Brown put his hand in his pocket for his black leather case in which the bills were; he felt, he searched, he examined, first one pocket, then the other, then both waistcoat pockets, but no leather case could he find. He looked terrified. It was the face of real terror, but the landlord conceived it to be that of guilt, and abused him heartily for putting his old tricks upon him; he swore he would not be imposed upon any longer, the money or a jail, there lay his choice.

Brown protested for once with great truth, that he had no intention to deceive; declared that he had actually brought the money, and knew not what

what was become of it, but the thing was far too unlikely to gain credit. Brown now called to mind that he had fallen asleep on the settle in the room where they had supped. This raised his spirits; for he had no doubt but the case had fallen out of his pocket; he said he would step to the public house and search for it, and would be back directly. Not one word of all this did the landlord believe, so inconvenient is it to have a bad character. He swore Brown should not stir out of his house without a constable, and made him wait while he sent for one. Brown, guarded by the constable, went back to the Blue Posts, the landlord charging the officer not to lose sight of the culprit. The caution was needless, Brown had not the least design of running away, so firmly persuaded was he that he should find his leather case.

But who can paint his dismay, when no tale or tidings of the leather case could be had! The master, the mistress, the boy, and the maid of the public house all protested they were innocent. His suspicions soon fell on the strollers with whom he had passed the night; and he now found out, for the first time, that a merry evening did not always produce a happy morning. He obtained a warrant, and proper officers were sent in pursuit of the strollers. No one however believed he had really lost any thing; and as he had not a shilling left to defray the expensive treat he had given, the master of the inn agreed with the other landlord in thinking this story was a trick to de-
fraud

fraud them both, and Brown remained in close custody. At length the officers returned, who said they had been obliged to let the strollers go, as they could not fix the charge on any one, and they had all offered to swear before a justice that they had seen nothing of the leather case. It was at length agreed that as he had passed the evening in a crowded barn, he had probably been robbed there, if at all; and among so many, who could pretend to guess at the thief?

Brown raved like a madman, he cried, tore his hair, and said he was ruined for ever. The abusive language of his old landlord, and his new creditor at the Blue Posts, did not lighten his sorrow. His landlord would be put off no longer. Brown declared he could neither find bail nor raise another shilling, and as soon as the forms of law were made out, he was sent to the county jail.

Here it might have been expected that hard living and much leisure would have brought him to reflect a little on his past follies. But his heart was not truly touched. The chief thing which grieved him at first was, his having abused the kindness of Stock, for to him he should appear guilty of a real fraud, where he had indeed been only vain, idle, and imprudent. And it is worth while here to remark, that vanity, idleness, and imprudence, often bring a man to ruin both soul and body, though silly people do not put them in the catalogue of heavy sins, and those who indulge in them are often reckoned honeſt merry fellows, with *good hearts.*

I wiſh I had room to tell my readers what befel Jack in his preſent doleful habitation, and what became of him afterwards. I promiſe them, however, that they ſhall certainly know the firſt of next month, when I hope they will not forget to inquire for the Fourth Part of the Shoemakers, or Jack Brown in priſon.

Z.

PART IV.

JACK BROWN IN PRISON.

I HOPE the reader has not forgotten where the third part of this hiſtory left off laſt month. It finiſhed with an account how Jack Brown, by keeping idle company, when he ſhould have been paying his debts, was robbed of his pocket-book while he was aſleep on the ſettle at the Blue Poſts. It was alſo told how the landlord not believing one word of his ſtory, ſent him to priſon for debts long due to him.

Brown was no ſooner lodged in his doleful habitation, and a little recovered from his firſt ſurpriſe, than he ſat down and wrote his friend Stock the whole hiſtory of the tranſaction. Mr. Stock, who had long known the exceeding lightneſs and diſſipation of his mind, did not ſo utterly
diſbelieve

disbelieve the story as all the other creditors did. To speak the truth, Stock was the only one among them who had good sense enough to know, that a man may be completely ruined, both in what relates to his property and his soul, without committing Old Bailey crimes. He well knew that idleness, vanity, and the love of *pleasure*, as it is falsely called, will bring a man to a morsel of bread, as surely as those things which are reckoned much greater sins; and that they undermine his principles as certainly, though not perhaps quite so fast.

Stock was too angry with what had happened to answer Brown's letter, or to seem to take the least notice of him. However, he kindly and secretly undertook a journey to the hard-hearted old Farmer, Brown's father, to intercede with him, and to see if he would do any thing for his son. Stock did not pretend to excuse Jack, or even to lessen his offences; for it was a rule of his never to disguise truth or to palliate wickedness. Sin was still sin in his eyes, though it were committed by his best friend; but though he would not soften the sin he felt tenderly for the sinner. He pleaded with the old Farmer on the ground, that his son's idleness and other vices would gather fresh strength in a jail. He told him, that the loose and worthless company which he would there keep would harden him in vice, and if he was now wicked he might there become irreclaimable.

But all his pleas were urged in vain. The Farmer was not to be moved. Indeed he argued with some justice, that he ought not to make his industrious children beggars to save one rogue from the gallows. Mr. Stock allowed the force of his reasoning, though he saw the father was less influenced by this principle of justice than by resentment on account of the old story of Smiler. People, indeed, should take care that what appears in their conduct to proceed from justice does not really proceed from revenge. Wiser men than Farmer Brown often deceive themselves, and fancy they act on better principles than they really do, for want of looking a little more closely into their own hearts, and putting down every action to its true motive. When we are praying against deceit we should not forget to take self-deceit into the account.

Mr. Stock at length wrote to poor Jack; not to offer him any help, that was quite out of the question, but to exhort him to repent of his evil ways; to lay before him the sins of his past life, and to advise him to convert the present punishment into a benefit, by humbling himself before God. He offered his interest to get his place of confinement exchanged for one of those improved prisons, where solitude and labour have been made the happy instruments of bringing many to a better way of thinking, and ended by saying, that if he ever gave any solid signs of real amendment he would still be his friend in spite of all that was past.

If

If Mr. Stock had sent him a good sum of money to procure his liberty, or even a trifle to make merry with his wretched companions, Jack would have thought him a friend indeed. But to send him nothing but dry advice, and a few words of empty comfort, was, he thought, but a cheap shabby way of shewing his kindness. Unluckily the letter came just as he was going to sit down to one of those direful merry-makings which are often carried on with brutal riot within the doleful walls of a jail on the entrance of a new prisoner, who is often expected to give a feast to the rest.

When his companions were heated with gin, Now, said Jack, I'll treat you with a sermon, and a very pretty preachment it is. So saying he took out Mr. Stock's kind and pious letter, and was delighted at the bursts of laughter it produced. What a canting dog, said one! Repentance, indeed! cried Tom Crew; No, no, Jack, tell this hypocritical rogue that if we have lost our liberty, it is only for having been jolly, hearty fellows, and we have more spirit than to repent of that I hope: all the harm we have done is living a little too fast, like honest bucks as we are. Aye, aye, said Jolly George, had we been such sneaking miserly fellows as Stock, we need not have come hither. But if the ill-nature of the laws has been so cruel as to clap up such fine hearty blades, we are no *felons* however. We are afraid of no Jack Ketch; and I see no cause to repent of any sin that's not hanging matter. As to those who are thrust into the condemned hole indeed, and have but a few hours to live, they *must* see the parson, and hear a sermon, and such stuff. But I do not know what such stout young fellows as we are have to do with repentance. And so, Jack, let us have that rare new catch which you learnt of the strollers that merry night when you lost your pocket-book.

Brown soon gave a fresh proof of the power of evil company, and of the quick progress of the heart of a sinner from bad to worse. Brown, who always wanted principle, soon grew to want feeling also. He joined in the laugh which was raised against Stock, and told many *good stories*, as they were called, in derision of the piety, sobriety, and self-denial of his old friend. He lost every day somewhat of those small remains of shame and decency which he had brought with him to the prison. He even grew reconciled to this wretched way of life, and the want of money seemed to him the heaviest evil in the life of a jail.

Mr. Stock finding, from the gaoler, that his letter had been treated with ridicule, would not write to him any more. He did not come to see him nor send him any assistance, thinking it right to let him suffer that want which his vices had brought upon him. But, as he still hoped that the time might come when he might be brought to a sense of his own evil courses, he continued

to

to have an eye upon him by means of the gaoler, who was an honeſt, kind-hearted man.

Brown ſpent one part of his time in thoughtleſs riot, and the other in gloom and ſadneſs. Company kept up his ſpirits; with his new friends he contrived to drown thought; but when he was alone he began to find that a *merry fellow*, when deprived of his companions and his liquor, is often a moſt forlorn wretch. Then it is, that even a merry fellow ſays of laughter, What is it? and of mirth it is madneſs.

As he contrived, however, to be as little alone as poſſible, his gaiety was commonly uppermoſt, till that loathſome diſtemper, called the Jail Fever, broke out in the priſon. Tom Crew, the ringleader in all their evil practices, was firſt ſeized with it. Jack ſtaid a little while with his comrade to aſſiſt and divert him, but of aſſiſtance he could give little, and the very thought of diverſion was now turned into horror. He ſoon caught the diſtemper, and that in ſo dreadful a degree, that his life was in great danger. Of thoſe who remained in health not a ſoul came near him, though he had ſhared his laſt farthing with them. He had juſt ſenſe enough left to feel this cruelty. Poor fellow! he did not know before that the friendſhip of the worldly is at an end when there is no more drink or diverſion to be had. He lay in the moſt deplorable condition; his body tormented with a dreadful diſeaſe, and his ſoul terrified and amazed at the approach of death: that death which he thought at ſo great a diſtance, a distance, and of which his comrades had assured him, that a young fellow of five and twenty was in no danger. Poor Jack! I cannot help feeling for him. Without a shilling! without a friend! without one comfort respecting this world, and, what is far more terrible, without one hope respecting the next.

Let not the young reader fancy that Brown's misery arose entirely from his altered circumstances. It was not merely his being in want, and sick, and in a prison, which made his condition so desperate. Many an honest man unjustly accused, many a persecuted Saint, many a holy Martyr has enjoyed sometimes more peace and content in a prison, than wicked men have ever tasted in the height of their prosperity. But to any such comforts poor Jack had left himself no right.

A Christian friend generally comes forward at the very time when worldly friends forsake the wretched. The other prisoners would not come near Brown, though he had often entertained and never offended them, even his own father was not moved with his sad condition. When Mr. Stock informed him of it, he answered, 'tis no more than he deserves. As he brews so he must bake. He has made his own bed, and let him lie in it. The hard old man had ever at his tongue's end some proverb of hardness, or frugality, which he contrived to turn in such a way as to excuse himself.

We

We shall now see how Mr. Stock behaved. He had his favourite sayings too, but they were chiefly on the side of kindness, mercy, or some other virtue. I must not, said he, pretend to call myself a Christian, if I do not requite evil with good. When he received the gaoler's letter with the account of Brown's sad condition, Will Simpson and Tommy Williams began to compliment him on his own wisdom and prudence, by which he had escaped Brown's misfortunes. He only gravely said, Blessed be GOD that I am not in the same misery. It is *He* who has made us to differ. But for *his* grace I might have been in no better condition. Now Brown is brought low by the hand of GOD, it is my time to go to him. What you, said Will, whom he cheated of your money? This is not a time to remember injuries, said Mr. Stock. How can I ask forgiveness for my own sins, if I withhold forgiveness from him? So saying, he ordered his horse, and set off to see poor Brown, thus proving that his was a religion not of words but of deeds.

Stock's heart nearly failed him as he passed through the prison. The groans of the sick and dying, and what to such a heart as his was still more moving, the brutal merriment of the healthy in such a place pierced his very soul. Many a silent prayer did he put up as he passed along, that GOD would yet be pleased to touch their hearts, and that now (during this infectious sickness) might be the accepted time. The gaoler observed him drop a tear, and asked the cause.

cause. I cannot forget, said he, that the most diffolute of these men is still my fellow-creature. The same GOD made them; the same SAVIOUR died for them; how then can I hate the worst of them? With my advantages they might have been much better than I am; without the blessing of GOD on my good Minister's instructions, I might have been worse than the worst of these. I have no cause for pride, much for thankfulness; *let us not be high-minded, but fear.*

It would have moved a heart of stone to have seen poor miserable Jack Brown lying on his wretched bed, his face so changed by pain, poverty, dirt and sorrow, that he could hardly be known for that merry soul of a jack boot, as he used to be proud to hear himself called. His groans were so piteous that it made Mr. Stock's heart ach. He kindly took him by the hand, though he knew the distemper was catching. How dost do Jack? said he, dost know me? Brown shook his head and said faintly, know you? aye, that I do. I am sure I have but one friend in the world who would come to see me in this woeful condition. O James! what have I brought myself to? What will become of my poor soul? I dare not look back, for that is all sin, nor forward, for that is all misery and woe.

Mr. Stock spoke kindly to him, but did not attempt to cheer him with false comfort, as is too often done. I am ashamed to see you in this dirty place, says Brown. As to the place Jack, replied the other, if it has helped to bring you
to

to a sense of your past offences, it will be no bad place for you. I am heartily sorry for your distress and your sickness; but if it should please GOD by them to open your eyes, and to shew you that sin is a greater evil than the prison to which it has brought you, all may yet be well. I had rather see you in this humble penitent state, lying on this dirty bed, in this dismal prison, than roaring and rioting at the Greyhound, the king of the company, with handsome cloaths on your back, and plenty of money in your pocket.

Brown wept bitterly and squeezed his hand, but was too weak to say much. Mr. Stock then desired the gaoler to let him have such things as were needful, and he would pay for them. He would not leave the poor fellow till he had given him with his own hands some broth which the gaoler had got ready for him, and some medicines which the doctor had sent. All this kindness cut Brown to the heart. He was just able to sob out my unnatural father leaves me to perish, and my injured friend is more than a father to me. Stock told him that one proof he must give of his repentance was, that he must forgive his father, whose provocation had been very great. He then said he would leave him for the present to take some rest, and desired him to lift up his heart to GOD for mercy. Dear James, replied Brown, do you pray for me. GOD perhaps may hear you, but he will never hear the prayer of such a sinner as I have been. Take care how you think so, said Stock. To believe

believe that GOD cannot forgive you would be still a greater sin than any you have yet committed against him. He then explained to him in a few words, as well as he was able, the nature of repentance, and forgiveness through a Saviour, and warned him earnestly against unbelief and hardness of heart.

Poor Jack grew much refreshed in body with the comfortable things he had taken; and a little cheered with Stock's kindness in coming so far to see, and to forgive such a forlorn outcast, sick of an infectious distemper, and locked within the walls of a prison. Surely, said he to himself, there must be some mighty power in a religion which can lead men to do such things! things so much against the grain as to forgive such an injury, and to risk catching such a distemper, but he was so weak he could not express this in words. He tried to pray, but he could not; at length, overpowered with weariness, he fell asleep.

When Mr. Stock came back, he was surprised to find him so much better in body; but his agonies of mind were dreadful, and he had now got strength to express part of the horrors which he felt. James, said he, (looking wildly) it is all over with me. I am a lost creature. Even your prayers cannot save me. Dear Jack, replied Mr. Stock, I am no minister; it does not become me to talk much to thee: but I know I may venture to say whatever is in the Bible. As ignorant as I am I shall be safe
enough

enough while I stick to that. Aye, said the sick man, you used to be ready enough to read to me, and I would not listen, or if I did it was only to make fun of what I heard, and now you will not so much as read a bit of a chapter to me.

This was the very point to which Stock longed to bring him. So he took a little Bible out of his pocket, which he always carried with him on a journey, and read slowly verse by verse, the 55th chapter of Isaiah. When he came to the sixth and seventh verses, poor Jack cried so much that Stock was forced to stop. The words were, " Let the wicked man forsake his way, and the unrighteous man his thoughts, and let him return unto the Lord." Here Brown stopped him, saying, Oh it is too late, too late for me. Let me finish the verse, said Stock, and you will see your error; you will see that it is never too late. So he read on—" let him return unto the Lord, and he will have mercy upon him, and to our God, and he will abundantly pardon." Here Brown started up, snatched the book out of his hand and cried out, Is that really there? No, no; that's of your own putting in, in order to comfort me; let me look at the words myself. No, indeed, said Stock, I would not for the world give you unfounded comfort, or put off any notion of my own for a scripture doctrine. But is it possible! cried the sick man, that God may really pardon me? Do'st think he can? Do'st think he will? I am sure of it, said Stock; I dare not give thee false hopes, or, indeed, any hopes of my own. But these are God's own words, and the only difficulty is to know when we are really brought into such a state as that the words may be applied to us.

Mr. Stock was afraid of saying more. He would not venture out of his depth; nor, indeed, was poor Brown able to bear more discourse just now. So he made him a present of the Bible, folding down such places as he thought might be best suited to his state, and took his leave, being obliged to return home that night. He left a little money with the gaoler, to add a few comforts to the allowance of the prison, and promised to return in a short time.

When he got home, he described the sufferings and misery of Brown in a very moving manner; but Tommy Williams, instead of being properly affected at it, only said, Indeed, Master, I am not very sorry; he is rightly served. How, Tommy, said Mr. Stock, (rather sternly), not sorry to see a fellow-creature brought to the lowest state of misery? one too whom you have known so prosperous? No, Master, I can't say I am; for Mr. Brown used to make fun of you, and laugh at you for being so godly, and reading your Bible.

Let me say a few words to you Tommy, said Mr. Stock. In the first place you should never watch for the time of a man's being brought low by trouble to tell of his faults. Next, you should

never

never rejoice at his trouble, but pity him, and pray for him. Laſtly, as to his ridiculing me for my religion, if I cannot ſtand an idle jeſt, I am not worthy the name of a Chriſtian.—*He that is aſhamed of me and my word,* do'ſt remember what follows, Tommy? Yes, Maſter, 'twas laſt Sunday's text,—*of him ſhall the Son of Man be aſhamed when he ſhall judge the world.*

Mr. Stock ſoon went back to the priſon. But he did not go alone. He took with him Mr. Thomas, the worthy Miniſter who had been the guide and inſtructor of his youth, who was ſo kind as to go at his requeſt and viſit this forlorn priſoner. When they got to Brown's door, they found him ſitting up in his bed with the Bible in his hand. This was a joyful ſight to Mr. Stock, who ſecretly thanked God for it. Brown was reading aloud; they liſtened; it was the fifteenth of Saint Luke. The circumſtances of this beautiful Parable of the Prodigal Son were ſo much like his own, that the ſtory pierced him to the ſoul; and he ſtopped every minute to compare his own caſe with that of the Prodigal. He was juſt got to the eighteenth verſe, *I will ariſe and go to my father,*—at that moment he ſpied his two friends; joy darted into his eyes. O dear Jem, ſaid he, it is *not* too late, I will ariſe and go to my father, my heavenly Father, and you, Sir, will ſhew me the way, won't you? ſaid he to Mr. Thomas, whom he recollected. I am very glad to ſee you in ſo hopeful a diſpoſition, ſaid the good Miniſter. O, Sir, ſaid Brown, what a place

place is this to receive you in! O, see to what I have brought myself!

Your condition, as to this world, is indeed very low, replied the good Divine. But what are mines, dungeons, or gallies, to that eternal hopeless prison to which your unrepented sins must soon have consigned you. Even in this gloomy prison, on this bed of straw, worn down by pain, poverty, and want, forsaken by your worldly friends, an object of scorn to those with whom you used to carouse and riot; yet here, I say, brought thus low, if you have at last found out your own vileness, and your utterly undone state by sin, you may still be more an object of favour in the sight of God, than when you thought yourself prosperous and happy; when the world smiled upon you, and you passed your days and nights in envied gaiety and unchristian riot. If you will but improve the present awful visitation; if you do but heartily renounce and abhor your present evil courses; if you even now turn to the Lord your Saviour with lively faith, deep repentance, and unfeigned obedience, I shall still have more hope of you than of many who are going on quite happy, because quite insensible. The heavy laden sinner, who has discovered the iniquity of his own heart, and his utter inability to help himself, may be restored to God's favour, and become happy, though in a dungeon. And be assured, that he who from deep and humble contrition dares not so much as lift up his eyes to heaven, when with a hearty faith he sighs out,
Lord

Lord be merciful to me a sinner, shall in no wise be cast out. These are the words of him who cannot lie.

It is impossible to describe the self-abasement, the grief, the joy, the shame, the hope, and the fear which filled the mind of this poor man. A dawn of comfort at length shone on his benighted mind. His humility and fear of falling back into his former sins, if he should ever recover, Mr. Thomas thought were strong symptoms of a sound repentance. He improved and cherished every good disposition he saw arising in his heart, and particularly warned him against self deceit, self-confidence, and hypocrisy.

One day, when Mr. Thomas and Mr. Stock came to see him, they found him more than commonly affected. His face was more ghastly pale than usual, and his eyes were red with crying. Oh, Sir, said he, what a sight have I just seen! Jolly George, as we used to call him, the ring-leader of all our mirth, who was at the bottom of all the fun, and tricks, and wickedness, that are carried on within these walls, Jolly George is just dead of the jail-distemper! He taken, and I left! I *would* be carried into his room to speak to him, to beg him to take warning by me, and that I might take warning by him. But what did I see! what did I hear! not one sign of repentance; not one dawn of hope. Agony of body, blasphemies on his tongue, despair in his soul; while I am spared and comforted with hopes of mercy and acceptance. Oh, if if all my old friends at the Greyhound could but then have seen Jolly George! A hundred sermons about death, Sir, don't speak so home, and cut so deep, as the sight of one dying sinner.

Brown grew gradually better in his health, that is, the fever mended, but the distemper settled in his limbs, so that he seemed likely to be a poor, weakly cripple the rest of his life. But as he spent much of his time in prayer, and in reading such parts of the Bible as Mr. Thomas directed, he improved every day in knowledge and piety, and of course grew more resigned to pain and infirmity.

Some months after this, his hard-hearted father, who had never been prevailed upon to fee him, or offer him the least relief, was taken off suddenly by a fit of apoplexy; and, after all his threatenings, he died without a will. He was one of those silly, superstitious men, who fancy they shall die the sooner for having made one; and who love the world and the things that are in the world so dearly, that they dread to set about any business which may put them in mind that they are not always to live in it. As, by this neglect, his father had not fulfilled his threat of cutting him off with a shilling, Jack, of course, went shares with his brothers in what their father left. What fell to him proved to be just enough, to discharge him from prison, and to pay all his debts, but he had nothing left. His joy at being thus enabled to make restitution was so great, that he thought little of his own wants. He did not defire to conceal the moſt trifling debt, nor to keep a ſhilling for himſelf.

Mr. Stock undertook to ſettle all his affairs. There did not remain money enough, after every creditor was ſatisfied, even to pay for his removal home. Mr. Stock kindly ſent his own cart for him with a bed in it, made as comfortable as poſſible, for he was too weak and lame to be removed any other way, and Mr. Stock gave the driver a particular charge to be tender and careful of him, and not to drive hard, nor to leave the cart a moment.

Mr. Stock would fain have taken him into his own houſe, at leaſt for a time, ſo convinced was he of his ſincere reformation both of heart and life; but Brown would not be prevailed on to be further burdenſome to this generous friend. He inſiſted on being carried to the pariſh workhouſe, which he ſaid was a far better place than he deſerved. In this houſe Mr. Stock furniſhed a ſmall room for him, and ſent him every day a morſel of meat from his own dinner. Tommy Williams begged that he might always be allowed to carry it, as ſome atonement for his having for a moment ſo far forgotten his duty, as rather to rejoice than ſympathize in Brown's misfortunes. He never thought of this fault without ſorrow, and often thanked his maſter for the wholeſome leſſon he then gave him, and he was the better for it all his life.

Mrs. Stock often carried poor Brown a bit of tea or a baſon of good broth herſelf. He was
quite

quite a cripple, and never able to walk out as long as he lived. Mr. Stock, Will Simpson, and Tommy Williams laid their heads together, and contrived a sort of barrow on which he was often carried to Church by some of his poor neighbours, of which Tommy was always one; and he requited their kindness, by reading a good book to them whenever they would call in, or teaching their children to sing Psalms or say the Catechism.

It was no small joy to him thus to be enabled to go to church. Whenever he was carried by the Greyhound, he was much moved, and used to put up a prayer full of repentance for the past, and praise for the present. Z.

THE PRODIGAL SON.

This Hymn was frequently sung by Jack Brown in the Workhouse.

BEHOLD the wretch whose lust and wine
    Have wasted his estate;
He begs a share among the swine,
    To taste the husks they eat.

I die with hunger here he cries,
    I starve in foreign lands;
My father's house has large supplies,
    And bounteous are his hands.

I'll go, and with a mournful tongue
 Fall down before his face,
Father I've done thy juſtice wrong,
 Nor can deſerve thy grace.

He ſaid, and haſten'd to his home,
 To ſeek his father's love;
The father ſaw the rebel come,
 And all his bowels move.

He ran, and fell upon his neck,
 Embrac'd and kiſs'd his ſon;
The rebel's heart with ſorrow breaks
 For ſins which he had done.

Take off his cloaths of ſhame and ſin,
 (The father gives command,)
Dreſs him in garments white and clean,
 With rings adorn his hand.

A day of feaſting I ordain,
 Let mirth and joy abound,
My ſon was dead and lives again,
 Was loſt and now is found.

PART V.

A Dialogue between James Stock and Will Simpſon, the Shoemakers, as they ſat at Work.

JAMES STOCK, and his journeyman Will Simpſon, as I informed my Readers in the Second Part of the Two Shoemakers, had re-
 ſolved

solved to work together one hour every evening, in order to pay for Tommy Williams's schooling. This circumstance brought them to be a good deal together when the rest of the men were gone home. Now it happened that Mr. Stock had a mighty way of endeavouring to turn all common events to some use; and he thought it right on the present occasion to make the only return in his power to Will Simpson for his great kindness. For, said he, if Will gives up so much of his time to help me to provide for this poor boy, it is the least I can do to try to turn part of that time to the purpose of promoting Will's spiritual good. Now as the bent of Stock's own mind was religious, it was easy to him to lead their talk to something profitable. He always took especial care however, that the subject should be introduced properly, chearfully, and without constraint. As he well knew that great good may be sometimes done by a prudent attention in seizing proper opportunities, so he knew that the cause of piety had been sometimes hurt by forcing serious subjects where there was clearly no disposition to receive them. I say he had found out that two things were necessary to the promoting of religion among his friends; a warm zeal to be always on the watch for occasions, and a cool judgment to distinguish which was the right time and place to make use of them. To know *how* to do good is a great matter, but to know *when* to do it is no small one.

Simpson

Simpson was an honest good-natured fellow; he was now become sober, and rather religiously disposed. But he was ignorant, he did not know much of the grounds of religion, or of the corruption of his own nature; he was regular at church, but was first drawn thither rather by his skill in psalm-singing than by any great devotion. He had left off going to the Greyhound, and often read the Bible, or some other good book on the Sunday evening. This he thought was quite enough; he thought the Bible was the prettiest history book in the world, and that religion was a very good thing for Sundays. But he did not much understand what business people had with it on working days. He had left off drinking because it had brought Williams to the grave, and his wife to dirt and rags; but not because he himself had seen the evil of sin. He now considered swearing and sabbath-breaking as scandalous and indecent, but he had not found out that both were to be left off because they are highly offensive to God, and grieve his Holy Spirit. As Simpson was less self-conceited than most ignorant people are, Stock had always a good hope that when he should come to be better acquainted with the word of God, and with the evil of his own heart, he would become one day a good Christian. The great hindrance to this was, that he fancied himself so already.

One evening Simpson had been calling to Stock's mind how disorderly the house and shop, where they

they were now sitting quietly at work, had formerly been, and he went on thus:

Will. How comfortably we live now, master, to what we used to do in Williams's time! I used then never to be happy but when we were keeping it up all night, but now I am as merry as the day is long. I find I am twice as happy since I am grown good and sober.

Stock. I am glad you are happy, Will, and I rejoice that you are sober; but I would not have you take too much pride in your own *goodness* for fear it should become a sin, almost as great as some of those you have left off. Besides, I would not have you make quite so sure that you *are* good.

Will. Not good, master! why don't you find me regular and orderly at work?

Stock. Very much so, and accordingly I have a great respect for you.

Will. I pay every one his own, seldom miss church, have not been drunk since Williams died, have handsome cloaths for Sundays, and save a trifle every week.

Stock. Very true, and very laudable it is; and to all this you may add that you very generously work an hour, for poor Tommy's education, every evening without fee or reward.

Will. Well, master, what can a man do more? If all this is not being good, I don't know what is.

Stock. All these things are very right as far as they go, and you could not well be a Christian without doing them. But I shall make you stare

stare perhaps when I tell you, you may do all these things, and many more, and yet be no Christian.

Will. No Christian! surely, master, I do hope that after all I have done, you will not be so unkind as to say I am no Christian.

Stock. God forbid that I should say so, Will. I hope better things of you. But come now, what do you think it is to be a Christian?

Will. What! why to be christened when one is a child, to learn the Catechism when one can read, to be confirmed when one is a youth, and to go to Church when one is a man.

Stock. These are all very proper things, and quite necessary. They make a part of a Christian's life. But for all that, a man may be exact in them all, and yet not be a Christian.

Will. Not be a Christian! ha! ha! ha! you are very comical, master.

Stock. No indeed, I am very serious, Will. At this rate it would be a very easy thing to be a Christian, and every man who went through certain forms would be a good man; and one man who observed these forms would be as good as another. Whereas, if we come to examine ourselves by the word of God, I am afraid there are but few comparatively whom our Saviour would allow to be real Christians. What is your notion of a Christian's practice?

Will. Why, he must not rob nor murder, nor get drunk. He must avoid scandalous things, and do as other decent orderly people do.

Stock.

Stock. It is easy enough to be what the world calls a Christian, but not to be what the Bible calls so.

Will. Why, master, we working men are not expected to be saints, and martyrs, and apostles, and ministers.

Stock. We are not. And yet, Will, there are not two sorts of Christianity; we are called to practise the same Religion which they practised, and something of the same spirit is expected in us which we reverence in them. It was not saints and martyrs only to whom our Saviour said that they must " crucify the world with its affections and lusts." We are called to " be holy" in our measure and degree, " as he who hath called us is holy." It was not only saints and martyrs who were told that they must be " like-minded with Christ"—That " they must do all to the glory of God"—That they must renounce the spirit of the world, and deny themselves." It was not to apostles only that Christ said, " they must have their conversation in Heaven." It was not to a few holy men set apart for the altar, that he said, " they must set their affections on things above"—That they " must not be conformed to the world."—No, it was to Fishermen, to Publicans, to Farmers, to Day-labourers, to poor Tradesmen, that he spoke when he told them, they must " love not the world, nor the things of the world"—" That they must renounce the hidden things of dishonesty, grow in grace, lay up for themselves treasures in Heaven."

Will.

Will. All this might be very proper for *them* to be taught, because they had not been bred up Christians, but Heathens or Jews: and Christ wanted to make them his followers, that is, Christians. But thank God we do not want to be taught all this, for we *are* Christians, born in a Christian country, of Christian parents.

Stock. I suppose then you fancy that Christianity comes to people in a Christian country by nature?

Will. I think it comes by a good education or a good example. When a fellow whoh as got any sense sees a man cut off in his prime by drinking, I think he will begin to leave it off. When he sees another man respected, like you, master, for honesty and sobriety, and going to Church, why he will grow honest and sober and go to Church; that is, he will see it is his advantage to be a Christian.

Stock. Will, what you say is the truth, but 'tis not the whole truth. You are right as far as you go, but you do not go far enough. The worldly advantages of piety, are, as you suppose, in general great. Credit, prosperity, and health, almost naturally attend on a religious life, both because a religious life supposes a sober and industrious life; and because a man who lives in a course of duty puts himself in the way of God's blessing. But a true Christian has a still higher aim in view, and will follow Religion even under circumstances, when it may hurt his credit and ruin his prosperity, if it should ever happen to be the will of God that he should be brought into such a trying state.

Will. Well, master, to speak the truth, if I go to Church on Sundays, and follow my work in the week, I must say I think that is being good.

Stock. I agree with you, that he who does both gives the best outward signs that he is good as you call it. But our going to Church, and even reading the Bible, are no proofs that we are as good as we need be, but rather that we do both these in order to make us better than we are. We do both on Sundays, as means, by God's blessing, to make us better all the week. We are to bring the fruits of that Chapter or of that Sermon into our daily life, and try to get our inmost heart and secret thoughts, as well as our daily conduct, amended by them.

Will. Why, sure master, you won't be so unreasonable as to want a body to be religious always? I can't do that neither. I'm not such a hypocrite as to pretend to it.

Stock. Yes, you can be so in every action of your life!

Will. What, master, always to be thinking about Religion?

Stock. No, far from it Will; much less to be always talking about it. But you must be always be acting under it's power and spirit.

Will. But surely 'tis pretty well if I do this when I go to Church; or while I am saying my prayers. Even you, master, as strict as you are,
would

would not have me always on my knees, nor always at church, I suppose: for then how would your work be carried on, and how would our town be supplied with shoes?

Stock. Very true, Will. 'Twould be no proof of our religion to let our customers go barefoot; but 'twould be a proof of our laziness, and we should starve as we ought to do. The business of the world must not only be carried on, but carried on with spirit and activity. We have the same authority for not being slothful in business as we have for being fervent in spirit. Religion has put godliness and laziness as wide asunder as any two things in the world; and what God has separated, let no man pretend to join. Indeed, the spirit of religion can have no fellowship with sloth, indolence, and self-indulgence. But still, a christian does not carry on his common trade quite like another man neither; for something of the spirit which he labours to attain at church, he carries with him into his worldly concerns. While there are some who set up for Sunday Christians, who have no notion that they are bound to be Weekday Christians too.

Will. Why, master, I do think, if God Almighty is contented with one day in seven, he won't thank you for throwing him the other six into the bargain. I thought he gave us them for our own use; and I am sure nobody works harder all the week than you do.

Stock. God, it is true, sets apart one day in seven for actual rest from labour, and for more immediate devotion to his service. But shew me that text, wherein he says, thou shalt love the Lord thy God on *Sundays*—Thou shalt keep my commandments on the *Sabbath Day*—To be carnally minded on *Sundays, is death*—Cease to do evil, and learn to do well *one day in seven*—Grow in grace on the *Lord's Day*—Is there any such text?

Will. No, to be sure there is not; for that would be encouraging sin in all the other days.

Stock. Yes, just as you do when you make religion a thing for the church and not for the world. There is no one lawful calling in pursuing which we may not serve God acceptably. You and I may serve him while we are stitching this pair of boots. Farmer Furrow, while he is plowing yonder field. Betsy West, over the way, whilst she is nursing her sick mother. Neighbour Incle, in measuring out his tapes and ribbons. I say, all these may serve God just as acceptably in those employments as at church, I had almost said more so.

Will. Aye, indeed—how can that be? Now your're too much on t'other side.

Stock. Because a man's trials in trade being often greater, they give him fresh means of glorifying God, and proving the sincerity of religion. A man who mixes in business, is naturally brought into continual temptations and difficulties. These will lead him, if he be a good man, to look more to God, than he perhaps would otherwise do. He sees temptations on the right hand

hand and on the left; he knows that there are snares all around him, this makes him watchful: he feels that the enemy within is too ready to betray him, this makes him humble himself; while a sense of his own difficulties makes him tender to the failings of others.

Will. Then you would make one believe, after all, that trade and business must be sinful in itself, since it brings a man into all these snares and scrapes.

Stock. No, no, Will; trade and business don't create evil passions—they were in the heart before—Only now and then they seem to lie snug a little—our concerns with the world bring them out into action a little more, and thus shew both others and ourselves what we really are. But then, as the world offers more trials on the one hand, so on the other it holds out more duties. If we are called to battle oftener, we have more opportunities of victory. Every temptation resisted, is an enemy subdued; and "he that ruleth his own spirit, is better than he that taketh a city."

Will. I don't quite understand you, master.

Stock. I will try to explain myself. There is no passion more called out by the transactions of trade than covetousness. Now, 'tis impossible to withstand such a master sin as that, without carrying a good deal of the spirit of religion into one's trade.

Will. Well, I own I don't yet see how I am to be religious when I'm hard at work, or busy settling an account. I can't do two things at once; 'tis as if I were to pretend to make a shoe and cut out a boot at the same moment.

Stock. I tell you both must subsist together. Nay, the one must be the motive to the other. God commands us to be industrious, and if we love him, the desire of pleasing him should be the main spring of our industry.

Will. I don't see how I can always be thinking about pleasing God.

Stock. Suppose, now, a man had a wife and children whom he loved, and wished to serve, would not he be often thinking about them while he was at work? and though he would not be *always* thinking about them, yet would not the very love he bore them be a constant spur to his industry? He would always be pursuing the same course from the same motive, though his words and even his thoughts must often be taken up in the common transactions of life.

Will. Well, I say first one, then the other; now for labour, now for religion.

Stock. I will shew that both must go together. I will suppose you were going to buy so many skins of our currier—that is quite a worldly transaction—you can't see what a spirit of religion has to do with buying a few calves' skins. Now, I tell you it has a great deal to do with it. Covetousness, a desire to make a good bargain, may rise up in your heart. Selfishness, a spirit of monopoly, a wish to get all, in order to distress others; these are evil desires, and must be subdued.

subdued. Some opportunity of unfair gain offers, in which there may be much sin, and yet little scandal. Here a Christian will stop short; he will recollect, "that he who maketh haste to be rich shall hardly be innocent." Perhaps the sin may be on the side of your dealer—*he* may want to overreach *you*—this is provoking—you are tempted to violent anger, perhaps to swear,—here is a fresh demand on you for a spirit of patience and moderation, as there was before for a spirit of justice and self-denial. If, by God's grace, you get the victory over these temptations, you are the better man for having been called out to them; always provided, that the temptations be not of your own seeking. If you give way, and sink under these temptations, don't go and say that trade and business have made you covetous, passionate, and profane. No, no; depend upon it, you were so before; you would have had all these evil seeds lurking in your heart, if you had been loitering about at home and doing nothing, with the additional sin of idleness into the bargain. When you are busy, the devil often tempts you; when you are idle, you tempt the devil. If business and the world call these evil tempers into action, business and the world call that religion into action too which teaches us to resist them. And in this you see the Week-day fruit of the Sunday's piety. 'Tis trade and business in the week which call us to put our Sunday readings, praying, and church-going into practice.

Will.

Will. Well, master, you have a comical way, some how, of coming over one. I never should have thought there would have been any religion wanted in buying and selling a few calves' skins. But, I begin to see there is a good deal in what you say.—And, whenever I am doing a common action, I will try to remember that it must be done after a godly sort.

Stock. I hear the clock strike nine—let us leave off our work. I will only observe farther, that one good end of our bringing religion into our business is, to put us in mind not to undertake more business than we can carry on consistently with our religion. I shall never commend that man's diligence, though it is often commended by the world, who is not diligent about the salvation of his soul. We are as much forbidden to be overcharged with the *cares* of life as with it's *pleasures.* I only wish to prove to you, that a discreet Christian may be wise for both worlds; that he may employ his hands without entangling his soul, and labour for the meat that perisheth without neglecting that which endureth unto eternal life; that he may be prudent for time, while he is wise for eternity.

Z.

THE HYMN.

O THAT the Lord wou'd guide my ways,
   To keep his statutes still!
O that my God wou'd give me grace
   To know and do his will!

Lord,

Lord, send thy spirit down to write
    Thy love upon my heart,
Nor let my tongue indulge deceit,
    Nor act a liar's part.

From vanity, Lord, turn mine eyes,
    Let no corrupt design,
No covetous desires arise
    Within this soul of mine.

Order my footsteps by thy word,
    And make my heart sincere;
Let sin have no dominion, Lord,
    But keep my conscience clear.

My soul hath gone too far astray,
    My feet too often slip;
I wou'd not, Lord, forget thy way,
    Bring back thy wand'ring sheep.

Make me to walk in thy commands,
    'Tis a delightful road;
Nor let my head, or heart, or hands,
    Offend against my God.

THE TWO WEALTHY FARMERS,

OR, THE HISTORY OF

Mr. BRAGWELL.

MR. Bragwell and Mr. Worthy happened to meet laſt year at Weyhill-Fair. They were glad to ſee each other as they had but ſeldom met of late; Mr. Bragwell having removed ſome years before from Mr. Worthy's neighbourhood, to a diſtant village where he had bought an eſtate.

Mr.

Mr. Bragwell was a substantial Farmer and Grazier. He had risen in the world by what worldly men call a run of good fortune. He had also been a man of great industry; that is, he had paid a diligent and constant attention to his own interest. He understood business, and had a knack of turning almost every thing to his own advantage. He had that sort of sense, which good men call cunning, and knaves call wisdom. He was too prudent ever to do any thing so wrong that the law could not take hold of him; yet he was not over scrupulous about the morality of an action, when the prospect of enriching himself by it was very great, and the chance of hurting his character was small. The corn he sent home to his customers was not always quite so good as the samples he had produced at market, and he now and then forgot to name some capital blemish in the horses he sold at fair. He scorned to be guilty of the petty frauds of cheating in weights and measures, for he thought that was a beggarly sin; but he valued himself on his skill in making a bargain, and fancied it shewed his knowledge of the world to take advantage of the ignorance of a dealer.

It was his constant rule to undervalue every thing he was about to buy, and to overvalue every thing he was about to sell; but as he prided himself on his character he avoided every thing that was very shameful, so that he was considered merely as a hard dealer, and a keen hand at a bargain. Now and then, when he had

G 6 been

been caught in pushing his own advantage too far, he contrived to get out of the scrape by turning the whole into a jest, saying it was a good take in, a rare joke, and that he had only a mind to divert himself with the folly of his neighbour who could be so easily imposed on.

Mr. Bragwell had one favourite maxim, namely, that a man's success in life was a sure proof of his wisdom; and that all failure and misfortune was the consequence of a man's own folly. As this opinion was first taken up by him from vanity and ignorance; so it was more and more confirmed by his own prosperity. He saw that he himself had succeeded greatly without either money or education to begin with, and he therefore now despised every man, however excellent his character or talents might be, who had not had the same success in life. His natural disposition was not particularly bad, but prosperity had hardened his heart. He made his own progress in life the rule by which the conduct of all other men was to be judged, without any allowance for their peculiar disadvantages, or the visitations of Providence. He thought, for his part, that every man of sense could command success on his undertakings, and controul and dispose the events of his own life.

But though he considered those who had had less success than himself, as no better than fools, yet he did not extend this opinion to Mr. Worthy, whom he looked upon not only as a good but wise man. They had been bred up when children

dren in the same house, but with this difference, that Worthy was the nephew of the master, and Bragwell the son of the servant.

Bragwell's father had been ploughman in the family of Mr. Worthy's uncle, a sensible man, who farmed a small estate of his own, and who having no children, bred up young Worthy as his son, instructed him in the business of husbandry, and at his death left him his estate. The father of Worthy was a pious clergyman who lived with his brother the farmer, in order to help out a narrow income. He had bestowed much pains on the instruction of his son, and used frequently to repeat to him a saying which he had picked up in a book written by one of the greatest men in this country,—that there were two things with which every man ought to be acquainted, RELIGION AND HIS OWN BUSINESS. While he therefore took care that his son should be made an excellent Farmer, he filled up his leisure hours in improving his mind; so that young Worthy had read more good books and understood them better than most men in his station. His reading however had been chiefly confined to husbandry and divinity, the two subjects which were of the most immediate importance to him.

The reader will see by this time that Mr. Bragwell and Mr. Worthy were likely to be as opposite to each other as two men could well be, who were nearly of the same age and condition, and who were neither of them without credit in the world. Bragwell indeed made far the greater figure,

figure, for he liked to *cut a dash*, as he called it. And while it was the study of Worthy to conform to his station, and to set a good example to those about him, it was the delight of Bragwell to vie in his way of life with men of larger fortune. He did not see how much this vanity raised the envy of his inferiors, the ill-will of his equals, and the contempt of his betters.

His wife was a notable stirring woman, but vain, violent, and ambitious; very ignorant, and very high-minded. She had married Bragwell before he was worth a shilling, and as she had brought him a good deal of money, she thought herself the grand cause of his rising in the world, and thence took occasion to govern him most completely. Whenever he ventured to oppose her she took care to put him in mind that he owed every thing to her, that had it not been for her he might still have been stumping after a plow-tail, or serving hogs in old Worthy's farm-yard, but that it was she who had made a gentleman of him. In order to set about making him a gentleman she had begun by teazing him till he had turned away all his poor relations who worked in the farm. She next drew him off from keeping company with his old acquaintance, and at last persuaded him to remove from the place where he had got his money. Poor woman! she had not sense and virtue enough to see how honourable it is for a man to raise himself in the world by fair means, and then to help forward his poor relations and friends; engaging
their

their services by his kindness, and endeavouring to keep want out of the family.

Mrs. Bragwell was an excellent mistress, according to her own notions of excellence, for no one could say that she ever lost an opportunity of scolding a servant, or was ever guilty of the weakness of overlooking a fault. Towards her two daughters her behaviour was far otherwise. In them she could see nothing but perfections; but her extravagant fondness for these girls was full as much owing to pride as to affection. She was bent on making a family, and having found out that she was too ignorant, and too much trained to the habits of getting money, ever to hope to make a figure herself, she looked to her daughters as the persons who were to raise the family of Bragwells; and in this hope she foolishly submitted to any drudgery for their sakes, and bore every kind of impertinence from them.

The first wish of her heart was to set them above their neighbours; for she used to say, what was the use of having substance, if her daughters might not carry themselves above girls who had nothing? To do her justice, she herself would be about early and late to see that the business of the house was not neglected. She had been bred to great industry, and continued to work when it was no longer necessary, both from early habit, and the desire of heaping up money for her daughters. Yet her whole notion of gentility was, that it consisted in being rich and idle; and though she was willing to be a drudge herself, she
resolved

resolved to make her daughters gentlewomen on this principle. To be well dressed and to do nothing, or nothing which is of any use, was what she fancied distinguished people in genteel life. And this is too common a notion of a fine education among some people. They do not esteem things by their use, but by their shew. They estimate the value of their children's education by the money it costs, and not by the knowledge and goodness it bestows. People of this stamp often take a pride in the expence of learning, instead of taking pleasure in the advantages of it. And the silly vanity of letting others see that they can afford any thing, often sets parents on letting their daughters learn not only things of no use, but things which may be really hurtful in their situation; either by setting them above their proper duties, or by taking up their time in a way inconsistent with them.

Mrs. Bragwell sent her daughters to a boarding school, where she instructed them to hold up their heads as high as any body; to have more spirit than *to be put upon* by any one; never to be pitiful about money, but rather to shew that they could spend with the best; to keep company with the richest girls in the school, and to make no acquaintance with Farmer's Daughters.

They came home at the usual age of leaving school, with a large portion of vanity grafted on their native ignorance. The vanity was added but the ignorance was not taken away. Of Religion they could not possibly learn any thing, since

since none was taught, for at that place it was considered as a part of education which belonged only to Charity Schools. Of knowledge they got just enough to laugh at their fond parents' rustic manners and vulgar language, and just enough taste to despise and ridicule every girl who was not as vainly dressed as themselves.

The mother had been comforting herself for the heavy expence of their bringing up, by looking forward to the pleasure of seeing them become fine ladies, and to the pride of marrying them above their station.

Their father hoped also that they would be a comfort to him both in sickness and in health. He had had no learning himself, and could write but poorly, and owed what skill he had in figures to his natural turn for business. He hoped that his daughters, after all the money he had spent on them, would now write his letters and keep his accounts. And as he was now and then laid up with a fit of the gout, he was enjoying the prospect of having two affectionate children to nurse him.

When they came home, however, he had the mortification to find, that though he had two smart showy ladies to visit him, he had neither dutiful daughters to nurse him, nor faithful stewards to keep his books, nor prudent children to manage his house. They neither soothed him by kindness when he was sick, nor helped him when he was busy. They thought the maid might take care of him in the gout as she did before.

before. And as to their skill in cyphering he soon found, to his cost, that though they knew how to *spend* both Pounds, Shillings, and Pence, yet they did not know so well how to cast them up.

Mrs. Bragwell one day being very busy in preparing a great dinner for the neighbours, ventured to request her daughters to assist in making the pastry. They asked her scornfully, whether she had sent them to Boarding School to learn to cook; and added, that they supposed she would expect them next to make puddings for the haymakers. So saying they coolly marched off to their music. When the mother found her girls were too polite to be of any use, she would take comfort in observing how her parlour was set out with their Fillagree and Flowers, their Embroidery and Cut paper. They spent the morning in bed, the noon in dressing, the evening at the Spinnet, and the night in reading Novels.

With all these fine qualifications it is easy to suppose, that as they despised their sober duties, they no less despised their plain neighbours. When they could not get to a horse race, a petty ball, or a strolling play, with some company as idle and as smart as themselves, they were driven for amusement to the Circulating-Library. Jack, the plow-boy, on whom they had now put a livery jacket, was employed half his time in trotting backwards and forwards with the most wretched trash the little neighbouring book shop could furnish. The choice was often left to Jack, who

who could not read, but who had general orders to bring all the new things, and a great many of them.

Things were in this state, or rather growing worse, for idleness and vanity are never at a stand; when these two wealthy farmers, Bragwell and Worthy met at Weyhill Fair, as was said before. After many hearty salutations had passed between them, it was agreed that Mr. Bragwell should spend the next day with his old friend, whose house was not many miles distant. Bragwell invited himself in the following manner, we have not had a comfortable day's chat for years, said he, and as I am to look at a drove of lean beasts in your neighbourhood, I will take a bed at your house, and we will pass the evening in debating as we used to do. You know I always loved a bit of an argument, and am reckoned not to make the worst figure at our club: I had not, to be sure, such good learning as you had, because your father was a parson, and you got it for nothing. But I can bear my part pretty well for all that. When any man talks to me about his learning, I ask if it has helped him to get a good estate; if he says no, then I would not give him a rush for it; for of what use is all the learning in the world if it does not make a man rich? But as I was saying I will come and see you to-morrow; but now don't let your wife put herself into a fuss for me. Don't alter your own plain way, for I am not proud I assure

assure you, nor above my old friends, though I thank GOD I am pretty well in the world.

To all this flourishing speech Mr. Worthy coolly answered, that certainly worldly prosperity ought never to make any man proud, since it is GOD who giveth strength to get riches, and without his blessing, *'tis in vain to rise up early and to eat the bread of carefulness.*

About the middle of the next day Mr. Bragwell reached Mr. Worthy's neat and pleasant dwelling. He found every thing in it the reverse of his own. It had not so many ornaments, but it had more comforts. And when he saw his friend's good old fashioned arm chair in a warm corner, he gave a sigh to think how his own had been banished to make room for his daughter's Piano Forte. Instead of made flowers in glass cases, and a tea chest and screen too fine to be used, which he saw at home, and about which he was cautioned, and scolded as often as he came near them, he saw a neat shelf of good books for the service of the family, and a small medicine chest for the benefit of the poor.

Mrs. Worthy and her daughters had prepared a plain but neat and good dinner. The tarts were so excellent that Bragwell felt a secret kind of regret that his own daughters were too genteel to do any thing so very useful. Indeed he had been always unwilling to believe that any thing which was very proper and very necessary, could be so extremely vulgar and unbecoming as his daughters were always declaring it to be. And his

his late experience of the little comfort he found at home, inclined him now still more strongly to suspect that things were not so right as he had been made to suppose. But it was in vain to speak; for his daughters constantly stopped his mouth by a favorite saying of theirs, better be out of the world than out of the fashion.

Soon after dinner the women went out to their several employments, and Mr. Worthy being left alone with his guest the following discourse took place.

Bragwell. You have a couple of sober, pretty looking girls, Worthy; but I wonder they don't tiff off a little more. Why my girls have as much fat and flour on their heads as would half maintain my reapers in suet pudding.

Worthy. Mr. Bragwell, in the management of my family, I don't consider what I might afford only, though that is one great point; but I consider also what is needful and becoming in a man of my station, for there are so many useful ways of laying out money, that I feel as if it were a sin to spend one unnecessary shilling. Having had the blessing of a good education myself, I have been able to give the like advantage to my daughters. One of the best lessons I have taught them is, to know themselves; and one proof that they have learnt this lesson is, that they are not above any of the duties of their station. They read and write well, and when my eyes are bad, they keep my accounts in a very pretty manner. If I had put them to learn what you call *genteel things,*

things, these might either have been of no use to them, and so both time and money might have been thrown away; or they might have proved worse than nothing to them by leading them into wrong notions, and wrong company. Though we don't wish them to do the laborious parts of the dairy work; yet they always assist their mother in the management of it. As to their appearance, they are every day nearly as you see them now, and on Sundays they are very neatly dressed, but it is always in a decent and modest way. There are no lappets, fringes, furbelows, and tawdry ornaments, fluttering about among my cheese and butter. And I should feel no vanity but much mortification if a stranger seeing Farmer Worthy's daughters at Church, should ask who those fine ladies were.

Bragwell. Now I own I should like to have such a question asked concerning my daughters. I like to make people stare and envy. It makes one feel one-self somebody. But as to yourself, to be sure you best know what you can afford. And indeed there is some difference between your daughters and the Miss Bragwells.

Worthy. For my part, before I engage in any expence, I always ask myself these two short questions, First, Can I afford it?—Secondly, Is it proper for me?

Bragwell. Do you so? Now I own I ask myself but one. For if I find I can afford it, I take care to make it proper for me. If I can pay for a thing, no one has a right to hinder me from having it.

Worthy. Certainly. But a man's own prudence and sense of duty, ought to prevent him from doing an improper thing, as effectually as if there were somebody to hinder him.

Bragwell. Now I think a man is a fool who is hindered from having any thing he has a mind to; unless, indeed, he is in want of money to pay for it; I'm no friend to debt. A poor man must want on.

Worthy. But I hope my children have learnt not to want any thing which is not proper for them. They are very industrious, they attend to business all day; and in the evening they sit down to their work and a good book. I think they live in the fear of GOD. I trust they are humble and pious, and I am sure they seem cheerful and happy. If I am sick, it is pleasant to see them dispute which shall wait upon me, for they say the maid cannot do it so tenderly as themselves.——

This part of the discourse staggered Bragwell. Vain as he was, he could not help feeling what a difference a religious and a worldly education made on the heart, and how much the former regulated even the natural temper. Another thing which surprised him was, that these girls, living a life of domestic piety, without any public diversions, should be so very cheerful and happy; while his own daughters who were never contradicted, and were indulged with continual

tinual amusements, were always sullen and ill-tempered. That they who were more humoured should be less grateful and less happy, disturbed him much. He envied Worthy the tenderness of his children, though he would not own it, but turned it off thus.

Bragwell. But my girls are too smart to make mopes of, that is the truth. Though ours is such a lonely village, 'tis wonderful to see how soon they get the fashions. What with the descriptions in the Magazines, and the pictures in the Pocket Books, they have them in a twinkling, and out-do their patterns all to nothing. I used to take in the County Journal, because it was useful enough to see how Oats went, the time of high water, and the price of Stocks. But when my ladies came home forsooth, I was soon wheedled out of that, and forced to take a London paper, that tells a deal about caps and feathers, and all the trumpery of the quality. When I want to know what Hops are a bag, they are snatching the paper to see what violet soap is a pound. And as to the dairy, they never care how Cow's milk goes, as long as they can get some stuff which they call Milk of Roses.

Worthy. But do your daughters never read?

Bragwell. Read! I believe they do too. Why our Jack, the Plow-boy, spends half his time in going to a shop in our Market town, where they let out books to read with marble covers. And they sell paper with all manner of colours on the edges, and gim-cracks, and powder-puffs, and wash-

wash-balls, and cards without any pips, and every thing in the world that's genteel and of no use. 'Twas but t'other day I met Jack with a basket full of these books, so having some time to spare, I sat down to see a little what they were about.

Worthy. Well, I hope you there found what was likely to improve your daughters, and teach them the true use of time.

Bragwell. O as to that, you are pretty much out. I could make neither head nor tail of it. It was neither fish, flesh, nor good red-herring. It was all about my Lord, and Sir Harry, and the Captain. But I never met with such nonsensical fellows in my life. Their talk was no more like that of my old landlord, who was a Lord you know, nor the Captain of our fencibles, than chalk is like cheese. I was fairly taken in at first, and began to think I had got hold of a *godly* book, for there was a deal about hope and despair, and heaven, and Angels, and torments, and everlasting happiness. But when I got a little on, I found there was no meaning in all these words, or if any, 'twas a bad meaning. Misery perhaps only meant a disappointment about a bit of a letter: and everlasting happiness meant two people talking nonsense together for five minutes. In short, I never met with such a pack of lies. The people talk such gibberish as no folks in their sober senses ever did talk; and the things that happen to them are not like the things that ever happen to any of my acquaintance. They are at home one minute, and beyond sea the next. Beggars to day, and Lords to morrow. Waiting maids in the morning, and Duchesses at night. You and I, Master Worthy, have worked hard many years, and think it very well to have scraped a trifle of money together, you a few hundreds I suppose, and I a few thousands. But one would think every man in these books, had the Bank of England in his scrutore. Then there's another thing which I never met with in true life. We think it pretty well, you know, if one has got one thing, and another has got another. I'll tell you how I mean. You are reckoned sensible, our Parson is learned, the Squire is rich, I am rather generous, one of your daughters is pretty, and both mine are genteel. But in these books, (except here and there one, whom they make worse than Satan himself) every man and woman's child of them, are all wise, and witty, and generous, and rich, and handsome, and genteel; and all to the last degree. Nobody is middling, or good in one thing, and bad in another, like my live acquaintance; but 'tis all up to the skies, or down to the dirt. I had rather read Tom Hickathrift, or Jack the Giant Killer, a thousand times.

Worthy. You have found out, Mr. Bragwell, that many of these books are ridiculous; I will go farther, and say, that to me they appear wicked also. And I should account the reading of them a great mischief, especially to people in
middling

middling and low life, if I only took into the account the great loss of time such reading causes, and the aversion it leaves behind for what is more serious and solid. But this, though a bad part, is not the worst. These books give false views of human life. They teach a contempt for humble and domestic duties; for industry, frugality, and retirement. Want of youth and beauty, is considered in them as ridiculous. Plain people, like you and me, are objects of contempt. Parental authority is set at nought. Nay, plots and contrivances against parents and guardians, fill half the volumes. They consider love as the great business of human life, and even teach that it is impossible to be regulated or restrained, and to the indulgence of this passion, every duty is therefore sacrificed. A country life, with a kind mother, or a sober aunt, is described as a state of intolerable misery. And one would be apt to fancy, from their painting, that a good country house is a prison, and a worthy father the gaoler. Vice is set off with every ornament which can make it pleasing and amiable; while virtue and piety are made ridiculous by tacking to them something that is silly, or absurd. Crimes which would be considered as hanging matter at the Old Bailey, are here made to take the appearance of virtue, by being mixed with some wild flight of unnatural generosity. Those crying sins, ADULTERY, GAMING, DUELS, and SELF-MURDER, are made so familiar, and the wickedness of them is so disguised, that even innocent girls get to lose their abhorrence, and to talk with complacency of *things which should not be so much as named by them.*

I should not have said so much on this mischief (continued Mr. Worthy,) from which I dare say, great folks fancy people in our station are safe enough, if I did not know, and lament that this corrupt reading is now got down even among some of the lowest class. And it is an evil which is spreading every day. Poor industrious girls, who get their bread by the needle, or the loom, spend half the night in listening to these books. Thus the labour of one girl is lost, and the minds of the rest are corrupted; for though their hands are employed in honest industry, which might help to preserve them from a life of sin, yet their hearts are at that very time polluted by scenes and descriptions which are too likely to plunge them into it. And I think I don't go too far, when I say, that the vain and shewy manner in which young women who have to work for their bread, have taken to dress themselves, added to the poison they draw from these books, contribute together to bring them to destruction, more than almost any other cause. Now tell me, don't you think these wild books will hurt your daughters?

Bragwell. Why I do think they are grown full of schemes and contrivances and whispers, that's the truth on't. Every thing is a secret. They always seem to be on the look out for something,

something, and when nothing comes on't, then they are sulky and disappointed. They will not keep company with their equals. They despise trade and farming, and I own, *I'm for the stuff.* I should not like for them to marry any, but a man of substance, if he was ever so smart. Now they will hardly sit down with a substantial country dealer. But if they hear of a recruiting party in our Market Town, on goes the finery—off they are. Some flimsy excuse is patched up. They want something at the book shop, or the milliner's, because I suppose there is a chance that some Jack-a-napes of an Ensign may be there buying sticking-plaister. In short I do grow a little uneasy, for I should not like to see all I have saved thrown away on a knapsack.

So saying they both rose, and walked out to view the farm. Mr. Bragwell affected greatly to admire the good order of every thing he saw; but never forgot to compare it with something larger and handsomer or better of his own. It was easy to see that *self* was his standard of perfection in every thing. All he possessed gained some increased value in his eyes from being his; and in surveying the property of his friend, he derived food for his vanity, from things which seemed least likely to raise it. Every appearance of comfort, of success, of merit, in any thing which belonged to Mr. Worthy, led him to speak of some superior advantage of his own, of the same kind. And it was clear that the chief part of the satisfaction he felt in walking over the farm of his friend, was caused by thinking how much larger his own was.

Mr. Worthy who felt a kindness for him, which all his vanity could not cure, was on the watch how to turn their talk to some useful point. And whenever people resolve to go into company with this view, it is commonly their own fault if some opportunity of turning it to account, does not offer.

He saw Bragwell was intoxicated with pride, and undone by prosperity, and that his family was in the high-road to ruin. He thought that if some means could be found to open his eyes on his own character, to which he was now totally blind, it might be of the utmost service to him. The more Mr. Worthy reflected, the more he wished to undertake this kind office. He was not sure that Mr. Bragwell would bear it, but he was very sure it was his duty to attempt it. Mr. Worthy was very humble, and very candid, and he had great patience and forbearance with the faults of others. He felt no pride at having escaped the same errors himself, for he knew who it was had *made them to differ*. He remembered that God had given him many advantages, a pious father, and a religious education; this made him humble under a sense of his own sins, and charitable towards the sins of others, who had not the same privileges.

Just as he was going to try to enter into a very serious conversation with his guest, he was stopped by the appearance of his daughter, who told them

them supper was ready.—This interruption obliges me to break off also, and I shall reserve what follows to the next month, when I promise to give my readers the second part of this History. Z.

PART II.

MY readers may remember that the first part of this history concluded with a walk taken by Mr. Bragwell and Mr. Worthy over the grounds of the latter, in which walk Mr. Bragwell, though he seemed to admire, took care to lower every thing he saw, by comparing it with something better which he had of his own. Soon after supper Mrs. Worthy left the room with her daughters, at her husband's desire; for it was his intention to speak more plainly to Bragwell than was likely to be agreeable to him to hear before others.

The two farmers being seated at their little table, each in a handsome old fashioned great chair, Bragwell began.

It is a great comfort, neighbour Worthy, at a certain time of life to be got above the world; my notion is, that a man should labour hard the first part of his days, and that he may then sit down and enjoy himself for the remainder. Now though I hate boasting, yet as you are my oldest friend I am about to open my heart to you. Let me tell you then I reckon I have worked as hard as any man in my time, and that I now begin to think I have a right to indulge a little. I have got my money with a good character, and I mean to spend it with credit. I pay every one his own, I set a good example, I keep to my church, I serve God, I honour the king, and I obey the laws of the land.

This is doing a great deal indeed, replied Mr. Worthy; but, added he, I doubt that more goes to the making up all these duties than men are commonly aware of. Suppose then that you and I talk the matter over coolly, we have the evening before us. What if we sit down together as two friends, and examine one another.

Bragwell who loved argument, and who was not a little vain both of his sense and his morality, accepted the challenge, and gave his word that he would take in good part any thing that should be said to him. Worthy was about to proceed when Bragwell interrupted him for a moment, by saying,—But stop, friend, before we begin I wish you would remember that we have had a long walk, and I want a little refreshment; have you no liquor that is stronger than this cyder? I am afraid it will give me a fit of the gout.

Mr. Worthy immediately produced a bottle of wine, and another of spirits, saying, that though he drank neither spirits nor even wine himself,

himself, yet his wife always kept a little of each as a provision in case of sickness or accidents.

Farmer Bragwell preferred the brandy, and began to taste it. Why, said he, this is no better than English, I always use foreign myself. I bought this for foreign, said Mr. Worthy. No, no, it is English spirits I assure you, but I can put you into a way to get foreign nearly as cheap as English. Mr. Worthy replied that he thought that was impossible.

Bragwell. O no, there are ways and means—a word to the wife—there is an acquaintance of mine that lives upon the south coast—you are a particular friend, and I will get you a gallon for a trifle.

Worthy. Not if it be smuggled Mr. Bragwell, though I should get it for six-pence a bottle.—Ask no questions, said the other, I never say any thing to any one, and who is the wiser?—And so this is your way of obeying the laws of the land, said Mr. Worthy,—here is a fine specimen of your morality.

Bragwell. Come, come, don't make a fuss abuut trifles. If *every one* did it indeed it would be another thing, but as to *my* getting a drop of good brandy cheap, why that can't hurt the revenue much.

Worthy. Pray Mr. Bragwell what should you think of a man who would dip his hand into a bag and take out a few guineas?

Bragwell.

Bragwell. Think! why I think that he should be hanged to be sure.

Worthy. But suppose that bag stood in the king's treasury?

Bragwell. In the king's treasury! worse and worse! What, rob the king's treasury! Well, I hope the robber will be taken up and executed, for I suppose we shall all be taxed to pay the damage.

Worthy. Very true. If one man takes money out of the treasury, others must be obliged to pay the more into it; but what think you if the fellow should be found to have stopped some money *in its way* to the treasury, instead of taking it out of the bag after it got there?

Bragwell. Guilty, Mr. Worthy; it is all the same in my opinion. If I was a juryman, I should say guilty, death.

Worthy. Hark ye Mr. Bragwell, he that deals in smuggled brandy, is the man who takes to himself the king's money in its way to the treasury, and he as much robs the government as if he dipt his hands into a bag of guineas in the treasury chamber. It comes to the same thing exactly. Here Bragwell seemed a little offended.—What, Mr. Worthy, do you pretend to say I am not an honest man because I like to get my brandy as cheap as I can? and because I like to save a shilling to my family? Sir, I repeat it, I do my duty to God and my neighbour. I say the Lord's prayer most days, I go to church on Sundays, I repeat my creed and keep

keep the ten commandments, and though I may now and then get a little brandy cheap, yet upon the whole, I will venture to say, I do as much as can be expected of any man.

Worthy. Come then, since you say you keep the commandments, you cannot be offended if I ask you whether you understand them.

Bragwell. To be sure I do. I dare say I do: look'ee Mr. Worthy, I don't pretend to much reading, I was not bred to it as you were. If my father had been a parson, I fancy I should have made as good a figure as some other folks, but I hope good sense and *a good heart* may teach a man his duty without much scholarship.

Worthy. To come to the point let us now go through the ten commandments, and let us take along with us those explanations of them which our Saviour gave us in his sermon on the mount.

Bragwell. Sermon on the mount! why the ten commandments are in the 20th chapter of Exodus. Come, come, Mr. Worthy, I know where to find the commandments as well as you do, for it happens that I am church-warden, and I can see from the altar-piece where the ten commandments are without your telling me, for my pew directly faces it.

Worthy. But I advise you to read the sermon on the mount, that you may see the full meaning of them.

Bragwell. What do you want to make me believe that there are two ways of keeping the commandments?

Worthy. No; but there may be two ways of understanding them.

Bragwell. Well; I am not afraid to be put to the proof; I defy any man to say I do not keep at least all the four first that are on the left side of the altar-piece.

Worthy. If you can prove that, I shall be more ready to believe you observe those of the other table; for he who does his duty to God, will be likely to do his duty to his neighbour also.

Bragwell. What! do you think that I serve two Gods? Do you think then that I make graven images, and worship stocks or stones? Do you take me for a Papist or an Idolator? —

Worthy. Don't triumph quite so soon, master Bragwell. Pray is there nothing in the world you prefer to God, and thus make an idol of? Do you not love your money, or your lands, or your crops, or your cattle, or your own will, and your own way, rather better than you love God? Do you never think of these with more pleasure than you think of Him, and follow them more eagerly than your religious duty?

Bragwell. O there's nothing about that in the 20th Chapter of Exodus.

Worthy. But Jesus Christ has said, "He that loveth father or mother more than me is not worthy of me." Now it is certainly a man's duty to love his father and mother, nay it would be wicked not to love them, and yet we must not love even these more than our Creator and

our

our Saviour. Well I think on this principle, your heart pleads guilty to the breach of the first and second commandments, let us proceed to the third.

Bragwell. That is about swearing, is it not?

Mr. Worthy, who had observed Bragwell guilty of much profaneness in using the name of his Maker, (though all such offensive words have been avoided in writing this history) now told him that he had been waiting the whole day for an opportunity to reprove him for his frequent breach of the third commandment.

Good L——d, I break the third commandment, said Bragwell, no indeed hardly ever. I once used to swear a little to be sure, but I vow to G——d I never do it now, except now and then, when I happen to be in a passion: and in such a case, why good G——d you know the sin is with those who provoke me, and not with me; but upon my soul I don't think I have sworn an oath these three months, no not I faith, as I hope to be saved.

Worthy. And yet you have broken this holy law no less than five or six times in the last speech you have made.

Bragwell. Lord bless me! Sure you mistake. Good heavens, Mr. Worthy, I call G——d to witness, I have neither cursed nor swore since I have been in the house.

Worthy. Mr. Bragwell, this is the way in which many who call themselves very good sort of people deceive themselves. What! is it no profanation

profanation of the name of God to use it lightly, irreverently, and familiarly as you have done? Our Saviour has not only told us not to swear by the immediate name of God, but he has said, " swear not at all, neither by heaven nor by the earth," and in order to prevent our inventing any other irreligious exclamations or expressions, he has even added, " but let your communication be yea, yea, and nay, nay, for whatsoever is more than this simple affirmation and denial cometh of evil."

Bragwell. Well, well, I must take a little more care I believe: I vow to heaven I did not know there had been so much harm in it; but my daughters seldom speak without using some of these words, and yet they wanted to make me believe the other day that it was monstrous vulgar to swear.

Worthy. Women, even gentlewomen, who ought to correct this evil habit in their fathers, and husbands, and children, are too apt to encourage it by their own practice. And indeed they betray the profaneness of their own minds also by it, for none who truly venerate the holy name of God, can either profane it in this manner themselves, or hear others do so without being exceedingly pained at it.

Bragwell. Well, since you are so hard upon me, I believe I must e'en give up this point—so let us pass on to the next, and here I tread upon sure ground, for as sharp as you are upon me, you can't accuse me of being a sabbath-breaker, since

since I go to church every Sunday of my life, unless on some very extraordinary occasion.

Worthy. For those occasions the gospel allows, by saying, " the sabbath was made for man and not man for the sabbath." Our own sickness, or attending on the sickness of others, are lawful impediments.

Bragwell. Yes, and I am now and then obliged to look at a drove of beasts, or to go a journey, or to take some medicine, or perhaps some friend may call upon me, or it may be very cold, or very hot, or very rainy.

Worthy. Poor excuses, Mr. Bragwell; I am afraid these will not pass on the day of judgment. But how is the rest of your Sunday spent?

Bragwell. O why, I assure you, I often go to church in the afternoon also, and even if I am ever so sleepy.

Worthy. And so you finish your nap at church, I suppose.

Bragwell. Why as to that, to be sure we do contrive to have something a little nicer than common for dinner on a Sunday; in consequence of which one eats, you know, a little more than ordinary; and having nothing to do on that day, one has more leisure to take a chearful glass; and all these things will make one a little heavy you know.

Worthy. And don't you take a little ride in the morning, and look at your sheep when the weather is good, and so fill your mind just before you go to church with thoughts of them; and
when

when you come away again don't you settle an account, or write a few letters of business?

Bragwell. I can't say but I do, but that is nothing to any body, as long as I set a good example by keeping to my church.

Worthy. And how do you pass your Sunday evenings?

Bragwell. My wife and daughters go a visiting of a Sunday afternoon. My daughters are glad to get out at any rate, and as to my wife, she says, that being ready dressed it is a pity to lose the opportunity, besides it saves her time on a week day; so then you see I have it all my own way, and when I have got rid of the ladies, who are ready to faint at the smell of tobacco, I can venture to smoak a pipe, and drink a sober glass of punch with half a dozen friends.

Worthy. Which punch being made of smuggled brandy, and drank on the Lord's day, in very vain, as well as profane and worldly company, you are enabled to break both the law of God, and that of your country at a stroke: and I suppose when you are got together, you speak of your cattle, or of your crops, after which perhaps you talk over a few of your neighbours' faults, and then you brag a little of your own wealth, or your own achievements.

Bragwell. Why you seem to know us so well, that any one would think you had been sitting behind the curtain, and yet you are a little mistaken too, for I think we have hardly said a word
for

for several of our last Sundays on any thing but politics.

Worthy. And do you find that you much improve your Christian charity by that subject?

Bragwell. Why to be sure we do quarrel 'till we are very near fighting, that is the worst on't.

Worthy. And then you call names, and swear a little I suppose.

Bragwell. Why when one is contradicted and put in a passion you know, flesh and blood can't bear it.

Worthy. And when all your friends are gone home, what becomes of the rest of the evening?

Bragwell. That is just as it happens, sometimes I read the newspaper; and as one is generally most tired on the days one does nothing, I go to bed earlier than on other days, that I may be more fit to get up to my business the next morning.

Worthy. So you shorten Sunday as much as you can, by cutting off a bit at both ends, I suppose; for I take it for granted, you lie a little later in the morning.

Bragwell. Come, come. We shan't get through the whole ten to-night if you stand snubbing one at this rate. You may pass over the fifth, for my father and mother have been dead since I was a boy, so I am clear of that scrape.

Worthy. There are, however, many relative duties in that commandment; unkindness to all kindred is forbidden.

Bragwell.

Bragwell. O, if you mean my turning off my nephew Tom, the plowboy, you must not blame me for that, it was all my wife's fault. He was as good a lad as ever lived to be sure, and my own brother's son, but my wife could not bear that a boy in a carter's frock should be about the house, calling her aunt. We quarrelled like dog and cat about it; and when he was turned away we did not speak for a week.

Worthy. Which was a fresh breach of the commandment; a worthy nephew turned out of doors, and a wife not spoken to for a week, are no very convincing proofs of your observance of the fifth commandment.

Bragwell. Well, I long to come to the sixth, for you don't think I commit murder I hope.

Worthy. I am not sure of that.

Bragwell. What kill any body?

Worthy. Why the laws of the land indeed, and the disgrace attending it, are almost enough to keep any man from actual murder; let me ask, however, do you never give way to unjust anger, and passion, and revenge? as for instance, do you never feel your resentment kindle against some of the politicians who contradict you on a Sunday night? and do you never push your animosity against somebody that has affronted you, further than the occasion will justify?

Bragwell. Hark'ee, Mr. Worthy, I am a man of substance, and nobody shall offend me without my being even with him. So as to injuring a man, if he affronts me first, there's nothing but good reason in that.

Worthy.

Worthy. Very well! only bear in mind that you wilfully break this commandment, whether you abuse your servant, are angry at your wife, watch for a moment to revenge an injury on your neighbour, or even wreak your passion on a harmless beast; for you have then the seeds of murder working in your breast; and if there were no law, no gibbet to check you, and no fear of disgrace neither, I am not sure where you would stop.

Bragwell. Why, Mr. Worthy, you have a strange way of explaining the commandments, so you set me down for a murderer, merely because I bear hatred to a man who has done me a hurt, and am glad to do him a like injury in my turn.—I am sure I should want spirit if I did not.

Worthy. I go by the scripture rule, which says, " he that hateth his brother is a murderer," and again, " love your enemies, bless them that curse you, and pray for them that despitefully use you and persecute you." Besides, Mr. Bragwell, you made it a part of your boast that you said the Lord's prayer every day, wherein you pray to God to forgive you your trespasses as you forgive them that trespass against you.—If therefore you do not forgive them that trespass against you, in that case, you pray daily that your own trespasses may never be forgiven.

Bragwell. Well, come let us make haste and get through these commandments. The next is, " Thou shalt not commit adultery," thank God neither I nor my family can be said to break the seventh commandment.

Worthy.

Worthy. Here again, remember how Christ himself hath said, "whoso looketh on a woman to lust after her, hath already committed adultery with her in his heart." These are no far-fetched expressions of mine, Mr. Bragwell, they are the words of Jesus Christ. I hope you will not charge him with having carried things too far, for if you do, you charge him with being mistaken in the religion he taught, and this can only be accounted for, by supposing him an impostor.

Bragwell. Why, upon my word, Mr. Worthy, I don't like these sayings of his, which you quote upon me so often, and that is the truth of it, and I can't say I feel much disposed to believe them.

Worthy. I hope you believe in Jesus Christ. I hope you believe that creed of yours, which you also boasted of your repeating so regularly.

Bragwell. Well, well. I'll believe any thing you say rather than stand quarrelling with you.

Worthy. I hope then, you will allow, that since it is committing adultery to look at a woman with even an irregular thought, it follows from the same rule, that all immodest dress in your daughters, or indecent jests and double meanings in yourself; all loose songs or novels; and all diversions also which have a like dangerous tendency, are forbidden by the seventh commandment; for it is most plain from what Christ has said, that it takes in not only the act but the inclination, the desire, the indulged imagination;

imagination; the act is only the last and highest degree of any sin, the topmost round as it were of a ladder, to which all the lower rounds are only as so many steps and stages.

Bragwell. Strict indeed, Mr. Worthy, but let us go on to the next; you won't pretend to say *I steal.* Mr. Bragwell, I trust, was never known to rob on the highway, to break open his neighbour's house, or to use false weights or measures.

Worthy. No, nor have you ever been under any temptation to do it, and yet there are a thousand ways of breaking the eighth commandment besides actual stealing; for instance, do you never hide the faults of the goods you sell, and heighten the faults of those you buy? Do you never take advantage of an ignorant dealer, and ask more for a thing than it is worth? Do you never turn the distressed circumstances of a man, who has something to sell, to your own unfair benefit, and thus act as unjustly by him as if you had stolen? Do you never cut off a shilling from a workman's wages, under a pretence which your conscience can't justify? Do you never pass off an unsound horse, for a sound one? Do you never conceal the real rent of your estate from the overseers, and thereby rob the poor-rates of their legal due?

Bragwell. Pooh! these things are done every day. I shan't go to set up for being better than my neighbours in these sort of things; these little matters will pass muster.—I don't set up for a reformer.

reformer.—If I am as good as the rest of my neighbours, no man can call me to account; I'm not worse, I trust, and I don't pretend to be better.

Worthy. You must be tried hereafter at the bar of God, and not by a jury of your fellow-creatures; and the scriptures are given us, in order to shew by what rule we shall be judged. How many or how few do as you do, is quite aside from the question; Jesus Christ has even told us to strive to enter in at the *strait* gate, so that we ought rather to take fright, from our being like the common run of people, than to take comfort from our being so.

Bragwell. Come, I don't like all this close work—it makes a man feel I don't know how—I don't find myself so happy as I did—I don't like this fishing in troubled waters—I'm as merry as a grig when I let these things alone—I'm glad we are got to the ninth. But I suppose I shall be lugged in there too, head and shoulders. Any one who did not know me, would really think I was a great sinner, by your way of putting things; I don't bear false witness however.

Worthy. You mean, I suppose, you would not swear away a man's life falsely before a magistrate, but do you take equal care not to slander or backbite him? Do you never represent a good action of a man you have quarrelled with, as if it were a bad one? or do you never make a bad one worse than it is, by your manner of telling it? even when you invent no false circumstance,

cumstance, do you never give such a colour, to those you relate, as to leave a false impression on the mind of the hearers? Do you never twist a story so as to make it tell a little better for yourself, and a little worse for your neighbour, than truth and justice warrant?

Bragwell. Why, as to that matter, all this is only natural.

Worthy. Aye, much too natural to be right, I doubt. Well, now we are got to the last of the commandments.

Bragwell. Yes, I have run the gauntlet finely through them all; you will bring me in guilty here I suppose, for the pleasure of going through with it, for you condemn without judge or jury, master Worthy.

Worthy. The culprit, I think, has hitherto pleaded guilty to the evidence brought against him. The tenth commandment, however, goes to the root and principle of evil, it dives to the bottom of things; this command checks the first rising of sin in the heart, teaches us to strangle it in the birth as it were, before it breaks out in those acts which are forbidden: as for instance, every man covets before he proceeds to steal, nay, many covet who dare not steal, lest they should suffer for it.

Bragwell. Why, lookee, Mr. Worthy, I don't understand these new-fashioned explanations; one should not have a grain of sheer goodness left, if every thing one does is to be frittered away at this rate; I am not, I own, quite so

good

good as I thought, but if what you say were true, I should be so miserable, I should not know what to do with myself. Why, I tell you, all the world may be said to break the commandments at this rate.

Worthy. Very true. All the world, and I myself also, are but too apt to break them, if not in the letter, at least in the spirit of them. Why then all the world are (as the scripture expresses it) " guilty before God." And if guilty, they should own they are guilty, and not stand up and justify themselves as you do, Mr. Bragwell.

Bragwell. Well, according to my notion, I am a very honest man, and honesty is the sum and substance of all religion, say I.

Worthy. All truth, honesty, justice, order, and obedience, grow out of the christian religion. The true christian acts, at all times, and on all occasions, from the pure and spiritual principle of love to God; on this principle, he is upright in his dealings, true to his word, kind to the poor, helpful to the oppressed. In short, if he truly loves God, he must do justice, and *can't help* loving mercy. Christianity is a uniform consistent thing. It does not allow us to make up for the breach of one part of God's law, by our strictness in observing another. There is no sponge in one duty, that can wipe out the spot of another sin.

Bragwell. Well, but at this rate, I should be always puzzling and blundering, and should never know for certain whether I was right or not, whereas I am now quite satisfied with myself, and have no doubts to torment me.

Worthy. One way of knowing whether we really desire to obey the whole law of God is this; when we find we have as great a regard to that part of it, the breach of which does not touch our own interest, as to that part which does. For instance, a man robs me; I am in a violent passion with him, and when it is said to me, doest thou well to be angry? I answer, I do well. *Thou shalt not steal* is a law of GOD, and this fellow has broken that law. Aye, but says conscience, 'tis *thy own property* which is in question.—He has broken *thy* hedge—he has stolen *thy* sheep—he has taken *thy* purse. Art thou therefore sure whether it is his violation of thy property, or of GOD's law, which provokes thee? I will put a second case—I hear another swear most grievously; or I meet him coming drunk out of an alehouse; or I find him singing a loose, profane song. If I am not as much grieved for this blasphemer, or this drunkard, as I was for the robber; if I do not take the same pains to bring him to a sense of his sin, which I did to bring the robber to justice, " how dwelleth the love of GOD in me?" Is it not clear that I value my own sheep more than God's commandments? That I prize my purse more than I love my Maker? In short, whenever I find out that I am more jealous for my own property than for GOD's law; more careful about my own reputation

tion than *his* honour, I always suspect I am got upon wrong ground, and that even my right actions are not proceeding from a right principle.

Bragwell. Why what in the world would you have me do?

Worthy. You must confess that your sins *are* sins. You must not merely call them sins, while you see no guilt in them; but you must confess them so as to hate and detest them; so as to be habitually humbled under the sense of them; so as to trust for salvation not in your freedom from them, but in the mercy of a Saviour; and so as to make it the chief business of your life to contend against them, and in the main to forsake them. And remember that if you seek for a deceitful gaiety, rather than a well grounded cheerfulness; if you prefer a false security to final safety, and now go away to your cattle and your farm, and dismiss the subject from your thoughts lest it should make you uneasy; I am not sure that this simple discourse may not appear against you at the day of account, as a fresh proof that you "loved darkness rather than light," and so increase your condemnation.

Mr. Bragwell was more affected than he cared to own. He went to-bed with less spirits and more humility than usual. He did not however care to let Mr. Worthy see the impression which it had made upon him; but at parting next morning, he shook him by the hand more

cordially

cordially than usual, and made him promise to return his visit in a short time.

What befel Mr. Bragwell and his family on his going home, may, perhaps, make the subject of a future history.   Z.

PART III.

MR. BRAGWELL, when he returned home from his visit to Mr. Worthy, as recorded in the Second Part of this History, found that he was not quite so happy as he had formerly been. The discourses of Mr. Worthy had broken in not a little on his comfort. And he began to suspect that he was not so completely in the right as his vanity had led him to believe. He seemed also to feel less satisfaction in the idle gentility of his own daughters, since he had been witness to the simplicity, modesty, and usefulness of those of Mr. Worthy. And he could not help seeing that the vulgar violence of his wife did not produce so much family happiness at home, as the humble piety and quiet diligence of Mrs. Worthy produced in the house of his friend.

Happy would it have been for Mr. Bragwell, if he had followed up those new convictions of his own mind, which would have led him to struggle against the power of evil principles in himself, and to have controuled the force of evil habits in his family. But his convictions were just strong enough to make him uneasy under his errors, without driving him to reform them. The slight impression soon wore off, and he fell back into his old practices. Still his esteem for Mr. Worthy was not at all abated by the plain dealing of that honest friend. It is true he dreaded his piercing eye. He felt that his example held out a constant reproof to himself. Yet such is the force of early affection and rooted reverence, that he longed to see him at his house. This desire, indeed, as is commonly the case, was made up of mixed motives. He wished for the pleasure of his friend's company; he longed for that favorite triumph of a vulgar mind, an opportunity of shewing him his riches; and he thought it would raise his credit in the world, to have a man of Mr. Worthy's character at his house.

Mr. Bragwell, it is true, still went on with the same eagerness in gaining money, and the same ostentation in spending it. But though he was as covetous as ever, he was not quite so sure that it was right to be so. While he was actually engaged abroad indeed, in transactions with his dealers, he was not very scrupulous about the means by which he *got* his money; and while he was indulging in festivity with his friends at home, he was easy enough as to the manner in which he *spent* it. But a man can neither be making bargains, nor making feasts always; there must be some intervals between these two

great

great objects for which worldly men may be said to live; and in some of these intervals the most worldly form, perhaps, some random plans of amendment. And though many a one may say in the fullness of enjoyment, " Soul take thine ease, eat, drink, and be merry;" yet hardly any man, perhaps, allows himself to say, even in the most secret moments, I will *never* retire from business—I will *never* repent—I will *never* think of death—Eternity shall *never* come into my thoughts. The most that such an one probably ventures to say is, I need not repent *yet*; I will continue such a sin a little longer, it will be time enough to think on the next world when I am no longer fit for the business or the pleasures of this.

Such was the case with Bragwell. He set up in his own mind a general distant sort of resolution, that *some years hence*, when he should be a *few years older*, and a *few* thousands richer; when a few more of his *present schemes should be compleated*, he would then think of altering his course of life. He would then certainly set about spending a religious old age; he would reform some practices in his dealings, or perhaps quit business intirely; he would think about reading good books, and when he had compleated such and such a purchase, he would even begin to give something to the poor, but at present he really had little to spare for charity. The very reason why he should have given more, was just the cause he assigned for not giving at all,

all, namely, the *hardness of the times.* The true grand source of charity,-self-denial, never came into his head. *Spend less* that you may *save* more, he would have thought a shrewd maxim enough. But *spend less* that you may *spare more,* never entered into his book of Proverbs.

At length the time came when Mr. Worthy had promised to return his visit. It was indeed a little hastened by notice that Mr. Bragwell would have, in the course of the week, a piece of land to sell by auction; and though Mr. Worthy believed the price was likely to be above his pocket, yet he knew it was an occasion which would be likely to bring the principal Farmers of that neighbourhood together, some of whom he wanted to meet. And it was on this occasion that Mr. Bragwell prided himself, that he should shew his neighbours so sensible a man as his dear friend Mr. Worthy.

Worthy arrived at his friend's house on the Saturday, time enough to see the house, and garden, and grounds of Mr. Bragwell by daylight. He saw with pleasure (for he had a warm and generous heart) those evident signs of his friend's prosperity, but as he was a man of a sober mind, and was a most exact dealer in truth, he never allowed his tongue the licence of immodest commendation, which he used to say either favoured of flattery or envy. Indeed he never rated mere worldly things so highly as to bestow upon them undue praise. His calm approbation

probation somewhat disappointed the vanity of Mr. Bragwell, who could not help secretly suspecting that his friend, as good a man as he was, was not quite free from envy. He felt, however, very much inclined to forgive this jealousy, which he feared the sight of his ample property, and handsome habitation, must naturally awaken in the mind of a man whose own possessions were so inferior. He practised the usual trick of ordinary and vulgar minds, that of pretending himself to find some fault with those things which were particularly deserving praise, when he found Worthy disposed to pass them over in silence.

When they came in to supper, he affected to talk of the comforts of Mr. Worthy's *little* parlour, by way of calling his attention to his own large one. He repeated the word *snug*, as applied to every thing at Mr. Worthy's, with the plain design to make comparisons favourable to his own more ample domains. He contrived, as he passed by to his chair, by a seeming accident, to push open the door of a large beaufet in the parlour, in which all the finery was most ostentatiously set out to view. He protested, with a look of satisfaction which belied his words, that for his part he did not care a farthing for all this trumpery; and then smiling and rubbing his hands, added with an air of no small importance, what a good thing it is, though for people of substance, that the tax on plate is taken off. You are a happy man, Mr. Worthy, you do not feel these things; tax or no tax it is all the same to you. He took care during this speech, by a cast of his eye, to direct Mr. Worthy's attention to a great profusion of the brightest cups, salvers, and tankards, and other shining ornaments, which crowded the beaufet. Mr. Worthy gravely answered; Mr. Bragwell, it was indeed a tax which could not affect so plain a man as myself, but as it fell on a mere luxury, and therefore could not hurt the poor, I was always sorry that it could not be made productive enough to be continued. A man in my middling situation, who is contented with a good glass of beer, poured from a handsome earthen mug, the glass, the mug, and the beer, all of English manufacture, will be but little disturbed at taxes on plate or on wine; but he will regret, as I do, that many of these taxes are so much evaded, that new taxes are continually brought on to make up the deficiencies of the old.

During supper the young ladies sat in disdainful silence, not deigning to bestow the smallest civility on so plain a man as Mr. Worthy. They left the room with their Mamma as soon as possible, being impatient to get away to ridicule their father's friend at full liberty.

The Dance; or, the Christmas Merry-making.

As soon as they were gone, Mr. Worthy asked Bragwell how his family comforts stood, and how his daughters, who, he said, were really

fine

fine young women, went on. O, as to that, replied Bragwell, pretty much like other men's handsome daughters, I suppose, that is, worse and worse. I really begin to apprehend that their fantastical notions have gained such a head, that after all the money I have scraped together, I shall never get them well married. Betsey has just lost as good an offer as any girl could desire, young Wilson, an honest, substantial grazier as any in the county. He not only knows every thing proper for his station, but is pleasing in his behaviour, and a pretty scholar into the bargain; he reads history books and voyages, of a winter's evening, to his infirm father, instead of going to the card assembly in our town; he neither likes drinking nor sporting, and is a sort of favourite with our Parson, because he takes in the weekly numbers of a fine Bible with Cuts, and subscribes to the Sunday School, and makes a fuss about helping the poor, these dear times, as they call them, but I think they are good times for *us*, Mr. Worthy. Well, for all this, Betsey only despised him, and laughed at him; but as he is both handsome and rich, I thought she might come round at last; and so I invited him to come and stay a day or two at Christmas, when we have always a little sort of merry making here. But it would not do. He scorned to talk that palavering stuff which she has been used to in the marble covered books I told you of. He told her, indeed, that it would be the happiness of his heart to live with her, which I own I thought

thought was as much as could be expected of any man. But Miss had no notion of marrying one who was only desirous of living with her. No, no, forsooth, her lover must declare himself ready to die for her, which honest Wilson was not such a fool as to offer to do. In the afternoon, however, he got a little into her favour by making out a Rebus or two, in the Lady's Diary, and she condescended to say, she did not think Mr. Wilson had been so good a scholar; but he soon spoilt all again. We had a bit of a hop in the evening. The young man, though he had not much taste for those sort of gambols, yet thought he could foot it a little in the old-fashioned way. So he asked Betsey to be his partner. But when he asked what dance they should call, Miss drew up her head, and in a strange gibberish, said she should dance nothing but a *Menuet de la Cour*, and ordered him to call it; Wilson stared, and honestly told her she must call it herself, for he could neither spell nor pronounce such outlandish words. I burst out a laughing, and told him; I supposed it was something like questions and commands, and if so, that was much merrier than dancing. Seeing her partner standing stock still, and not knowing how to get out of the scrape, the girl began by herself, and fell to swimming, and sinking, and capering, and flourishing, and posturing, for all the world just like the man on the slack rope at our fair. But seeing Wilson standing like a stuck pig, and we all laughing at her, she resolved to

wreak

wreak her malice upon him; so, with a look of rage and disdain, she advised him to go down country bumkin, with the dairy maid, who would make a much fitter partner, as well as wife, for him, than she could do. I am quite of your mind, Miss, said he, with more spirit than I thought was in him; you may make a good partner for a dance, but you would make a sad one to go through life with. I will take my leave of you, Miss, with this short story. I I had lately a pretty large concern in hay-jobbing, which took me to London. I waited a good while in the Hay-market for my dealer, and, to pass away the time, I stepped into a sort of singing play-house there, where I was grieved to the heart to see young women painted and dizened out, and capering away just as you have been doing. I thought it bad enough in them, and wondered the quality could be entertained with such indecent mummery. But little did I think to meet with the same paint, finery, and tricks, in a farm house. I will never marry a woman who despises me, nor the station in which I should place her, and so I take my leave.— Poor girl, how she *was* provoked! to be publicly refused, and turned off, as it were, by a grazier! But it was of use to some of the other girls, who have not held up their heads quite so high since, nor painted quite so red, but have condescended to speak to their equals.

But how I run on! I forget it is Saturday night, and that I ought to be paying my workmen, who are all waiting for me without.

Saturday Night; or the Workmens' Wages.

As soon as Mr. Bragwell had done paying his men, Mr. Worthy said to him, I have made it a habit, and I hope not an unprofitable one, of trying to turn to some moral use, not only all the events of daily life, but all the employments of it too. And though it occurs so often, I hardly know one that sets me a thinking more seriously than the ordinary business you have been just discharging. Aye, said Bragwell, it sets me thinking too, and seriously, as you say, when I observe how much the price of wages is increased. Yes, yes, you are ready enough to think of that, said Worthy, but you say not a word of how much the value of your land is increased, and that the more you pay, the more you can afford to pay. But the thoughts I spoke of are quite of another cast. When I call in my labourers, on a Saturday night, to pay them, it often brings to my mind the great and general day of account, when I, and you, and all of us, shall be called to our grand and awful reckoning, when we shall go to receive *our* wages, master and servants, farmer and labourer. When I see that one of my men has failed of the wages he should have received, because he has been idling at a fair; another has lost a day by a drinking bout, a third confesses that, though he had task work, and might have earned still more, yet he has been careless, and has not his full pay to receive; this,

this, I say, sometimes sets me on thinking whether I also have made the most of my time. And when I come to pay even the more diligent who have worked all the week; when I reflect that even these have done no more than it was their duty to do, I cannot help saying to myself, night is come; Saturday night is come. No repentance, or diligence on the part of these poor men can now make a bad week's work good. This week is gone into eternity. To-morrow is the season of rest; working time is over. My life also will soon be swallowed up in eternity; soon the space allotted me for diligence, for labour, will be over. Soon will the grand question be asked, "What hast thou done? Didst thou use thy working days to the end for which they were given?" With some such thoughts I commonly go to bed, and they help to quicken me to a keener diligence for the next week.

Some account of a Sunday in Mr. Bragwell's Family.

Mr. Worthy had been for so many years used to the sober ways of his own well ordered family, that he greatly disliked to pass a Sunday in any house of which Religion was not the governing principle. Indeed, he commonly ordered his affairs, and regulated his journies with an eye to this object. To pass a Sunday in an irreligious family, said he, is always unpleasant, often unsafe. I seldom find I can do
them

them any good, and they may perhaps do me some harm. At least, I am giving a sanction to their manner of passing it, if I pass it in the same manner. If I reprove them, I subject myself to the charge of singularity, and of being " righteous over much;" if I do *not* reprove them, I confirm and strengthen them in evil. And whether I reprove them or not, I certainly partake of their guilt if I spend it as they do.

He had, however, so strong a desire to be useful to Mr. Bragwell, that he at length determined to break through his common practice, and pass the Sunday at his house. Mr. Worthy was surprised to find that though the church bell was going, the breakfast was not ready, and expressed his wonder how this should be the case in so industrious a family. Bragwell made some aukward excuses. He said his wife worked her servants so hard all the week, that even she, as notable as she was, a little relaxed from the strictness of her demands on Sunday mornings; and he owned that in a general way, no one was up early enough for church. He confessed that his wife commonly spent the morning in making puddings, pies, and cakes, to last through the week, as Sunday was the only leisure time she and her maids had. Mr. Worthy soon saw an uncommon bustle in the house. All hands were busy. It was nothing but baking and boiling, and frying, and roasting, and running, and scolding, and eating. The boy was kept from church to clean the plate, the man to gather the fruit,
the

the mistress to make he cheese cakes, the maids to dress the dinner, and the young ladies to dress themselves.

The truth was, Mrs. Bragwell, who had heard much of the order and good management of Mr. Worthy's family, but who looked down with disdain upon them as far less rich than herself, was resolved to indulge her vanity on the present occasion. She was determined to be even with Mrs. Worthy, in whose praises Bragwell had been so loud, and felt no small pleasure in the hope of making her guest uneasy, when he should be struck with the display both of her skill and her wealth. Mr. Worthy was indeed struck to behold as large a dinner as he had been used to see at a Justice's meeting. He, whose frugal and pious wife had accustomed him only to such a plain Sunday's dinner as could be dressed without keeping any one from church, when he surveyed the loaded table of his friend, instead of feeling that envy which these grand preparations were meant to raise, felt nothing but disgust at the vanity of his friend's wife, mixed with much thankfulness for the piety of his own.

After having made the dinner wait a long time, the Miss Bragwells marched in, dressed as if they were going to the Assize-Ball; they looked very scornful at having been so hurried; though they had been dressing ever since they got up, and their fond father, when he saw them so fine, forgave all their impertinence, and cast an eye of triumph on Mr. Worthy, who felt he had

never

never loved his own humble daughters so well as at that moment.

In the afternoon, the whole party went to church. To do them justice, it was indeed their common practice once a day, when the weather was good, and the road was neither dusty nor dirty, when the Minister did not begin too early, when the young ladies had not been disappointed of their new bonnets on the Saturday night, and when they had no smart company in the house who rather wished to stay at home. When this last was the case, which, to say the truth, happened pretty often, it was thought a piece of good manners to conform to the humour of the guests. Mr. Bragwell had this day forborne to ask any of his usual company, well knowing that their vain and worldly conversation would only serve to draw on him some new reprimand from his friend.

Mrs. Bragwell and her daughters picked up, as usual, a good deal of acquaintance at church. Many compliments passed, and much of the news of the week was retailed before the service began. They waited with impatience for the reading the lessons as a licensed season, for whispering, and the subject begun during the lessons, was finished while they were singing. The young ladies made an appointment for the afternoon with a friend in the next pew, while their Mamma took the opportunity of enquiring the character of a dairy maid, which she observed with

with a compliment to her own good management, would save time on a week-day.

Mr. Worthy, who found himself quite in a new world, returned home with his friend alone. In the evening he ventured to ask Bragwell, if he did not, on a Sunday night, at least, make it a custom to read and pray with his family. Bragwell told him, he was sorry to say he had no family at home, else he should like to do it for the sake of example. But as his servants worked hard all the week, his wife was of opinion that they should then have a little holiday. Mr. Worthy pressed it home upon him, whether the utter neglect of his servants' principles was not likely to make a heavy article in his final account: and asked him if he did not believe that the too general liberty of meeting together, jaunting, and diverting themselves, on Sunday evenings, was not often found to produce the worst effects on the morals of servants and the good order of families? I put it to your conscience, said he, Mr. Bragwell, whether Sunday, which was meant as a blessing and a benefit, is not, as it is commonly kept, turned into the most mischievous part of the week, by the selfish kindness of masters, who, not daring to set their servants about any public work, allot them that day to follow their own devices, that they themselves may with more rigour refuse them a little indulgence and a reasonable holiday in the working part of the week, which a good servant has now and then a fair right to expect. Those
masters

masters who will give them half, or all the Lord's day, will not spare them a single hour of a working day. *Their* work *must* be done; God's work may be let alone.

Mr. Bragwell owned that Sunday had produced many mischiefs in his own family. That the young men and maids, having no eye upon them, frequently went to improper places with other servants, turned adrift like themselves. That in these parties the poor girls were too frequently led astray, and the men got to public houses, and fives-playing. But it was none of his business to watch them. His family only did as others do; indeed it was his wife's concern; and as she was so good a manager on other days, that she would not spare them an hour to visit a sick father or mother, it would be hard, she said, if they might not have Sunday afternoon to themselves, and she could not blame them for making the most of it. Indeed, she was so indulgent in this particular, that she often excused the men from going to church that they might serve the beasts, and the maids that they might get the milking done before the holiday part of the evening came on. She would not indeed hear of any competition between doing *her* work and taking their pleasure; but when the difference lay between their going to church and taking their pleasure, he *must* say that for his wife, she always inclined to the good-natured side of the question. She is strict enough in keeping them sober, because drunkenness is a costly

costly sin; and to do her justice, she does not care how little they sin at her expence.

Well, said Mr. Worthy, I always like to examine both sides fairly, and to see the different effects of opposite practices; now, which plan produces the greatest share of comfort to the master, and of profit to the servants in the long run? Your servants, 'tis likely, are very much attached to you; and very fond of living where they get their own way in so great a point.

O, as to that, replied Bragwell, you are quite out. My house is a scene of discord, mutiny, and discontent. And though there is not a better manager in England than my wife, yet she is always changing her servants, so that every quarter-day is a sort of gaol-delivery at my house; and when they go off, as they often do, at a moment's warning, to own the truth, I often give them money privately, that they may not carry my wife before the Justice to get their wages.

I see, said Mr. Worthy, that all your worldly compliances do not procure you even worldly happiness. As to my own family, I take care to let them see that their pleasure is bound up with their duty, and that what they may call my strictness, has nothing in view but their safety and happiness. By this means, I commonly gain their love as well as secure their obedience. I know, that with all my care, I am liable to be disappointed, "from the corruption that is in the world through sin." But whenever this happens, so far from encouraging me in remissness,

remissness, it only serves to quicken my zeal. If, by God's blessing, my servant turns out a good Christian, I have been an humble instrument in his hand of saving a soul committed to my charge.

Mrs. Bragwell came home, but brought only one of her daughters with her, the other, she said, had given them the slip, and was gone with a young friend, and would not return for a day or two. Mr. Bragwell was greatly displeased; as he knew that young friend had but a slight character, and kept bad acquaintances. Mrs. Bragwell came in, all hurry and bustle, saying, if her family did not go to bed with the Lamb on Sundays, when they had nothing to do, how could they rise with the Lark on Mondays, when so much was to be done.

Mr. Worthy had this night much matter for reflexion. We need not, said he, go into the great world to look for dissipation and vanity. We can find both in a farm house. As for me and my house, continued he, we will serve the Lord every day, but especially on Sundays. It is the day which the Lord hath made: hath made for himself; we will rejoice in it, and consider the religious use of it not only as a duty but as a privilege.

The next morning Mr. Bragwell and his friend set out early for the Golden Lion. What passed on this little journey, my readers shall hear next month. Z.

PART

PART IV.

IT was mentioned in the last part of this History, that the chief reason which had drawn Mr. Worthy to visit his friend just at the present time, was, that Mr. Bragwell had a small estate to sell by auction. Mr. Worthy, though he did not think he should be a bidder, wished to be present, as he had business to settle with one or two persons, who were expected at the Golden Lion on that day, and he had put off his visit till he had seen the sale advertised in the County Paper.

Mr. Bragwell and Mr. Worthy set out early on the Monday morning, on their way to the Golden Lion, a small inn, in a neighbouring market town. As they had time before them, they had agreed to ride slowly, that they might converse on some useful subject; but here, as usual, they had two opinions about the same thing. Mr. Bragwell's notion of an useful subject was, something by which money was to be got, and a good bargain struck. Mr. Worthy was no less a man of business than his friend. His schemes were wise, and his calculations just; his reputation for integrity and good sense made him the common judge and umpire in his neighbours' affairs, while no one paid a more exact attention to every transaction of his own. But the

the business of getting money was not with him the first, much less was it the whole concern of the day. Every morning when he rose, he remembered that he had a Maker to worship, as well as a family to maintain. Religion, however, never made him neglect business, though it sometimes led him to postpone it. He used to say, no man had any reason to expect God's blessing through the day who did not ask it in the morning; nor was he likely to spend the day in the fear of God, who did not begin it with his worship. But he had not the less sense, spirit, and activity, when he was among men abroad, because he had first served God at home.

As these two Farmers rode along, Mr. Worthy took occasion, from the fineness of the day, and the beauty of the country through which they passed, to turn the discourse to the goodness of God, and our infinite obligations to him. He knew that the transition from thanksgiving to prayer would be natural and easy, and he therefore slid, by degrees, into that important subject: and he observed, that secret prayer was a duty of universal obligation, which every man had it in his power to fulfil; and which he seriously believed was the ground-work of all religious practice, and of all devout affections.

Mr. Bragwell felt conscious that he was very negligent and irregular in the performance of this duty; indeed, he considered it as a mere ceremony, or at least, as a duty which might give way to the slightest temptation of drowsiness at night,

night, or of business in the morning. As he knew he did not live in the conscientious performance of this practice, he tried to ward off the subject, knowing what a home way his friend had of putting things. After some evasion, he at last said, he certainly thought private prayer a good custom, especially for people who have time; and those who were sick, or old, or out of business, could not do better; but that for his part, he believed much of these sort of things was not expected from men in active life.

Mr. Worthy. I should think, Mr. Bragwell, that those who are most exposed to temptation stand most in need of prayer; now there are few, methinks, who are more exposed to temptation than men in business, for those must be in most danger, at least, from the world, who have most to do with it. And if this be true, ought we not to prepare ourselves in the closet for the trials of the market, the field, and the shop? It is but putting on our armour before we go out to battle.

Bragwell. For my part, I think example is the whole of religion, and if the master of a family is orderly, and regular, and goes to church, he does every thing which can be required of him, and no one has a right to call him to account for any thing more.

Worthy. Give me leave to say, Mr. Bragwell, that highly as I rate a good example, still I must set a good principle above it. I know I must keep good order indeed, for the sake of others;
but

but I must keep a good conscience for my own sake. To God I owe secret piety, I must therefore pray to him in private.—To my family I owe a christian example, and for that, among other reasons, I must not fail to go to church.

Bragwell. You are talking, Mr. Worthy, as if I were an enemy to Christianity. Sir, I am no Heathen. Sir, I belong to the Church; I go to Church; I always drink prosperity to the Church. You yourself, as strict as you are, in never missing it twice a day, are not a warmer friend to the Church than I am.

Worthy. That is to say, you know its value as an institution, but you do not seem to know that a man may be very irreligious under the best religious institutions; and that even the most excellent of them are but *means* of being religious, and are no more religion itself than brick and mortar are prayers and thanksgivings. I shall never think, however high their profession, and even however regular their attendance, that those men truly respect the Church, who bring home little of that religion which is taught in it into their own families, or their own hearts; or, who make the whole of Christianity to consist in their attendance there. Excuse me, Mr. Bragwell.

Bragwell. Mr. Worthy, I am persuaded that religion is quite a proper thing for the poor; and I don't think that the multitude can ever be kept in order without it; and I am a sort of
a poli-

a politician you know. We *must* have bits, and bridles, and restraints for the vulgar.

Worthy. Your opinion is very just, as far as it goes, but it does not go far enough, since it does not go to the root of the evil, for while you value yourself on the soundness of this principle as a politician, I wish you also to see the reason of it as a Christian; depend upon it, if religion be good for the community at large, it is equally good for every family; and what is right for a family is equally right for each individual in it. You have therefore yourself brought the most unanswerable argument why you ought to be religious yourself, by asking how we shall keep others in order without religion. For, believe me, Mr. Bragwell, there is no particular clause to except you in the Gospel. There are no exceptions there in favour of any one class of men. The same restraints which are necessary for the people at large are equally necessary for men of every order, high and low, rich and poor, bond and free, learned and ignorant. If Jesus Christ died for no one particular rank, class, or community, there is no one rank, class, or communion, exempt from the obedience to his laws enjoined by the Gospel. May I ask you, Mr. Bragwell, what is your reason for going to Church?

Bragwell. Sir, I am shocked at your question. How can I avoid doing a thing so customary and so creditable? Not go to Church, indeed! What do you take me for, Mr. Worthy? I am afraid you suspect me to be a Papist, or a Heathen,

then, or of some religion or other that is not what it should be.

Worthy. If a foreigner were to hear how violently one set of Christians in this country often speak against another, how earnest would he suppose us all to be in religious matters: and how astonished to discover that many a man has perhaps little other proof to give of the sincerity of his own religion, except the violence with which he hates the religion of another party. It is not *irreligion* which such men hate; but the religion of the man, or the party, whom they are set against: now hatred is certainly no part of the religion of the Gospel. Well, you have told me why you go to Church; now pray tell me, why do you confess there on your bended knees every Sunday, that "you have erred and strayed from God's ways?" "that there is no health in you?" "that you have done what you ought not to do?" "and that you are a miserable sinner?"

Bragwell. Because it is in the Common Prayer Book, to be sure, a book which I have heard you yourself say was written by wise and good men, the pillars of the Protestant Church.

Worthy. But have you no other reason?

Bragwell. No, I can't say I have.

Worthy. When you repeat that excellent form of confession, do you really feel that you *are* a miserable sinner?

Bragwell. No, I can't say I do: But that is no objection to my repeating it, because it may suit the case of many who are so. I suppose the good

good Doctors who drew it up, intended that part for wicked people only, such as drunkards, and thieves, and murderers; for I imagine they could not well contrive to make the same prayer quite suit an honest man and a rogue; and so I suppose they thought it safer to make a good man repeat a prayer which suited a rogue, than to make a rogue repeat a prayer which suited a good man; and you know it is so customary for every body to repeat the general confession, that it can't hurt the credit of the most respectable persons, though every respectable person must know they have no particular concern in it.

Worthy. Depend upon it, Mr. Bragwell, those good Doctors you speak of, were not quite of your opinion; they really thought that what you call honest men were grievous sinners in a certain sense, and that the best of us stand in need of making that humble confession. Mr. Bragwell, do you believe in the fall of Adam?

Bragwell. To be sure I do, and a sad thing for Adam it was; why, it is in the Bible, is it not? It is one of the prettiest chapters in Genesis. Don't *you* believe it, Mr. Worthy?

Worthy. Yes, truly I do. But I don't believe it *merely* because I read it in Genesis; though I know, indeed, that I am bound to believe every part of the word of God. But I have still an additional reason for believing in the fall of the first man.

Bragwell. Have you, indeed? Now, I can't guess what that can be.

Worthy. Why, my own obfervation of what is within myfelf teaches me to believe it. It is not only the third chapter of Genefis which convinces me of the truth of the fall, but alfo the finful inclinations which I find in my own heart correfponding with it. This is one of thofe leading truths of Chriftianity of which I can never doubt a moment; firft, becaufe it is abundantly expreffed or implied in Scripture; and next becaufe the confcioufnefs of the evil nature I carry about with me confirms the doctrine beyond all doubt. Befides, is it not faid in Scripture, that by one man fin entered into the world, and that " all we, like fheep, have gone aftray; that by one man's dif- obedience many were made finners;" and fo again in twenty more places that I could tell you of.

Bragwell. Well; I never thought of this. But is not this a very melancholy fort of doc- trine, Mr. Worthy?

Worthy. It is melancholy, indeed, if we ftop here. But while we are deploring this fad truth, let us take comfort from another, that " As in Adam all die, fo in Chrift fhall all be made alive."

Bragwell. Yes; I remember I thought thofe very fine words, when I heard them faid over my poor father's grave. But as it was in the Burial of the Dead, I did not think of taking it to myfelf; for I was then young and hearty, and in little danger of dying, and I have been so busy ever since, that I have hardly had time to think of it.

Worthy. And yet the service pronounced at the burial of all who die, is a solemn admonition to all who live. It is there said, as indeed the Scripture says also, "I am the resurrection and the life; whosoever *believeth in me* shall never die, but I will raise him up at the last day." Now, do you think you *believe in Christ*, Mr. Bragwell?

Bragwell. To be sure I do; why you are always fancying me an Atheist.

Worthy. In order to believe in Christ, we must believe first in our own guilt and our own unworthiness; and when we do this we shall see the use of a Saviour, and not till then.

Bragwell. Why, all this is a new way of talking. I can't say I ever meddled with such subjects before in my life. But now, what do you advise a man to do upon your plan of Religion?

Worthy. Why, all this leads me back to the ground from which we set out, I mean the duty of prayer; for if we believe that we have an evil nature within us, and that we stand in need of God's grace to help us, and a Saviour to redeem us, we shall be led of course to pray for what we so much need; and without this conviction we shall not be led to pray.

Bragwell. Well; but don't you think, Mr. Worthy, that you good folks who make so much of prayer, have lower notions than we have of the wisdom of the Almighty? You think he wants to be informed of the things you tell him; whereas, I take it for granted, that he knows them already, and that, being so good as he is, he will give me every thing he sees fit to give me, without my asking it.

Worthy. God, indeed, who knows all things, knows what we want before we ask him; but still has he not said, that "with prayer and supplication we must make known our requests unto him." Prayer is the way in which God hath said that his favour must be sought. It is the channel through which he hath declared it is his sovereign will and pleasure that his blessings should be conveyed to us. What ascends up in prayer descends again to us in blessings. It is like the rain which just now fell, and which had been drawn up from the ground in vapours to the clouds before it descended from them to the earth in that refreshing shower. Besides, prayer has a good effect on our minds; it tends to excite a right disposition towards God in us, and to keep up a constant sense of our dependance. But above all, it is the way to get the good things we want. "Ask," says the Scripture, "and ye shall receive."

Bragwell. Now that is the very thing which I was going to deny. For the truth is, men do not always get what they ask; I believe if I could get a good crop for asking it, I should pray oftener than I do.

Worthy. Sometimes, Mr. Bragwell, men "ask and receive not, because they ask amiss." They ask

ask worldly blessings, perhaps, when they should ask spiritual ones. Now the latter, which are the good things I spoke of, are always granted to those who pray to God for them, though the former are not. I have observed in the case of some worldly things I have sought for, that the grant of my prayer would have caused the misery of my life; so that God equally consults our good in what he withholds, and in what he bestows.

Bragwell. And yet you continue to pray on, I suppose?

Worthy. Certainly; but then I try to mend as to the object of my prayers. I pray for God's blessing and favour, which is better than riches.

Bragwell. You seem very earnest on this subject.

Worthy. To cut the matter short; I ask then, whether prayer is not positively commanded in the Gospel. When this is the case, we can never dispute about the necessity or the duty of a thing, as we may when there is no such command. Here, however, let me just add also, that a man's prayers may be turned to no small use in the way of discovering to him whatever is amiss in his life.

Bragwell. How so, Mr. Worthy?

Worthy. Why, suppose now, you were to try yourself by turning into the shape of a prayer every practice in which you allow yourself. For instance, let the prayer in the morning be a sort of preparation for the deeds of the day, and the prayer at night a sort of observation on those deeds. You, Mr. Bragwell, I suspect are a little inclined to covetousness; excuse me, Sir. Now suppose after you have been during a whole day a little too eager to get rich, suppose, I say, you were to try how it would sound to beg of God at night on your knees, to give you still more money, though you have already so much that you know not what to do with it. Suppose you were to pray in the morning, "O Lord, give me more riches, though those I have are a snare and a temptation to me;" and ask him in the same solemn manner to bless all the grasping means you intend to make use of in the day, to add to your substance?

Bragwell. Mr. Worthy, I have no patience with you for thinking I could be so wicked.

Worthy. Hear me out, Mr. Bragwell; you turned your good nephew, Tom Broad, out of doors, you know; you owned to me it was an act of injustice. Now suppose on the morning of your doing so you had begged of God in a solemn act of prayer, to prosper the deed of cruelty and oppression, which you intended to commit that day. I see you are shocked at the thought of such a prayer. Well, then, would not hearty prayer have kept you from committing that wicked action? In short, what a life must that be, no act of which you dare beg God to prosper and bless. If once you can bring yourself to believe that it is your bounden duty to pray for God's blessing on your day's work, you

you will certainly grow careful about passing such a day as you may safely ask his blessing upon. The remark may be carried to sports, diversions, company. A man, who once takes up the serious use of prayer, will soon find himself obliged to abstain from such diversions, occupations, and societies, as he cannot reasonably desire that God will bless to him; and thus he will see himself compelled to leave off either the practice or the prayer. Now, Mr. Bragwell, I need not ask you which of the two he that is a real Christian will give up, sinning or praying.

Mr. Bragwell began to feel that he had not the best of the argument, and was afraid he was making no great figure in the eyes of his friend. Luckily, however, he was relieved from the difficulty into which the necessity of making some answer must have brought him, by finding they were come to the end of their little journey: and he never beheld the Bunch of Grapes, which decorated the Sign of the Golden Lion, with more real satisfaction.

I refer my readers for the transactions at the Golden Lion, and for the sad Adventures which afterwards befel Mr. Bragwell's family, to the Fifth Part of the History of the Two Wealthy Farmers. Z.

PART V.

Bragwell in a Passion at hearing of his Daughter's Marriage.

MR. BRAGWELL and Mr. Worthy alighted at the Golden Lion. It was market-day: the inn, the yard, the town, was all alive. Mr. Bragwell was quite in his element. Money, company, and good cheer, alway set his spirits afloat. He felt himself the principal man in the scene. He had three great objects in view, the sale of his land, the letting Mr. Worthy see how much

much he was looked up to by so many substantial people, and the shewing these people what a wise man his most intimate friend, Mr. Worthy, was. It was his way to try to borrow a little credit from every person, and every thing he was connected with, and by that credit to advance his interest and increase his wealth.

The Farmers met in a large room, and while they were transacting their various concerns, those whose pursuits were the same, naturally herded together. The Tanners were drawn to one corner, by the common interest which they took in bark and hides. A useful debate was carrying on at another little table, whether the practice of *sowing* wheat or of *planting* it were most profitable. Another set were disputing whether horses or oxen were best for plows. Those who were concerned in Canals, sought the company of other Canallers; while some, who were interested in the new bill for Inclosures, wisely looked out for such as knew most about waste lands.

Mr. Worthy was pleased with all these subjects, and picked up something useful on each. It was a saying of his, that most men understood some one thing, and that he who was wise would try to learn from every man something on the subject he best knew; but Mr. Worthy made a further use of the whole. What a pity is it, said he, that Christians are not as desirous to turn their time to good account as men of business are! When shall we see religious persons as anxious to derive profit from the experience of others,

others, as these Farmers? When shall we see them as eager to turn their time to good account? While I approve these men for not being *slothful in business*, let me improve the hint, by being also *fervent in spirit*.

Shewing how much *wiser the children of this generation are than the children of light.*

When the hurry was a little over, Mr. Bragwell took a turn on the Bowling-green. Mr. Worthy followed him, to ask why the sale of the estate was not brought forward. Let the Auctioneer proceed to business, said he; the company will be glad to get home by day-light. I speak mostly with a view to others, for I do not think of being a purchaser myself.—I know it, said Bragwell, or I would not be such a fool as to let the cat out of the bag. But is it really possible (proceeded he, with a smile of contempt) that you should think I will sell my estate before dinner? Mr. Worthy, you are a clever man at books, and such things; and perhaps can make out an account on paper in a handsomer manner than I can. But I never found much was to be got by fine writing. As to figures, I can carry enough of them in my head to add, divide, and multiply, more money than your learning will ever give you the fingering of. You may beat me at a book, but you are a very child at a bargain. Sell my land before dinner, indeed!

Mr. Worthy was puzzled to guess how a man was to shew more wisdom by selling a piece of ground at one hour than at another, and desired

an

an explanation. Bragwell felt rather more contempt for his understanding than he had ever done before. Look'ee, Mr. Worthy, said he, I do not know that knowledge is of any use to a man unless he has sense enough to turn it to account. Men are my books, Mr. Worthy, and it is by reading, spelling, and putting them together to good purpose, that I have got up in the world. I shall give you a proof of this to-day. These Farmers are most of them come to the Lion with a view of purchasing this bit of land of mine, if they should like the bargain. Now, as you know a thing can't be any great bargain both to the buyer and the seller too, to them and to me, it becomes me, as a man of sense, who has the good of his family at heart, to secure the bargain to myself. I would not cheat any man, Sir, but I think it fair enough to turn his weakness to my own advantage; there is no law against that, you know; and this is the use of one man's having more sense than another. So, whenever I have a bit of land to sell, I always give a handsome dinner, with plenty of punch and strong beer. We fill up the morning with other business, and I carefully keep back any talk about the purchase till we have dined. At dinner we have, of course, a bit of politics. This puts most of us into a passion, and you know anger is thirsty. Besides, " Church and King" naturally bring on a good many other toasts. Now, as I am Master of the Feast, you know, it would be shabby in me to save my liquor, so I push about the glass one way,

way, and the tankard the other, till all my company are as merry as kings. Every man is delighted to see what a fine hearty fellow he has to deal with, and Mr. Bragwell receives a thousand compliments. By this time they have gained as much in good humour as they have lost in sober judgment, and this is the proper moment for setting the Auctioneer to work, and this I commonly do to such good purpose, that I go home with my purse a score or two of pounds heavier than if they had not been warmed by their dinner. In the morning men are cool and suspicious, and have all their wits about them; but a chearful glass cures all distrust. And, what is lucky, I add to my credit as well as my pocket, and get more praise for my dinner, than blame for my bargain.

Mr. Worthy was struck with the absurd vanity which could tempt a man to own himself guilty of an unfair action for the sake of shewing his wisdom. He was beginning to express his disapprobation, when they were told dinner was on table. They went in, and were soon seated. All was mirth and good cheer. Every body agreed that no one gave such hearty dinners as Mr. Bragwell. Nothing was pitiful where he was Master of the Feast. Bragwell, who looked with pleasure on the excellent dinner before him, and enjoyed the good account to which he should turn it, heard their praises with delight, and cast an eye on Worthy, as much as to say, Who is the wise man now? Having a mind, for his own
credit,

credit, to make his friend talk, he turned to him, saying, Mr. Worthy, I believe no people in the world enjoy life more than men of our class. We have money and power, we live on the fat of the land, and have as good a right to gentility as the best.

As to gentility, Mr. Bragwell, replied Worthy, I am not sure that this is among the wisest of our pretensions. But I will say, that ours is a creditable and respectable business. In ancient times, Farming was the employment of Princes and Patriarchs; and, now-a-days, an honest, humane, sensible, English yeoman, I will be bold to say, is not only a very useful, but an honourable character. But then, he must not merely think of *enjoying life*, as you call it, but he must think of living up to the great ends for which he was sent into the world. A Wealthy Farmer not only has it in his power to live well, but to do much good. He is not only the father of his own family, but of his workmen, his dependants, and the poor at large, especially in these hard times. He has it in his power to raise into credit all the parish offices which have fallen into disrepute, by getting into bad hands; and he can convert, what have been falsely thought mean offices, into very important ones, by his just and Christian-like manner of filling them. An upright Juryman, a conscientious Constable, a humane Overseer, an independent Elector, an active Superintendant of a Work-house, a just Arbitrator in public disputes, a kind Counsellor in private troubles; such a one, I say, fills up a station in society no less necessary; and, as far as it reaches, scarcely less important than that of a Magistrate, a Sheriff of a County, or even a Member of Parliament. That can never be a slight or a degrading office, on which the happiness of a whole parish may depend.

Bragwell, who thought the good sense of his friend reflected credit on himself, encouraged Worthy to go on, but he did it in his own vain way. Aye, very true, Mr. Worthy, said he, you are right; a leading man in our class ought to be looked up to as an example, as you say; in order to which, he should do things handsomely and liberally, and not grudge himself, or his friends, any thing, casting an eye of complacency on the good dinner he had provided. True, replied Mr. Worthy, he should be an example of simplicity, sobriety, and plainness of manners. But he will do well, added he, not to affect a frothy gentility, which will set but clumsily upon him. If he has money, let him spend prudently, lay up moderately for his children, and give liberally to the poor. But let him rather seek to dignify his own station, by his virtues, than to get above it by his vanity. If he acts thus, then, as long as this country lasts, a Farmer of England will be looked upon as one of its most valuable members; nay more, by this conduct he may contribute to make England last the longer. The riches of the Farmer, corn and cattle, are the true riches of a nation; but let
him

him remember, that though corn and cattle *enrich* a country, nothing but justice, integrity, and religion, can *preserve* it.

Young Wilson, the worthy grazier, whom Miss Bragwell had turned off because he did not understand French dances, thanked Mr. Worthy for what he had said, and hoped he should be the better for it as long as he lived, and desired his leave to be better acquainted. Most of the others declared they had never heard a finer speech, and then, as is usual, proceeded to shew the good effect it had on them, by loose conversation, hard drinking, and whatever could counteract all that Worthy had said.

Mr. Worthy was much concerned to hear Mr. Bragwell, after dinner, whisper to the waiter, to put less and less water into every fresh bowl of punch.—This was his way; if the time they had to sit was long, then the punch was to be weaker, as he saw no good in wasting money to make it stronger than the time required. But if time pressed, then the strength was to be increased in due proportion, as a small quantity must then intoxicate them as much in a short time as would be required of a greater quantity had the time been longer. This was one of Mr. Bragwell's nice calculations, and this was the sort of skill on which he so much valued himself.

At length the guests were properly primed for business; just in that convenient stage of intoxication which makes men warm and rash, yet keeps short of that absolute drunkenness, which disqualifies

disqualifies for business. The Auctioneer set to work. All were bidders, and, if possible, all would have been purchasers, so happily had the feast and the punch operated. They bid on with a still increasing spirit, till they had got so much above the value of the land, that Bragwell, with a wink and a whisper, said, Who would sell his land fasting? Eh! Worthy? At length the estate was knocked down, at a price very far above its worth.

As soon as it was sold, Bragwell again said softly to Worthy; Five from fifty, and there remain forty-five. The dinner and drink won't cost me five pounds, and I have got fifty more than the land was worth. Spend a shilling to gain a pound, this is what I call practical Arithmetic, Mr. Worthy.

Mr. Worthy was glad to get out of this scene; and seeing that his friend was quite sober, he resolved, as they rode home, to deal plainly with him. Bragwell had found out, among his calculations, that there were some sins which could only be committed, by a prudent man, one at a time. For instance, he knew that a man could not well get rich, and get drunk, at the same moment, so that he used to practise one first, and the other after; but he had found out that some vices made very good company together; thus, while he had watched himself in drinking, lest he should become as unfit to sell, as his guests were to buy, he had indulged, without measure, in the good dinner he had provided. Mr. Worthy,

thy, I say, seeing him able to bear reason, rebuked him for this day's proceedings, with some severity. Bragwell bore his reproofs with that sort of patience which arises from an opinion of one's own wisdom, and a recent flush of prosperity. He behaved with that gay, good humour which grows out of vanity and good luck. You are too squeemish, Mr. Worthy, said he, I have done nothing discreditable. These men came with their eyes open. There is no compulsion used. They are free to bid, or to let it alone. I make them welcome, and I shall not be thought a bit the worse of by them, to-morrow, when they are sober. Others do it besides me, and I shall never be ashamed of any thing, as long as I have custom on my side.

Worthy. I am sorry, Mr. Bragwell, to hear you support such practices by such arguments. There is not, perhaps, a more dangerous snare to the souls of men than is to be found in that word CUSTOM. It is a word invented to reconcile corruption with credit, and sin with safety. But no custom, no fashion, no combination of men, to set up a false standard, can ever make a wrong action right. That a thing is often done, is so far from a proof of its being right, that it is the very reason which will set a thinking man to inquire if it be not really wrong, lest he should be following " a multitude to do evil." Right is right, though only one man in a thousand pursues it, and wrong will be for ever wrong, though it be the allowed practice of the other nine hundred

dred and ninety-nine. If this shameful custom is really common, which I can hardly believe, that is a fresh reason why a conscientious man should set his face against it. And I must go so far as to say, (you will excuse me, Mr. Bragwell,) that I see no great difference, in the eye of conscience, whatever there may be in the eye of law, between your making a man first lose his reason, and then getting fifty guineas out of his pocket, *because* he has lost it; and your picking the fifty guineas out of his pocket, if you had met him dead drunk in his way home to-night. Nay, he who meets a man already drunk and robs him, commits but one sin, while he who makes him drunk first, that he may rob him afterwards, commits two.

Bragwell gravely replied, Mr. Worthy, while I have the practice of people of credit to support me, and the law of the land to protect me, I see no reason to be ashamed of any thing I do.— Mr. Bragwell, answered Worthy, a truly honest man is not always looking sharp about him, to see how far custom and the law will bear him out; if he be honest on principle he will consult the law of his conscience, and if he be a Christian, he will consult the written law of God.

Notwithstanding this rebuff, Mr. Bragwell got home in high spirits, for no arguments could hinder him from feeling that he had the fifty guineas in his purse. As soon as he came in, he gaily threw the money he had received on the table, and desired his wife to lock it up. Instead of of receiving it with her ufual fatisfaction, fhe burft into a violent fit of paffion, and threw it back to him. You may keep your cafh yourfelf, faid fhe. It is all over: we want no more money. You are a ruined man! A wicked creature, fcraping and working as we have done for her! Bragwell trembled, but durft not afk what he dreaded to hear. His wife fpared him the trouble, by crying out, as foon as her rage permitted, Polly is gone off! Poor Bragwell's heart funk within him; he grew fick and giddy, and as his wife's rage fwallowed up her grief, fo, in his grief, he almoft forgot his anger. The purfe fell from his hand, and he caft a look of anguifh upon it, finding, for the firft time, that money cou'd not relieve his mifery.

Mr. Worthy, who, though much concerned, was lefs difcompofed, now called to mind, that the young lady had not returned with her mother and fifter the night before: he begged Mrs. Bragwell to explain this fad ftory. She, inftead of foothing her hufband, fell to reproaching him. It is all your fault, faid fhe, you were a fool for your pains. If I had had my way, the girls never would have kept company with any but men of fubftance, and then they could not have been ruined. Mrs. Bragwell, faid Worthy, if fhe has chofen a bad man, it would be ftill a misfortune, even though he had been rich. O, that would alter the cafe, faid fhe; *a fat forrow is better than a lean one.* But to marry a beggar! there is no fin like that. Here Mifs Betfey, who
ftood

stood sullenly by, put in a word, and said, her sister, however, had not disgraced herself by having married a Farmer or a Tradesman, she had, at least, made choice of a Gentleman. What marriage! what Gentleman, cried the afflicted father. Tell me the worst! He was now informed that his darling daughter was gone off with a strolling player, who had been acting in the neighbouring villages lately. Miss Betsy again put in, saying, he was no stroller, but a gentleman in disguise, who only acted for his own diversion. Does he so, said the now furious Bragwell, then he shall be transported for mine. At this moment a letter was brought him from his new son-in-law, who desired his leave to wait upon him, and implore his forgiveness. He owned he had been shopman to a haberdasher, but thinking his person and talents ought not to be thrown away upon trade, and being also a little behind hand, he had taken to the stage with a view of making his fortune. That he had married Miss Bragwell entirely for love, and was sorry to mention so paltry a thing as money, which he despised, but that his wants were pressing; his landlord, to whom he was in debt, having been so vulgar as to threaten to send him to prison. He ended with saying, I have been obliged to shock your daughter's delicacy, by confessing my unlucky real name; I believe I owe part of my success with her to my having assumed that of Augustus Frederic Theodosius. She is inconsolable at this confession, which,

which, as you are now my father, I must also make to you, and subscribe myself, with many blushes, by the vulgar name of your dutiful son,
TIMOTHY INCLE.

O, cried the afflicted father, as he tore the letter in a rage, Miss Bragwell married to a strolling actor! How shall I bear it? Why, I would not bear it at all, cried the enraged mother, I would never see her, I would never forgive her. I would let her starve at one corner of the barn, while that rascal, with all those Pagan, Popish names, was ranting away at the other. Nay, said Miss Betsey, if he is only a shopman, and if his name be really Timothy Incle, I would never forgive her neither. But who would have thought it by his looks, and by his monstrous genteel behaviour? no, he never can have so vulgar a name.

Come, come, said Mr. Worthy, were he really an honest haberdasher, I should think there was no other harm done, except the disobedience of the thing. Mr. Bragwell, this is no time to blame you, or hardly to reason with you. I feel for you sincerely. I ought not, perhaps, just at present, to reproach you for the mistaken manner in which you have bred up your daughters, as your error has brought its punishment along with it. You now see, because you now feel, the evil of a false education. It has ruined your daughter; your whole plan unavoidably led to some such end. The large sums you spent to qualify them, as you thought, for a high station,

tion, could do them nothing but harm, while your habits of life properly confined them to company of a lower station. While they were better dreſt than the daughters of the firſt gentry, they were worſe taught, as to real knowledge, than the daughters of your plowmen. Their vanity has been raiſed by exceſſive finery, and kept alive by exceſſive flattery. Every evil temper has been foſtered by indulgence. Their pride has never been controuled; their ſelf-will has never been ſubdued. Their idleneſs has laid them open to every temptation, and their abundance has enabled them to gratify every deſire. Their time, that precious talent, has been entirely waſted. Every thing they have been taught to do is of no uſe, while they are utterly unacquainted with all which they ought to have known. I deplore Miſs Polly's falſe ſtep. That ſhe ſhould have married a run-away ſhopman, turned ſtroller, I truly lament. But, for what huſband was ſhe qualified? For the wife of a Farmer ſhe was too idle. For the wife of a Tradeſman ſhe was too expenſive. For the wife of a Gentleman ſhe was too ignorant. You, yourſelf, was moſt to blame. You expected her to act wiſely, though you never taught her that *fear of God which is the beginning of wiſdom.* I owe it to you, as a friend, and to myſelf as a Chriſtian, to declare, that your practices in the common tranſactions of life, as well as your preſent misfortune, are almoſt the natural conſequences

sequences of those false principles which I protested against when you were at my house*.

Mrs. Bragwell attempted several times to interrupt Mr. Worthy, but her husband would not permit it. He felt the force of all his friend said, and encouraged him to proceed. Mr. Worthy thus went on. It grieves me to say how much your own indiscretion has contributed even to bring on your present misfortune. You gave your countenance to this very company of strollers, though you knew they are acting in defiance to the laws of the land, to say no worse. They go from town to town, and from barn to barn, stripping the poor of their money, the young of their innocence, and all of their time. Do you remember with how much pride you told me that you had bespoke *The Bold Stroke for a Wife*, for the benefit of this very Mr. Frederic Theodosius? To this pernicious ribaldry you not only carried your own family, but wasted I know not how much money in treating your workmen's wives and children, in these hard times too, when they have scarcely bread to eat, or a shoe on their feet. And all this only that you might have the absurd pleasure of seeing those flattering words, *By Desire of Mr. Bragwell*, stuck up in Print at the Public-house, on the Blacksmith's shed, at the Turnpike-gate, and on the Barn-door.

Mr. Bragwell acknowledged that his friend's rebuke was but too just, and he looked so very

---

* See Second Part of Two Farmers.

contrite as to raise the pity of Mr. Worthy, who, in a mild voice, thus went on. What I have said is not so much to reproach you with the ruin of one daughter, as from a desire to save the other. Let Miss Betsey go home with me. I do not undertake to be her gaoler, but I will be her friend. She will find in my daughters kind companions, and in my wife a prudent guide. I know she will dislike us at first, but I do not despair in time of convincing her that a sober, humble, useful, pious life, is as necessary to make us happy on earth, as it is to fit us for heaven.

Poor Miss Betsey, though she declared it would be *frightful dull*, and *monstrous vulgar*, and *dismal melancholy*, yet was she so terrified at the discontent and grumbling which she would have to endure at home, that she sullenly consented. She had none of that filial tenderness which led her to wish to stay and sooth and comfort her afflicted father! All she thought about was to get out of the way of her mother's ill humour, and to carry so much finery with her as to fill the Miss Worthies with envy and respect. Poor girl! She did not know that envy was a feeling they never indulged; and that fine cloaths was the last thing to draw their respect. Mr. Worthy took her home next day. When they reached his house, they found there young Wilson, Miss Betsey's old admirer. She was much pleased at this, and resolved to treat him well. But her good or ill treatment now signified but little. This young Grazier reverenced Mr. Worthy's character,

character, and ever since he had met him at the Lion, had been thinking what a happiness it would be to marry a young woman bred up by such a father. He had heard much of the modesty and discretion of both the daughters, but his inclination now determined him in favour of the elder.

Mr. Worthy, who knew him to be a young man of good sense and sound principles, allowed him to become a visitor at his house, but deferred his consent to the marriage till he knew him more thoroughly. Mr. Wilson, from what he saw of the domestic piety of this family, improved daily both in the knowledge and practice of religion, and Mr. Worthy soon formed him into a most valuable character. During this time Miss Bragwell's hopes had revived, but though she appeared in a new dress almost every day, she had the mortification of being beheld with great indifference by one whom she had always secretly liked. Mr. Wilson married before her face a girl who was greatly her inferior in fortune, person, and appearance, but who was humble, frugal, meek, and pious. Miss Bragwell now strongly felt the truth of what Mr. Wilson had once told her, that a woman may make an excellent partner for a dance, who would make a very bad one for life.

Hitherto Mr. Bragwell and his daughters had only learnt to regret their folly and vanity, as it had produced them mortification in this life; whether they were ever brought to a more serious sense of their errors, may be seen in a future part of this history.
Z.

PART VI.

MR. BRAGWELL was so much afflicted at the disgraceful marriage of his daughter, who ran off with Timothy Incle, the strolling-player, that he never fully recovered his spirits. His chearfulness which had arisen from an high opinion of himself, had been confirmed by a constant flow of uninterrupted success; and that is a sort of chearfulness which is very liable to be impaired, because it lies at the mercy of every accident and cross event in life. But though his pride was now disappointed, his misfortunes had not taught him any humility, because he had not discovered that they were caused by his own fault; nor had he acquired any patience or submission, because he had not learnt that all afflictions come from the hand of God to awaken us to a deep sense of our sins, and to draw off our hearts from the perishing vanities of this life. Besides, Mr. Bragwell was one of those people, who, even if they would be thought to bear with tolerable submission such trials as appear to be sent more immediately from Providence, yet think they have a sort of right to rebel at every misfortune which befals them through the fault of a fellow-creature; as if our fellow-creatures were not the agents and instruments by which Providence often sees fit to try or to punish us.

This

This imprudent daughter, Bragwell would not be brought to see or forgive, nor was the degrading name of Mrs. Incle ever allowed to be pronounced in his hearing. He had loved her with an excessive and undue affection; and while she gratified his vanity by her beauty and finery, he deemed her faults of little consequence; but when she disappointed his ambition by a disgraceful marriage, all his natural affection only served to increase his resentment. Yet, though he regretted her crime less than his own mortification, he never ceased in secret to lament her loss. She soon found out she was undone, and wrote in a strain of bitter repentance to ask his forgiveness. She owned that her husband, whom she had supposed to be a man of fashion in disguise, was a low person in distressed circumstances. She implored that her father, though he refused to give her husband that fortune for which alone it was now too plain he had married her, would at least allow her some subsistence, for that Mr. Incle was much in debt, and she feared in danger of a gaol. The father's heart was half melted at this account, and his affection was for a time awakened. But Mrs. Bragwell opposed his sending her any assistance. She always made it a point of duty never to forgive; " for she said it only encouraged those who had done wrong once to do worse next time. For her part she had never yet been guilty of so mean and pitiful a weakness as to forgive any one; for to pardon an injury always shewed either want of spirit to feel it, or want of power to resent it. She was resolved she would never squander the money for which she had worked early and late, on a baggage who had thrown herself away on a beggar, while she had a daughter single who might raise her family by a great match." I am sorry to say that Mrs. Bragwell's anger was not owing to the undutifulness of the daughter, or the worthlessness of the husband; poverty was in her eyes the grand crime. The doctrine of forgiveness, as a religious principle, made no more a part of Mr. Bragwell's system than of his wife's, but in natural feeling, particularly for this offending daughter, he much exceeded her.

In a few months, the youngest Miss Bragwell desired leave to return home from Mr. Worthy's. She had, indeed, only consented to go thither as a less evil of the two than staying in her father's house after her sister's elopement. But the sobriety and simplicity of Mr. Worthy's family were irksome to her. Habits of vanity and idleness were become so rooted in her mind, that any degree of restraint was a burthen; and though she was outwardly civil, it was easy to see that she longed to get away. She resolved, however, to profit by her sister's faults; and made her parents easy by assuring them she never would throw herself away on a *man who was worth nothing*. Encouraged by these promises, which were all that her parents thought they could

could in reason expect, her father allowed her to come home.

Mr. Worthy, who accompanied her, found Mr. Bragwell gloomy and dejected. As his house was no longer a scene of vanity and festivity, Mr. Bragwell tried to make himself and his friend believe that he was grown religious; whereas he was only become discontented. As he had always fancied that piety was a melancholy gloomy thing, and as he felt his own mind really gloomy, he was willing to think that he was growing pious. He had, indeed, gone more constantly to church, and had taken less pleasure in feasting and cards, and now and then read a chapter in the Bible; but all this was because his spirits were low, and not because his heart was changed. The outward actions were more regular, but the inward man was the same. The forms of religion were resorted to as a painful duty; but this only added to his misery, while he was utterly ignorant of its spirit and its power. He still, however, reserved religion as a loathsome medicine, to which he feared he must have recourse at last, and of which he even now considered every abstinence from pleasure, or every exercise of piety as a bitter dose. His health also was impaired, so that his friend found him in a pitiable state, neither able to receive pleasure from the world, which he so dearly loved, nor from religion which he so greatly feared. He expected to have been much commended by Worthy for the change in his way of life; but

Worthy, who saw that the alteration was only owing to the loss of animal spirits, and to the casual absence of temptation, was cautious of flattering him too much. " I thought, Mr. Worthy," said he, " to have received more comfort from you. I was told too, that religion was full of comfort, but I do not much find it." You were told the truth, replied Worthy, Religion is full of comfort, but you must first be brought into a state fit to receive it before it can become so; you must be brought to a deep and humbling sense of sin. To give you comfort while you are puffed up with high thoughts of yourself, would be to give you a strong cordial in a high fever. Religion keeps back her cordials till the patient is lowered and emptied; emptied of self, Mr. Bragwell. If you had a wound, it must be examined and cleansed, aye, and probed too, before it would be safe to put on a healing plaister. Curing it to the outward eye, while it was corrupt at bottom, would only bring on a mortification, and you would be a dead man while you trusted that the plaister was curing you. You must be, indeed, a Christian, before you can be entitled to the comforts of Christianity.—I am a Christian, said Bragwell, many of my friends are Christians, but I do not see it has done us much good.—Christianity itself, answered Worthy, cannot make us good unless it be applied to our hearts. Christian privileges will not make us Christians unless we make use of them. On that shelf I fee stands your medicine. The doctor orders you to take it. "*Have* you taken it?"—Yes, replied Bragwell. Are you the better for it? said Worthy.—I think I am, he replied.—But, added Worthy, are you the better because the doctor has ordered it merely, or because you have also taken it?—What a foolish question, cried Bragwell. Why, to be sure the doctor might be the best doctor, and his physic the best physic in the world; but if it stood for ever on the shelf, I could not expect to be cured by it. My doctor is not a mountebank. He does not pretend to cure by a charm. The physic is good, and as it suits my case, though it is bitter, I take it.—You have now, said Worthy, explained undesignedly the reason why Religion does so little good in the world. It is not a mountebank; it does not work by a charm; but offers to cure your worst corruptions by wholesome, though sometimes bitter prescriptions. But you will not take them; you will not apply to God with the same earnest desire to be healed with which you apply to your doctor; you will not confess your sins to the one as honestly as you tell your symptoms to the other, nor read your Bible with the same faith and submission with which you take your medicine. In reading it, however, you must take care not to apply to yourself the comforts which are not suited to your case. You must, by the grace of God, be brought into a condition to be entitled to the promises, before you can expect the comfort of them. Conviction is not conversion; that worldly discontent which is the effect of worldly disappointment, is not that *godly sorrow which worketh repentance*. Besides, while you have been pursuing all the gratifications of the world, do not complain that you have not all the comforts of Religion too. Could you live in the full enjoyment of both, *the Bible would not be true*.

Bragwell now seemed resolved to set about the matter in earnest, but he resolved in his own strength; and, unluckily, the very day Mr. Worthy took leave, there happened to be a grand ball at the next town, on account of the assizes. An assize-ball is a scene to which gentlemen and ladies periodically resort to celebrate the crimes and calamities of their fellow-creatures by dancing and music, and to divert themselves with feasting and drinking, while unhappy wretches are receiving sentence of death.

To this ball Miss Bragwell went, dressed out with a double portion of finery, pouring out on her own head the whole band-box of feathers and flowers her sister had left behind her. While she was at the ball her father formed many plans of religious reformation; he talked of lessening his business, that he might have more leisure for devotion; though not *just now*, while the markets were so high; and then he began to think of sending a handsome subscription to the infirmary; though, on second thoughts, he concluded he need not be *in a hurry*, but leave

it

it in his will; but to give, and repent, and reform, were three things he was bent upon. But when his daughter came home at night, so happy and so fine, and telling how she had danced with Squire Squeeze the great corn contractor, and how many fine things he had said to her, Mr. Bragwell felt the old spirit of the world return in its full force. A marriage with Mr. Dashall Squeeze, the contractor, was beyond his hopes, for Mr. Squeeze was supposed from a very low beginning to have got rich during the war. As for Mr. Squeeze he had picked up as much of the history of his partner between the dances as he desired, he was convinced there would be no money wanting, for Miss Bragwell, who was now looked on as an only child, must needs be a great fortune, and he was too much used to advantageous contracts to let this slip. As he was gaudily dressed, and possessed all the arts of vulgar flattery, Miss Bragwell eagerly caught at his proposal to wait on her father next day. Squeeze was quite a man after Bragwell's own heart, a genius at getting money, a fine dashing fellow at spending it. He told his wife that this was the very sort of man for his daughter, for he got money like a Jew and spent it like a Prince; but whether it was fairly got, or wisely spent, he was too much a man of the world to inquire. Mrs. Bragwell was not so run away with by appearances, but she desired her husband to be careful and quite sure that it was the right Mr. Squeeze, and no impostor. But being assured that Betsey would certainly keep her carriage, she never gave herself one thought with what sort of man she was to ride in it. To have one of her daughters drive in her own coach, filled up all her ideas of human happiness. The marriage was celebrated with great splendor, and Mr. and Mrs. Squeeze set off for London, where they had a house.

Mr. Bragwell now tried to forget that he had any other daughter, and if some thoughts of the resolutions he had made of entering on a more religious course, would sometimes force themselves upon him, they were put off, like the repentance of Felix, *to a more convenient season*, and finding he was likely to have a grandchild, he became more worldly and ambitious than ever, thinking this a just pretence for adding house to house, and field to field; and there is no stratagem by which men more deceive themselves than when they make even unborn children a pretence for that rapine, or that hoarding, of which their own covetousness is the true motive. Whenever he ventured to write to Mr. Worthy about the wealth, the gaiety, and the grandeur of Mr. and Mrs. Squeeze, that faithful friend honestly reminded him of the vanity and uncertainty of worldly greatness, and the error he had been guilty of in marrying his daughter before he had taken time to inquire into the real character of the man, saying, that he could not help foreboding, that the happiness of a match made at a ball might have an end. Notwithstanding, Mr. Bragwell had paid down a larger fortune than was prudent, for fear Mr. Squeeze should fly off, yet he was surprised to receive very soon a pressing letter from him, desiring him to advance a considerable sum, as he had the offer of an advantageous purchase, which he must lose for want of money. Bragwell was staggered, and refused to comply; but his wife told him he must not be shabby to such a gentleman as 'Squire Squeeze, for that she heard on all sides such accounts of their grandeur, their feasts, their carriages, and their liveries, that she and her husband ought even to deny themselves comforts to oblige such a generous son, who did all this in honour of their daughter; besides, if he did not send the money soon, they might be obliged to lay down their coach, and then she should never be able to shew her face again. At length Mr. Bragwell lent him the money on his bond: he knew Squeeze's income was large, for he had carefully enquired into this particular, and for the rest he took his word. Mrs. Squeeze also got great presents from her mother, by representing to her how expensively they were forced to live to keep up their credit, and what honour she was conferring on the family of the Bragwell's by spending their money in such grand company. Among many other letters she wrote her the following:—

" *To Mrs. Bragwell.*

" You can't imagine, dear mother, how charmingly we live—I lye a-bed almost all day, and am

up

up all night; but it is never dark for all that, for we burn such numbers of candles all at once, that the sun would be of no use at all in London.—Then I am so happy! for we are never quiet a moment, Sundays or working-days, nay, I should not know which was which, only that we have most pleasure on a Sunday, because it is the only day in which people have nothing to do but divert themselves.—Then the great folks are all so kind, and so good, they have not a bit of pride, for they will come and eat and drink, and win my money just as if I was their equals; and if I have got but a cold, they are so very unhappy that they send to know how I do; and though I suppose they can't rest till the footman has told them, yet they are so polite, that if I have been dying they seem to have forgot it next time we meet, and not to know but they have seen me the day before. Oh! they are true friends; and for ever smiling, and so fond of one another, that they like to meet and enjoy one another's company by hundreds, and always think the more the merrier.

Your dutiful daughter,

BETSEY SQUEEZE."

The style of her letters, however, altered in a few months. She owned that though things went on gayer and grander than ever, yet she hardly ever saw her husband, except her house was full of company, and cards, or dancing was going

going on; that he was often so busy he could not come all night, that he always borrowed the money her mother sent her when he was going out on this nightly business; and that the last time she had asked *him* for money, he cursed, and swore, and bid her apply to the old farmer and his rib, who were made of money. This letter Mrs. Bragwell concealed from her husband.

At length on some change in public affairs, Mr. Squeeze, who had made an overcharge of some thousand pounds in one article, lost his contract; he was found to owe a large debt to government, and his accounts must be made up immediately. This was impossible, he had not only spent his large income without making any provision for his family, but had contracted heavy debts by gaming and other vices. His creditors poured in upon him. He wrote to Bragwell to borrow another sum; but without hinting at the loss of his contract. These repeated demands made Bragwell so uneasy, that instead of sending him the money, he resolved to go himself secretly to London, and judge by his own eyes how things were going on, as his mind strangely misgave him. He got to Mr. Squeeze's house about eleven at night, and knocked gently, concluding that they must needs be gone to bed. But what was his astonishment to find the hall was full of men; he pushed through in spite of them, though to his great surprise they insisted on knowing his name. This affronted him: he refused, saying, I am not ashamed of my name,

it

it will pass for thousands in any market in the West of England. Is this your London manners, not to let a man of my credit in without knowing his name indeed! What was his amazement to see every room as full of card-tables, and of fine gentlemen and ladies as it would hold; all was so light, and so gay, and so festive, and so grand, that he reproached himself for his suspicions, thought nothing too good for them, and resolved secretly to give Squeeze another five hundred pounds to help to keep up so much grandeur and happiness. At length seeing a footman he knew, he asked him where were his master and mistress; for he could not pick them out among the company; or rather his ideas were so confused with the splendour of the scene, that he did not know whether they were there or not. The man said that his master had just sent for his lady up stairs, and he believed that he was not well. Mr. Bragwell said he would go up himself and look for his daughter, as he could not speak so freely to her before all that company. He went up and knocked at the chamber door, and its not being opened, made him push it with some violence. He heard a bustling noise within, and again made a fruitless attempt to open the door. At this the noise increased, and Mr. Bragwell was struck to the heart at the sound of a pistol from within. He now kicked so violently against the door that it burst open, when the first sight he saw was his daughter falling to the ground in a fit, and Mr. Squeeze

Squeeze dying by a shot from a pistol which was dropping out of his hand. Mr. Bragwell was not the only person whom the sound of the pistol had alarmed. The servants, the company, all heard it, and all ran up to this scene of horror. Those who had the best of the game took care to bring up their tricks in their hands, having had the prudence to leave the very few who could be trusted, to watch the stakes, while those who had a prospect of losing, profited by the confusion and threw up their cards. All was dismay and terror. Some ran for a surgeon, others examined the dying man, while some removed Mrs. Squeeze to her bed, while poor Bragwell could neither see nor hear, nor do any thing. One of the company took up a letter which lay open upon the table, addressed to him, they read it, hoping it might explain the horrid mystery. It was as follows:

"*To Mr. Bragwell.*

" Sir,

" Fetch home your daughter, I have ruined her, myself, and the child, to which she every hour expects to be a mother. I have lost my contract. My debts are immense. You refuse me money: I must die then; but I will die like a man of spirit. They wait to take me to prison, I have two executions in my house; but I have ten card tables in it. I would die as I have lived. I invited all this company, and have drank

drank hard since dinner to get primed for the dreadful deed. My wife refuses to write to you for another thousand, and she must take the consequences. *Vanity* has been my ruin. It has caused all my crimes. Whoever is resolved to live beyond his income is liable to every sin. He can never say to himself, thus far shalt thou go and no farther. Vanity led me to commit acts of rapine, that I might live in splendor; vanity makes me commit self-murder, because I will not live in poverty. The new philosophy says, that death is an eternal sleep; but the new philosophy lies. Do you take heed: it is too late for me. The dreadful gulf yawns to swallow me—I plunge into perdition. There is no repentance in the grave, no hope in hell.

Your's

Dashall Squeeze."

The dead body was removed, and Mr. Bragwell remaining almost without speech, or motion, the company began to think of retiring, much out of humour at having their party so disagreeably broken up; they comforted themselves, however, that as it were *so early*, for it was now scarcely twelve, they could finish their evening at another party or two; so completely do habits of *pleasure*, as it is called, harden the heart, and steel it not only against virtuous impressions, but against natural feeelings. Now it was, that those who had nightly rioted at the expence of those wretched

wretched people were the first to abuse them. Not an offer of assistance was made to this poor forlorn woman; not a word of kindness, or of pity, nothing but censure was now heard. Why must those upstarts ape people of quality? though as long as these upstarts could feast them, their vulgarity, and their bad character had never been produced against them. " As long as thou dost well unto thyself, men shall speak good of thee." One guest who, unluckily, had no other house to go to, coolly said, as he walked off,—Squeeze might as well have put off shooting himself till the morning. It was monstrous provoking that he could not wait an hour or two.

As every thing in the house was seized, Mr. Bragwell prevailed on his miserable daughter, weak as she was, next morning to set out with him for the country. His acquaintance with polite life was short, but he had seen a great deal in a little time. They had a slow and a sad journey. In about a week, Mrs. Squeeze lay-in of a dead child, she herself languished a few days and then died; and the afflicted parents saw the two darling objects of their ambition, for whose sakes they had made *too much haste to be rich*, carried to the land where all things are forgotten. Mrs. Bragwell's grief, like her other passions, was extravagant; and poor Bragwell's sorrow was rendered so bitter by self-reproach, that he would quite have sunk under it, had he not thought of his old expedient in distress, that of of sending for Mr. Worthy to comfort him. It was Mr. Worthy's way, to warn people of those misfortunes which he saw their faults must needs bring on them, but not to reproach, or desert them when the misfortunes came. He had never been near Bragwell, during the short, but flourishing, reign of the Squeezes; for he knew that prosperity made the ears deaf, and the heart hard to good counsel; but as soon as he heard his friend was in trouble he set out to go to him. Bragwell burst into a violent fit of tears when he saw him, and when he could speak, said, This trial is more than I can bear. Mr. Worthy kindly took him by the hand, and when he was a little composed, said, I will tell you a short story. There was in ancient times a famous man who was a slave. His master, who was very good to him, one day gave him a bitter melon, and bade him eat it; he eat it up without one word of complaint. How was it possible, said the master, for you to eat so very nauseous and disagreeable a fruit? The slave replied, My good master, I have received so many favours from your bounty, that it is no wonder if I should once in my life eat one bitter melon from your hands. This generous answer so struck the master, that the history, says he, gave him his liberty. With such submissive sentiments, my friend, should man receive his portion of sufferings from God, from whom he receives so many blessings. You in particular have received much

good

good at the hand of God, shall you not receive evil also?

O Mr. Worthy, said Bragwell, this blow is too heavy for me, I cannot survive this shock. I do not desire it, I only desire to die. We are very apt to talk most of dying when we are least fit for it, said Worthy. This is not the language of that submission which makes us prepare for death, but of that despair which makes us out of humour with life. O, Mr. Bragwell, you are indeed disappointed of the grand ends which made life so delightful to you; but till your heart is humbled, till you are brought to a serious conviction of sin, till you are brought to see what is the true end of life, you can have no hope in death. You think you have no business on earth, because those for whose sake you too eagerly heaped up riches are no more. But is there not under the canopy of heaven some afflicted being whom you may yet relieve, some modest merit which you may bring forward, some helpless creature you may save by your advice, some perishing christian you may sustain by your wealth? When you have no sins of your own to repent of, no mercies of God to be thankful for, no miseries of others to relieve, then, and not till then, I consent you should sink down in despair, and call on death to relieve you.

Mr. Worthy attended his afflicted friend to the funeral of his unhappy daughter and her babe. The solemn service, the committing his late gay
and

and beautiful daughter to darkness, to worms, and to corruption, the sight of the dead infant, for whose sake he had resumed all his schemes of vanity and covetousness, when he thought he had got the better of them, the melancholy conviction that all human prosperity ends in *ashes to ashes and dust to dust*, had brought down Mr. Bragwell's self-sufficient and haughty soul into something of that humble frame in which Mr. Worthy had wished to see it. As soon as they returned home he was beginning to seize the favourable moment for fixing these serious impressions, when they were unseasonably interrupted by the parish officer, who came to ask Mr. Bragwell what he was to do with a poor dying woman who was travelling the country with her child, and was taken in a fit under the church-yard wall? At first they thought she was dead, said the man, but finding she still breathed, they have carried her into the workhouse till she could give some account of herself. Mr. Bragwell was impatient at the interruption, which was indeed unseasonable, and told the man he was at that time too much overcome by sorrow to attend to business, but he would give him an answer to-morrow. But my friend, said Mr. Worthy, the poor woman may die to-night; your mind is indeed not in a frame for worldly business, but there is no sorrow too great to forbid our attending the calls of duty. An act of christian charity will not disturb but improve the seriousness of your spirit, and though you cannot dry your own tears, God may, in great mercy, permit you to dry thofe of another. This may be one of thofe occafions for which I told you life was worth keeping. Do let us fee this woman. Bragwell was not in a ftate either to confent or refufe, and his friend drew him to the workhoufe, about the door of which ftood a crowd of people. She is not dead, faid one, fhe moves her head. But fhe wants air, faid they all, while they all, according to cuftom, pufhed fo clofe upon her that it was impoffible fhe fhould get any. A fine boy of two or three years old ftood by her, crying, Mammy is dead, mammy is ftarved. Mr. Worthy made up to the poor woman, holding his friend by the arm: in order to give her air he untied a large black bonnet which hid her face, when Mr. Bragwell, at that moment cafting his eyes on her, faw in this poor ftranger the face of his own run-away daughter, Mrs. Incle. He groaned, but could not fpeak, and as he was turning away to conceal his anguifh, the little boy fondly caught hold of his hand, lifping out—O ftay, and give mammy fome bread. His heart yearned towards the child, he grafped his little hand in his, while he forrowfully faid to Mr. Worthy, It is too much, fend away the people. It is my dear naughty child, *my punifhment is greater than I can bear.* Mr. Worthy defired the people to go and leave the ftranger to them; but by this time fhe was no ftranger to any of them. Pale and meagre as was her face, and poor and fhabby as was her

drefs,

dress, the proud and flaunting Miss Polly Bragwell was easily known by every one present. They went away, but with the mean revenge of little minds, they paid themselves by abuse, for all the airs and insolence they had once endured from her. Pride must have a fall, said one. I remember when she was too good to speak to a poor body, said another; where are her flounces and her furbelows now? It is come home to her at last. Her child looks as if he would be glad of the worst bit she formerly denied us.

In the mean time Mr. Bragwell had sunk in an old wicker chair which stood behind, and groaned out, Lord forgive my hard heart! Lord subdue my proud heart, "create a clean heart, O God, and renew a right spirit within me." This was perhaps the first word of genuine prayer he had ever offered up in his whole life. Worthy overheard it, and his heart rejoiced, but this was not a time for talking, but doing. He asked Bragwell what was to be done with the unfortunate woman, who now seemed to recover fast, but she did not see them, for they were behind. She embraced her boy, and faintly said, my child what shall we do? *I will arise and go to my father, and say unto him, father I have sinned against heaven and before thee.* This was a joyful sound to Mr. Worthy, who began to hope that her heart might be as much changed for the better as her circumstances were altered for the worse, and he valued the goods of fortune so little, and contrition of soul so much, that he began to think the chang change on the whole might be a happy one. The boy then sprung from his mother and ran to Bragwell, saying, Do be good to mammy. Mrs. Incle looking round, now perceived her father; she fell at his feet, saying, O forgive your guilty child, and save your innocent one from starving. Bragwell sunk down by her, and prayed God to forgive both her and himself in terms of genuine sorrow. To hear words of real penitence and heart-felt prayer from this once high-minded father and vain daughter, was music to Worthy's ears, who thought this moment of outward misery was the only joyful one he had ever spent in the Bragwell family. He was resolved not to interfere, but to let the father's own feelings work out the way in which he was to act. Bragwell said nothing, but slowly led to his own house, holding the little boy by the hand, and pointing to Worthy to assist the feeble steps of his daughter, who once more entered her father's doors; but the dread of seeing her mother quite overpowered her. Mrs. Bragwell's heart was not changed, but sorrow had weakened her powers of resistance, and she rather suffered her daughter to come in, than gave her a kind reception. She was more astonished than pleased; and, even in this trying moment, was more disgusted with the little boy's mean cloaths, than delighted with his rosy face. As soon as she was a little recovered, Mr. Bragwell desired his daughter to tell him how she happened to be at that place just at that time.

In a weak voice she began, My tale, Sir, is short, but mournful.—Now I am very sorry that my Readers must wait for this short but mournful tale, till next month.

PART VII.

I LEFT your house, my dear father, said Mrs. Incle, with a heart full of vain triumph. I had no doubt but my husband was a great man who had put on that disguise to obtain my hand. Judge then what I felt to find that he was a needy impostor, who wanted my money but did not care for me. This discovery, though it mortified, did not humble me. I had neither affection to bear with the man who had deceived me, nor religion to improve by the disappointment. I have found that change of circumstances does not change the heart, till God is pleased to do it. My misfortunes only taught me to rebel more against him. I thought God unjust; I accused my father, I was envious of my sister, I hated my husband; but never once did I blame myself. My husband picked up a wretched subsistence by joining himself to any low scheme of idle pleasure that was going on. He would follow a mountebank, carry a dice-box, or fiddle at a fair. He was always taunting me for that gentility on which I so much valued myself.

myself. If I had married a poor working girl, said he, she could now have got her bread; but a fine lady, without money, is a burthen to her husband, and a plague to society. Every trial which affection might have made lighter, we doubled by animosity; at length my husband was detected in using false dice; he fought with his accuser, both were seized by a press-gang, and sent to sea. I was now left to the wide world, and miserable as I had thought myself before, I soon found there were higher degrees of misery. I was near my time, without bread for myself, or hope for my child. I set out on foot in search of the village where I had heard my husband say his friends lived. It was a severe trial to my proud heart to stoop to those low people, but hunger is not delicate, and I was near perishing. My husband's parents received me kindly, saying, that though they had nothing but what they earned by their labour, yet I was welcome to share their hard fare, for they trusted that God who sent mouths would send meat also. They gave me a small room in their cottage, and many necessaries, which they denied themselves.

O, my child, interrupted Bragwell, every word cuts me to the heart. These poor people gladly gave thee of their little, while thy rich parents left thee to starve.

How shall I own, continued Mrs. Incle, that all this goodness could not soften my heart, for God had not yet touched it. I received all their kindness as a favour done to them. When my father

father brought me home any little dainty which he could pick up, and my mother kindly dressed it for me, I would not condescend to eat it with them, but devoured it sullenly in my little garret alone, suffering them to fetch and carry every thing I wanted. As my haughty behaviour was not likely to gain their affection, it was plain they did not love me: and as I had no notion that there were any other motives to good actions but fondness, or self-interest, I was puzzled to know what could make them so kind to me, for of the powerful and constraining law of christian charity I was quite ignorant. To cheat the weary hours, I looked about for some books, and found, among a few others of the same cast, *Doddridge's Rise and Progress of Religion in the Soul.* But all those books were addressed to *sinners*; now as I knew I was not a sinner, I threw them away in disgust. Indeed they were ill suited to a taste formed by novels, to which reading I chiefly trace my ruin, for, vain as I was, I should never have been guilty of so wild a step as to run away, had not my heart been tainted, and my imagination inflamed, by those pernicious books.

At length my little George was born. This added to the burthen I had brought on this poor family, but it did not diminish their kindness, and we continued to share their scanty fare without any upbraiding on their part, or any gratitude on mine. Even this poor baby did not soften my heart; I wept over him indeed day and night, but they were tears of despair; I was
always

always idle, and wasted those hours in sinful murmurs at his fate, which I should have employed in trying to maintain him. Hardship, grief, and impatience, at length brought on a fever. Death seemed now at hand, and I felt a gloomy satisfaction in the thought of being rid of my miseries, to which I fear was added, a sullen joy to think that you, Sir, and my mother, would be plagued to hear of my death when it would be too late, and in this your grief, I anticipated a gloomy sort of revenge. But it pleased my merciful God not to let me thus perish in my sins. My poor mother-in-law sent for a good clergyman, who pointed out to me the danger of dying in that hard and unconverted state so forcibly, that I shuddered to find on what a dreadful precipice I stood. He prayed with me, and for me, so earnestly, that at length God, who is sometimes pleased to magnify his own glory in awakening those who are dead in trespasses and sins, was pleased, of his free grace, to open my blind eyes, and soften my stony heart. I saw myself a sinner, and prayed to be delivered from the wrath of God, in comparison of which the poverty and disgrace I now suffered appeared as nothing. To a soul convinced of sin, the news of a Redeemer was a joyful sound. Instead of reproaching Providence, or blaming my parents, or abusing my husband, I now learnt to condemn myself, to adore that God who had not cut me off in my ignorance, to pray for pardon for the past, and grace for the time to come.

I now desired to submit to penury and hunger in this world, so that I might but live in the fear of God here, and enjoy his favour in the world to come. I now learnt to compare my present light sufferings, the consequence of my own sin, with those bitter sufferings of my Saviour which he endured for my sake, and I was ashamed of murmuring. But self-ignorance, conceit, and vanity, were so rooted in me, that my progress was very gradual, and I had the sorrow to feel, how much the power of long bad habits keeps down the growth of religion in the heart, even after it has begun to take root. I was so ignorant of divine things, that I hardly knew words to frame a prayer; but when I got acquainted with the Psalms, I there learnt how to pour out the fulness of my heart, while in the Gospel I rejoiced to see what great things God had done for my soul.

I now took down once more from the shelf *Deddridge's Rise and Progress*, and, oh! with what new eyes did I read it! I now saw clearly, that not only the thief, and the drunkard, the murderer, and the adulterer, are sinners, for that I knew before; but I found that the unbeliever, the selfish, the proud, the worldly-minded, all, in short, who live without God in the world, are sinners. I did not now apply the reproofs I met with, to my husband, or my father, or other people, as I used to do, but brought them home to myself. In this book I traced, with strong emotions, and close self-application, the sinner

through

through all his course; his first awakening, his convictions, repentance, joys, sorrows, backsliding, and recovery, despondency, and delight, to a triumphant death-bed; and God was pleased to make it a chief instrument in bringing me to himself. Here it is, continued Mrs. Incle, untying her little bundle, and taking out a book, accept it, my dear father, and I will pray that God may bless it to you as He has done to me.

When I was able to come down, I passed my time with these good old people, and soon won their affection. I was surprized to find they had very good sense, which I never had thought poor people could have; but, indeed, worldly persons do not know how much religion, while it mends the heart, enlightens the understanding also. I now regretted the evenings I had wasted in my solitary garret, when I might have passed them in reading the Bible with these good folks. This was their refreshing cordial after a weary day, which sweetened the pains of want and age. I one day expressed my surprize that my unfortunate husband, the son of such pious parents, should have turned out so ill: the poor old man said with tears, I fear we have been guilty of the sin of Eli; our love was of the wrong sort. Alas! like him, *we honoured our son more than God*, and God has smitten us for it. We shewed him what was right, but through a false indulgence, we did not correct him for what was wrong. We were blind to his faults. He was a handsome boy, with sprightly parts; we took too much delight in those outward things. He soon got above our management, and became vain, idle, and extravagant, and when we sought to restrain him, it was then too late. We humbled ourselves before God; but he was pleased to make our sin become its own punishment. Timothy grew worse and worse; till he was forced to abscond for a misdemeanor; after which we never saw him, but have heard of him changing from one idle way of life to another, *unstable as water:* he has been a footman, a soldier, a shopman, and a strolling actor. With deep sorrow we trace back his vices to our ungoverned fondness; that lively and sharp wit, by which he has been able to carry on such a variety of wild schemes, might, if we had used him to reproof in his youth, have enabled him to have done great service for God and his country. But our flattery made him wise in his own conceit; and there is more hope of a fool than of him. We indulged our own vanity, and have destroyed his soul.

Here Mr. Worthy stopped Mrs. Incle, saying, that whenever he heard it lamented that the children of pious parents often turned out so ill, he could not help thinking that there must be frequently something of this sort of error in the bringing them up: he knew, indeed, some instances to the contrary, in which the best means had failed; but he believed, that from Eli the priest, to Incle the labourer, more than half the failures of this sort might be traced to some mistake,

take, or vanity, or bad judgment, or sinful indulgence in the parents.

I now looked about, continued Mrs. Incle, in order to see in what way I could assist my poor mother, regretting more heartily than she did, that I knew no one thing that was of any use. I was so desirous of humbling myself before God and her, that I offered even to try to wash.—You wash! exclaimed Bragwell, starting up with great emotion, Heaven forbid that with such a fortune and education, Miss Bragwell should be seen at a washing-tub. This vain father, who could bear to hear of her distresses and her sins, could not bear to hear of her washing. Mr. Worthy stopped him, saying, As to her fortune, you know, you refused to give her any; and, as to her education, you see it had not taught her how to do any thing better. I am sorry you do not see in this instance, the beauty of Christian humility. For my own part, I set a greater value on such an active proof of it, than on a whole volume of professions. Mr. Bragwell did not quite understand this, and Mrs. Incle went on. What to do to get a penny I knew not. Making of fillagree, or fringe, or card-purses, or cutting out paper, or dancing and singing, was of no use in our village. The shopkeeper, indeed, would have taken me, if I had known any thing of accounts; and the clergyman could have got me a nursery-maid's place, if I could have done good plain-work. I made some aukward attempts to learn to spin and knit, when my mother's wheel or knitting lay by, but I spoilt both through my ignorance. At last I luckily thought upon the fine netting I used to make for my trimmings, and it struck me that I might turn this to some little account. I procured some twine, and worked early and late to make nets for fishermen, and cabbage-nets. I was so pleased that I had at last found an opportunity to shew my good-will by this mean work, that I regretted my little George was not big enough to contribute his share to our support by travelling about to sell my nets.

Cabbage-nets! exclaimed Bragwell; there is no bearing this.—Cabbage-nets! My grandson hawk cabbage-nets! How could you think of such a scandalous thing?—Sir, said Mrs. Incle mildly, I am now convinced that nothing is scandalous which is not wicked. Besides, we were in want; and necessity, as well as piety, would have reconciled me to this mean trade. Mr. Bragwell groaned, and bade her go on.

In the mean time, my little George grew a fine boy; and I adored the goodness of God, who, in the sweetness of maternal love, had given me a reward for many sufferings. Instead of indulging a gloomy distrust about the fate of this child, I now resigned him to the will of God. Instead of lamenting because he was not likely to be rich, I was resolved to bring him up with such notions as might make him contented to be poor. I thought, if I could
subdue

subdue all vanity and selfishness in him, I should make him a happier man than if I had thousands to bestow on him; and I trusted, that I should be rewarded for every painful act of present self-denial, by the future virtue and happiness of my child. Can you believe it, my dear father, my days now past not unhappily? I worked hard all day, and that alone is a source of happiness beyond what the idle can guess. After my child was asleep at night, I read a chapter in the Bible to my parents, whose eyes now began to fail them. We then thanked God over our frugal supper of potatoes, and talked over the holy men of old, the saints, and the martyrs, who would have thought our homely fare a luxury. We compared our peace, and liberty, and safety, with their bonds, and imprisonment, and tortures; and should have been ashamed of a murmur. We then joined in prayer, in which my absent parents and my husband were never forgotten, and went to rest in charity with the whole world, and at peace in our own souls.

Oh! my forgiving child! interrupted Mr. Bragwell, sobbing, and didst thou really pray for thy unnatural father, and lie down in rest and peace? Then, let me tell thee, thou wast better off than thy mother and I were.—But no more of this; go on.

Whether my father-in-law had worked beyond his strength, in order to support me and my child, I know not; but he was taken dangerously ill. While he lay in this state, we received

ceived an account that my husband was dead in the West-Indies of the yellow fever, which has carried off such numbers of our countrymen; we all wept together, and prayed that his awful death might quicken us in preparing for our own. This shock, joined to the fatigue of nursing her sick husband, soon brought my poor mother to death's door. I nursed them both, and felt a satisfaction in giving them all I had to bestow, my attendance, my tears, and my prayers. I, who was once so nice and so proud, so disdainful in the midst of plenty, and so impatient under the smallest inconvenience, was now enabled to glorify God by my activity and my submission. Though the sorrows of my heart were enlarged, I cast my burthen on him who cares for the weary and heavy laden. After having watched by these poor people the whole night, I sat down to breakfast on my dry crust and coarse dish of tea, without a murmur; my greatest grief was, lest I should bring away the infection to my dear boy. I prayed to know what it was my duty to do between my dying parents, and my helpless child. To take care of the sick and aged, seemed to be my duty. So I offered up my child to him who is the father of the fatherless, and he spared him to me.

The chearful piety with which these good people breathed their last, proved to me, that the temper of mind with which the pious poor commonly meet death, is the grand compensation

sation made them by Providence for all the hardships of their inferior condition. If they have had few joys and comforts in life already, and have still fewer hopes in store, is not all fully made up to them by their being enabled to leave this world with stronger desires of heaven, and without those bitter regrets after the good things of this life, which add to the dying tortures of the worldly rich? To the forlorn and destitute death is not terrible, as it is to him who *sits at ease in his possessions*, and who fears that this night his soul shall be required of him.

Mr. Bragwell felt this remark more deeply than his daughter meant he should. He wept and bade her proceed.

I followed my departed parents to the same grave, and wept over them, but not as one who had no hope. They had neither houses nor lands to leave me, but they left me their Bible, their blessing, and their example, of which I humbly trust I shall feel the benefits when all the riches of this world shall have an end. Their few effects, consisting of some poor household goods, and some working-tools, hardly sufficed to pay their funeral expences. I was soon attacked with the same fever, and saw myself, as I thought, dying the second time; my danger was the same, but my views were changed. I now saw eternity in a more awful light than I had done before, when I wickedly thought death might be gloomily called upon as a refuge from every common trouble. Though I had still reason to
be

be humbled on account of my sin, yet, through the grace of God, I saw Death stripped of his sting, and robbed of his terrors, *through him, who loved me, and had given himself for me*; and in the extremity of pain, *my soul rejoiced in God my Saviour.*

I recovered, however, and was chiefly supported by the kind clergyman's charity. When I felt myself nourished and cheered by a little tea or broth, which he daily sent me from his own slender provision, my heart smote me, to think how I had daily sat down at home to a plentiful dinner, without any sense of thankfulness for my own abundance, or without enquiring whether my poor sick neighbours were starving; and I sorrowfully remembered, that what my poor sister and I used to waste through daintiness, would now have comfortably fed myself and child. Believe me, my dear mother, a labouring man who has been brought low by a fever, might often be restored to his work some weeks sooner, if on his recovery he was nourished and strengthened by a good bit from a farmer's table. Less than is often thrown to a favourite spaniel would suffice, so that the expence would be almost nothing to the giver, while to the receiver it would bring health, and strength, and comfort.

By the time I was tolerably recovered, I was forced to leave the house. I had no human prospect of subsistence. I humbly asked of God to direct my steps, and to give me entire obedience

dience to his will. I then cast my eyes mournfully on my child, and though prayer had relieved my heart of a load which without it would have been intolerable; my tears flowed fast, while I cried out in the bitterness of my soul, *How many hired servants of my father have bread enough, and to spare, and I perish with hunger.* This text appeared a kind of answer to my prayer, and gave me courage to make one more attempt to soften you in my favour. I resolved to set out directly to find you, to confess my disobedience, and to beg a scanty pittance, with which I and my child might be meanly supported in some distant country, where we should not disgrace our more happy relations. We set out and travelled as fast as my weak health and poor George's little feet and ragged shoes would permit. I brought a little bundle of such work and necessaries as I had left, by selling which we subsisted on the road.—I hope, interrupted Bragwell, there were no cabbage-nets in it?—At least, said her mother, I hope you did not sell them near home.—No; I had none left, said Mrs. Incle, or I should have done it. I got many a lift in a waggon for my child and my bundle, which was a great relief to me. And here I cannot help saying, I wish drivers would not be too hard in their demands, if they help a poor sick traveller on a mile or two; it proves a great relief to weary bodies and naked feet; and such little cheap charities may be considered as *the cup of cold water*, which, if given on right grounds,

shall

shall not lose its reward. Here Bragwell sighed, to think that when mounted on his fine bay mare, or driving his neat chaise, it had never once crossed his mind that the poor way-worn foot traveller was not equally at his ease, or that shoes were a necessary accommodation. Those who want nothing are apt to forget how many there are who want every thing.—Mrs. Incle went on: I got to this village about seven this evening, and while I sat on the church-yard wall to rest and meditate how I should make myself known at home, I saw a funeral; I enquired whose it was, and learnt it was my sister's. This was too much for me. I sunk down in a fit, and knew nothing that happened to me from that moment, till I found myself in the workhouse with my father and Mr. Worthy.

Here Mrs. Incle stopped. Grief, shame, pride, and remorse, had quite overcome Mr. Bragwell. He wept like a child; and said, he hoped his daughter would pray for him; for that he was not in a condition to pray for himself, though he found nothing else could give him any comfort. His deep dejection brought on a fit of sickness: O! said he, I now begin to feel an expression in the sacrament which I used to repeat without thinking it had any meaning, the *remembrance of my sins is grievous, the burthen of them is intolerable.* O, it is awful to think what a sinner a man may be, and yet retain a decent character! How many thousands are in my condition, taking to themselves all the credit of
their

their prosperity, instead of giving God the glory! Heaping up riches to their hurt, instead of dealing their bread to the hungry. O, let those who hear of the Bragwell family, never say that *vanity is a little sin.* In *me* it has been the fruitful parent of a thousand sins, selfishness, hardness of heart, forgetfulness of God. In one of my sons vanity was the cause of rapine, injustice, extravagance, ruin, self-murder. Both my daughters were undone by vanity, though it only wore the more harmless shape of dress, idleness, and dissipation. The husband of my daughter Incle it destroyed, by leading him to live above his station, and to despise labour. Vanity ensnared the souls even of his pious parents; for while it led them to wish to see their son in a better condition, it led them to allow him such indulgences as were unfit for his own. O, you who hear of us, humble yourselves under the mighty hand of God; resist high thoughts; let every imagination be brought into obedience to the Son of God. If you set a value on finery, look into that grave; behold the mouldering body of my Betsey, who now says to *Corruption, thou art my father, and to the worm thou art my mother and my sister.* Look at the bloody and brainless head of her husband. O, Mr. Worthy, how does Providence mock at human foresight! I have been greedy of gain, that the son of Mr. Squeeze might be a great man; he is dead; while the child of Timothy Incle, whom I had doomed to beggary, will be my heir. Mr. Worthy, to you I commit

mit this boy's education; teach him to value his immortal soul more, and the good things of this life less, than I have done. Bring him up in the fear of God, and in the government of his passions. Teach him that unbelief and pride are at the root of all sin. I have found this to my cost. I trusted in my riches; I said, tomorrow shall be as this day and more abundant. I did not remember that *for all these things God would bring me to judgment*. I am not sure that I believed in a judgment.

Bragwell at length grew better, but he never recovered his spirits. The conduct of Mrs. Incle through life was that of an humble Christian. She sold all her sister's finery, which her father had given her, and gave the money to the poor, saying, it did not become one who professed penitence, to return to the gaieties of life. Mr. Bragwell did not oppose this; not that he had fully acquired a just notion of the self-denying spirit of religion, but having a head not very clear at making distinctions, he was never able, after the sight of Squeeze's mangled body, to think of gaiety and grandeur, without thinking at the same time, of a pistol and bloody brains; for, as his first introduction into gay life had presented him with all these objects at one view, he never afterwards could separate them in his mind. He even kept his fine beaufet of plate always shut, because it brought to his mind the grand unpaid-for sideboard that he had seen laid out for Mr. Squeeze's supper, to the remembrance

membrance of which he could not help tacking debts, prisons, executions, and self-murder.

Mr. Bragwell's heart had been so buried in the love of the world, and evil habits were become so rooted in him, that the progress he made in religion was very slow; yet he earnestly prayed and struggled against vanity; and when his unfeeling wife declared she could not love the boy unless he was called by their name instead of Incle, Mr. Bragwell would never consent, saying, he stood in need of every help against pride. He also got the letter which Squeeze wrote just before he shot himself framed and glazed; this he hung up in his chamber, and made it a rule to go and read it as often as he found his heart disposed to VANITY.   Z.

THE HISTORY OF TOM WHITE,

THE POSTILION.

TOM WHITE was one of the beſt drivers of a poſt-chaiſe on the Bath road. Tom was the ſon of an honeſt labourer at a little village in Wiltſhire: he was an active induſtrious boy, and as ſoon as he was big enough he left his father, who was burthened with a numerous family, and
went

went to live with Farmer Hodges, a sober worthy man in the same village. He drove the waggon all the week; and on Sundays, though he was now grown up, the farmer required him to attend the Sunday-school, carried on under the inspection of Dr. Shepherd, the worthy Vicar, and always made him read his Bible in the evening after he had served his beasts; and would have turned him out of his service if he had ever gone to the ale-house for his own pleasure.

Tom by carrying some waggon-loads of faggots to the Bear-inn, at Devizes, soon made many acquaintances in the stable-yard. He soon leant to compare his own carter's frock, and shoes thick set with nails, with the smart red jacket, and tight boots of the post-boys, and grew ashamed of his own homely dress; he was resolved to drive a chaise, to get money, and to see the world. Foolish fellow! he never considered, that, though it is true, a waggoner works hard all day, yet he gets a quiet evening, and undisturbed rest at night. However, as there must be chaise-boys as well as plow-boys, there was no great harm in the change. The evil company to which it exposed him, was the chief mischief. He left farmer Hodges, though not without sorrow, at quitting so kind a master, and got himself hired at the Black Bear.

Notwithstanding the temptations to which he was now exposed, Tom's good education stood by him for some time. At first he was frightened to hear the oaths and wicked words which are too often uttered in a stable-yard. However, though he thought it very wrong, he had not the courage to reprove it, and the next step to being easy at seeing others sin, is to sin ourselves. By degrees he began to think it manly, and a mark of spirit in others to swear; though the force of good habits was so strong, that at first when he ventured to swear himself it was with fear, and in a low voice. But he was soon laughed out of his sheepishness, as they called it; and though he never became so prophane and blasphemous as some of his companions, (for he never swore in cool blood, or in mirth as so many do,) yet he would too often use a dreadful bad word when he was in a passion with his horses. And here I cannot but drop a hint on the great folly, as well as wickedness, of being in a great rage with poor beasts, who, not having the gift of reason, cannot be moved like human creatures, with all the wicked words that are said to them; though these dumb creatures, unhappily, having the gift of feeling, suffer as much as human creatures can do, at the cruel and unnecessary beatings given them. He had been bred up to think that drunkenness was a great sin, for he never saw farmer Hodges drunk in his life, and where a farmer is sober himself his men are less likely to drink, or if they do, the master can reprove them with the better grace.

Tom was not naturally fond of drink, yet for the sake of being thought merry company, and a hearty fellow, he often drank more than he ought. As he had been used to go to church twice on a Sunday, while he lived with the farmer, who seldom used his horses on that day, except to carry his wife to church behind him: Tom felt a little uneasy when he was sent the very first Sunday a long journey with a great family; for I cannot conceal the truth, that too many gentlefolks will travel when there is no necessity for it on a Sunday, and when Monday would answer the end just as well. This is a great grief to all good and sober people, both rich and poor; and it is still more inexcusable in the great, who have every day at their command. However, he kept his thoughts to himself, though he could not now and then help thinking how quietly things were going on at the farmer's, whose waggoner on a Sunday led as easy a life as if he had been a gentleman. But he soon lost all thoughts of this kind, and did not know a Sunday from a Monday. Tom went on prosperously, as it is called, for three or four years, got plenty of money, but saved not a shilling. As soon as his horses were once in the stable, whoever would might see them fed for Tom.—He had other fish to fry.—Fives, cards, cudgel-playing, laying wagers, and keeping loose company, each of which he at first disliked, and then practised, ran away with all his money, and all his spare time; and though he was generally in the way as soon as the horses were ready, (because if there was no driving there was no pay,) yet he did not care whether the carriage was clean, or the horses looked well, if the harness was whole, or the horses were shod. The certainty that the gains of to-morrow would make up for the extravagance of to-day, made him quite thoughtless and happy, for he was young, active, and healthy, and never foresaw that a rainy day might come, when he would want what he now squandered.

One day being a little flustered with liquor as he was driving his return chaise through Brentford, he saw just before him another empty carriage, driven by one of his acquaintance: he whipped up his horses, resolving to outstrip the other, and swearing dreadfully that he would be at the Red Lion first—for a pint,—done, cried the other—a wager.—Both cut and spurred the poor beasts with the usual fury, as if their credit had been really at stake, or their lives had depended on this foolish contest. Tom's chaise had now got up to that of his rival, and they drove along-side of each other with great fury and many imprecations. But in a narrow part, Tom's chaise being in the middle, with his antagonist on one side, and a cart driving against him on the other, the horses reared, the carriages got entangled; Tom roared out a great oath to the other to stop, which he either could not, or would not, but returned an horrid imprecation that he would win the wager if he was alive.

Tom's

Tom's horses took fright, and he was thrown to the ground with great violence. As soon as he could be got from under the wheels, he was taken up senseless; his leg was broke in two places, and his body much bruised. Some people whom the noise had brought together, put him into the post-chaise, in which the waggoner kindly assisted, but the other driver seemed careless and indifferent, and drove off, observing with a brutal coolness, I am sorry I have lost my pint; I should have beat him hollow, had it not been for this *little accident*. Some gentlemen who came out of the inn, after reprimanding this savage, inquired who he was, wrote to inform his master, and got him discharged: resolving that neither they nor any of their friends would ever employ him, and he was long out of place, and nobody ever cared to be driven by him.

Tom was taken to one of those excellent hospitals with which London abounds. His agonies were dreadful, his leg was set, and a high fever came on. As soon as he was left alone to reflect on his condition, his first thought was that he should die, and his horror was inconceivable.—Alas! said he, what will become of my poor soul? I am cut off in the very commission of three great sins:—I was drunk, I was in a horrible passion, and I had oaths and blasphemies in my mouth.—He tried to pray, but he could not, his mind was all distraction, and he thought he was so very wicked that God not forgive him; becaufe, fays he, I have finned againſt light and knowledge, and a fober education, and good examples; I was bred in the fear of God, and the knowledge of Chriſt, and I deſerve nothing but puniſhment.—At length he grew light-headed, and there was little hopes of his life. Whenever he came to his ſenſes for a few minutes, he cried out, O! that my old companions could now ſee me, ſurely they would take warning by my ſad fate, and repent before it is too late.

By the bleſſing of God on the ſkill of the ſurgeon, and the care of the nurſes, he, however, grew better in a few days. And here let me ſtop to remark, what a mercy it is that we live in a chriſtian country, where the poor, when ſick, or lame, or wounded, are taken as much care of as any gentry; nay in ſome reſpects more, becauſe in hoſpitals, and infirmaries, there are more doctors and ſurgeons to attend, than moſt private gentlefolks can afford to have at their own houſes, whereas *there never was an hoſpital in the whole heathen world.* Bleſſed be God for this, among the thouſand other excellent fruits of the Chriſtian Religion!

It was eight weeks before Tom could be taken out of bed. This was a happy affliction; for by the grace of God, this long ſickneſs and ſolitude, gave him time to reflect on his paſt life. He began ſeriouſly to hate thoſe darling ſins which had brought him to the brink of ruin. He could now pray heartily; he confeſſed and lamented

mented his iniquities with many tears, and began to hope that the mercies of God, through the merits of a Redeemer, might yet be extended to him on his sincere repentance. He resolved never more to return to the same evil courses, but he did not trust in his own strength, but prayed that God would give him grace for the future, as well as pardon for the past. He remembered, and he was humbled at the thought, that he used to have short fits of repentance, and to form resolutions of amendment, in his wild and thoughtless days, and often when he had a bad head-ach after a drinking bout, or had lost his money at all-fours, he vowed never to drink or play again. But as soon as his head was well, and his pockets recruited, he forgot all his resolutions. And how should it be otherwise? for he trusted in his own strength, he never prayed to God to strengthen him, nor ever avoided the next temptation. He did not know that it is the grace of God which bringeth us to repentance.

The case was now different. Tom began to find that *his strength was perfect weakness*, and that he could do nothing without the Divine assistance, for which he prayed heartily and constantly. He sent home for his Bible, and Prayerbook, which he had not opened for two years, and which had been given him when he left the Sunday School. He spent the chief part of his time in reading them, and derived great comfort, as well as great knowledge, from them.

The study of the Bible filled his heart with gratitude to God, who had not cut him off in the midst of his sins, but had given him space for repentance; and the agonies he had lately suffered with his broken leg increased his thankfulness, that he had escaped the more dreadful pain of eternal misery. And here let me remark what encouragement this is for rich people to give away Bibles and good books, and not to lose all hope, though, for a time, they see little, or no good effect from it. According to all appearance, Tom's were never likely to do him any good, and yet his generous benefactor who had cast his bread upon the waters, found it after many days, for this Bible, which had lain untouched for years, was at last made the means of his reformation. God will work in his own good time, and in his own way.

As soon as he got well, and was discharged from the hospital, Tom began to think he must return to get his bread. At first he had some scruples about going back to his old employ: but, says he, sensibly enough, gentlefolks must travel, travellers must have chaises, and chaises must have drivers: 'tis a very honest calling, and I don't know that goodness belongs to one sort of business more than another; and he who can be good in a state of great temptation, provided the calling be lawful, and the temptations are not of his own seeking, and he be diligent in prayer, may be better than another man for aught I know: and *all that belongs to us is, to do*

our

our duty in that state of life in which it shall please God to call us.' Tom had rubbed up his catechism at the hospital, and 'tis a pity that people don't look at their catechism sometimes when they are grown up; for it is full as good for men and women as it is for children; nay better, for though the answers contained in it are intended for children to *repeat*, yet the duties enjoined in it are intended for men and women to put in *practice*.

Tom now felt grieved that he was obliged to drive on Sundays. But people who are in earnest, and have their hearts in a thing, can find helps in all cases. As soon as he had set down his company at their stage, and had seen his horses fed, says Tom, A man who takes care of his horses, will generally think it right to let them rest an hour or two at least. In every town it is a chance but there may be a church open during part of that time. If the prayers should be over, I'll try hard for the sermon; and if I dare not stay to the sermon, it is a chance but I may catch the prayers; it is worth trying for, however; and as I used to think nothing of making a push, for the sake of getting an hour to gamble, I need not grudge to take a little pains extraordinary to serve God. By this watchfulness he soon got to know the hours of service at all the towns on the road he travelled, and while the horses fed, Tom went to church; and it became a favourite proverb with him, that *prayers and provender hinder no man's journey*; and

I beg leave to recommend Tom's maxim to all travellers, whether master or servant, carrier or coachman.

At first his companions wanted to laugh and make sport of this—but when they saw that no lad on the road was up so early or worked so hard as Tom: when they saw no chaise so neat, no glasses so bright, no harness so tight, no driver so diligent, so clean, or so civil, they found he was no subject to make sport at. Tom indeed was very careful in looking after the linch pins; in never giving his horses too much water when they were hot; nor, whatever was his haste, would he ever gallop them up hill, strike them across the head, or when tired, cut and flash them, or gallop over the stones, as soon as he got into a town, as some foolish fellows do. What helped to cure Tom of these bad practices, was, that remark he met with in the Bible, that *a good man is merciful to his beast.* He was much moved one day on reading the Prophet Jonah, to observe what compassion the great God of heaven and earth had for poor beasts: for one of the reasons there given, why the Almighty was unwilling to destroy the great city of Nineveh was, *because there was much cattle in it.* After this, Tom never could bear to see a wanton stroke inflicted. Doth God care for horses, said he, and shall man be cruel to them?

Tom soon grew rich for one in his station; for every gentleman on the road would be driven by no other lad if *careful Tom* was to be had.

Being

Being diligent, he *got* a great deal of money; being frugal, he *spent* but little; and having no vices, he *wasted* none. He soon found out that there was some meaning in that text which says, that *Godliness hath the promise of the life that now is, as well as of that which is to come:* for the same principles which make a man sober and honest, have also a natural tendency to make him healthy and rich; while a drunkard and a spendthrift can hardly escape being sick, and a beggar in the end. Vice is the parent of misery here as well as hereafter.

After a few years Tom begged a holiday, and made a visit to his native village; his good character had got thither before him. He found his father was dead, but during his long illness Tom had supplied him with money, and by allowing him a trifle every week, had had the honest satisfaction of keeping him from the parish. Farmer Hodges was still living, but being grown old and infirm, he was desirous to retire from business. He retained a great regard for his old servant, Tom; and finding he was worth money, and knowing he knew something of country business, he offered to let him a small farm at an easy rate, and promised his assistance in the management for the first year, with the loan of a small sum of money, that he might set out with a pretty stock. Tom thanked him with tears in his eyes, went back and took a handsome leave of his master, who made him a present of a horse and cart, in acknowledgement of his long and faithful services; for, says he, I have saved many horses by Tom's care and attention, and I could well afford to do the same by every servant who did the same by me; and should be a richer man at the end of every year by the same generosity, provided I could meet with just and faithful servants who deserved the same rewards.

Tom was soon settled in his new farm, and in less than a year had got every thing neat and decent about him. Farmer Hodges's long experience and friendly advice, joined to his own industry and hard labour, soon brought the farm to great perfection. The regularity, sobriety, peaceableness, and piety of his daily life, his constant attendance at Church twice every Sunday, and his decent and devout behaviour when there, soon recommended him to the notice of Dr. Shepherd, who was still living, a pattern of zeal, activity, and benevolence, to all parish Priests. The doctor soon began to hold up Tom, or, as we must now more properly term him, Mr. Thomas White, to the imitation of the whole parish, and the frequent and condescending conversation of this worthy Clergyman, contributed no less than his preaching to the improvement of his new parishioner in piety.

Farmer White soon found out that a dairy could not well be carried on without a mistress, and began to think seriously of marrying; he prayed to God to direct him in so important a business. He knew that a tawdry, vain, dressy girl,

girl, was not likely to make good cheese and butter, and that a worldly, and ungodly woman would make a sad wife and mistress of a family. He soon heard of a young woman of excellent character, who had been bred up by the vicar's lady, and still lived in the family as upper maid. She was prudent, sober, industrious, and religious. Her neat, modest, and plain appearance at church, (for she was seldom seen any where else out of her master's family) was an example to all persons in her station, and never failed to recommend her to strangers, even before they had an opportunity of knowing the goodness of her character. It was her character, however, which recommended her to farmer White. He knew that *favour is deceitful, and beauty is vain, but a woman that feareth the Lord, she shall be praised:*—aye, and not only praised, but chosen too, says Farmer White, as he took down his hat from the nail on which it hung, in order to go and wait on Dr. Shepherd, to break his mind and ask his consent; for he thought it would be a very unhandsome return for all the favours he was receiving from his Minister, to decoy away his faithful servant from her place without his consent.

This worthy gentleman, though sorry to lose so valuable a member of his little family, did not scruple a moment about parting with her, when he found it would be so greatly to her advantage. Tom was agreeably surprised to hear she had saved fifty pounds by her frugality. The doctor married them himself, Farmer Hodges being present.

In the afternoon of the wedding day, Dr. Shepherd condescended to call on Farmer and Mrs. White, to give a few words of advice on the new duties they had entered into; a common custom with him on those occasions. He often took an opportunity to drop, in the most kind and tender way, a hint on the great indecency of making marriages, christenings, and above all, funerals, days of riot and excess, as is too often the case in country villages. The expectation that the vicar might possibly drop in, in his walks, on these festivities, sometimes restrained excessive drinking, and improper conversation, even among those who were not restrained by higher motives, as farmer and Mrs. White were.

What the doctor said was always in such a cheerful, good-humoured way, that it was sure to increase the pleasure of the day, instead of damping it. Well, farmer, said he, and you, my faithful Sarah, any other friend might recommend peace and agreement to you on your marriage; but I, on the contrary, recommend cares and strifes*. The company stared—but Sarah, who knew that her old master was a facetious gentleman, and always had some good meaning behind, looked serious. Cares and strifes, Sir, said the farmer, what do you mean?

---

* See Dodd's Sayings.

I mean

I mean, said he, for the first, that your cares shall be who shall please God most, and your strifes, who shall serve him best, and do your duty most faithfully. Thus, all your cares and strifes being employed to the highest purposes, all petty cares and worldly strifes shall be at an end.

Always remember, both of you, that you have, both of you, a better friend than each other.—The company stared again, and thought no woman could have so good a friend as her husband. As you have chosen each other from the best motives, continued the doctor, you have every reasonable ground to hope for happiness; but as this world is a soil, in which troubles and misfortunes will spring up; troubles from which you cannot save one another: then remember, 'tis the best wisdom to go to that friend who is always near, always willing, and always able, to help you, and that friend is God.

Sir, said Farmer White, I humbly thank you for all your kind instructions, of which I shall now stand more in need than ever, as I shall have more duties to fulfil. I hope the remembrance of my past offences will keep me humble, and the sense of my remaining sin will keep me watchful. I set out in the world, Sir, with what is called a good natural disposition, but I soon found, to my cost, that without God's grace, that will carry a man but a little way. A good temper is a good thing, but nothing but the fear of God can enable one to bear up against temptation, evil company, and evil passions. The misfortune of breaking my leg, as I then thought it, has proved the greatest blessing of my life. It shewed me my own weakness, the value of the Bible, and the goodness of GOD. How many of my brother drivers have I seen since that time, cut off in the prime of life by drinking, or by some sudden accident, while I have not only been spared, but blessed and prospered. O Sir! it would be the joy of my heart, if some of my old comrades, good-natured, civil fellows, (whom I can't help loving) could see, as I have done, the danger of evil courses before it is too late. Though they may not hearken to you, Sir, or any other *Minister*, they may believe *me*, because I have been one of them: and I can speak from experience, of the great difference there is, even as to worldly comfort, between a life of sobriety and a life of sin. I could tell them, Sir, not as a thing I have read in a book, but as a truth I feel in my own heart, that to fear GOD and keep his commandments, will not only bring a man peace at the last, but will make him happy *now*. And I will venture to say, Sir, that all the stocks, pillories, prisons, and gibbets in the land, though so very needful to keep bad men in order, yet will never restrain a good man from committing evil, half so much as that single text, "how shall I do this great wickedness, and sin against God?" Dr. Shepherd condescended to approve of what the farmer had said, kindly shook him by the hand, and took leave.

Thomas

Thomas White had always been fond of singing, but he had for many years despised that vile trash which is too often sung in a stable-yard. One Sunday evening he heard his mistress at the Bear read some verses out of a fine book called the Spectator. He was so struck with the picture it contains of the great mercies of GOD, of which he had himself partaken so largely, that he took the liberty to ask her for these verses, and she being a very good-natured woman, made her daughter write out for the postilion the following

HYMN ON DIVINE PROVIDENCE.

When all thy mercies, O my GOD,
  My rising soul surveys,
Transported with the view I'm lost,
  In wonder, love, and praise.

O how shall words with equal warmth
  The gratitude declare,
That glows within my ravish'd heart?
  But thou canst read it there.

Thy PROVIDENCE my life sustain'd,
  And all my wants redrest,
When in the silent womb I lay,
  And hung upon the breast.

To all my weak complaints and cries,
  Thy mercy lent an ear,
Ere yet my feeble thoughts had learnt
  To form themselves in prayer.

Unnumber'd

Unnumber'd comforts to my soul
   Thy tender care bestow'd,
Before my infant heart conceiv'd
   From whom those comforts flow'd.

When in the slipp'ry path of YOUTH
   With heedless steps I ran,
Thine arm, unseen, convey'd me safe,
   And led me up to MAN.

Thro' hidden dangers, toils, and deaths,
   It gently clear'd my way,
And thro' the pleasing snares of vice,
   More to be fear'd than they.

When worn with sickness, oft hast THOU
   With health renew'd my face;
And when in sins and sorrow sunk,
   Reviv'd my soul with grace.

THY bounteous hand with worldly bliss,
   Has made my cup run o'er;
And in a kind and faithful friend,
   Has doubl'd all my store.

Ten thousand thousand precious gifts,
   My daily thanks employ,
Nor is the least a thankful heart
   That tastes those gifts with joy.

Thro' every period of my life
   Thy goodness I'll pursue;
And after death, in distant worlds,
   The glorious theme renew.

> When nature fails, and day and night
>   Divide thy works no more,
> My ever grateful heart, O LORD!
>   Thy mercy shall adore.
>
> Thro' all ETERNITY to Thee
>   A joyful song I'll raise,
> For O ETERNITY's too short
>   To utter all Thy Praise.

PART II.

THE WAY TO PLENTY.

Written in 1795, the Year of Scarcity.

TOM WHITE, as we have shewn in the first part of this history, from an idle post-boy was become a respectable farmer. GOD had blessed his industry, and he had prospered in the world. He was sober and temperate, and, as was the natural consequence, he was active and healthy. He was industrious and frugal, and he became prosperous in his circumstances. This is in the ordinary course of Providence. But it is not a certain and necessary rule. GOD *maketh his sun to shine on the just and the unjust.* A man who uses every honest means of thrift and industry, will, in most cases, find success attend his labours. But still the *race is not always to the swift, nor the battle to the strong.* God is sometimes pleased, for wise ends, to disappoint all the worldly hopes of the most upright man. His corn may be smitten by a blight; his barns may be consumed by fire; his cattle may be carried off by distemper. And to these, and other misfortunes, he is as liable as the spendthrift or the knave. Success is the *common* reward of industry, but if it were its *constant* reward, the industrious would be tempted to look no further than the present state. They would lose one strong ground of their faith. It would set aside the Scripture scheme. This world would then be looked on as a state of reward, instead of a state of trial, and we should forget to look to a day of final retribution.

Farmer *White* never took it into his head, that because he paid his debts, worked early and late, and ate the bread of carefulness, he was therefore to come into no *misfortune like other folk*, but was to be free from the common trials and troubles of life. He knew that prosperity was far from being a sure mark of God's favour, and had read in good books, and especially in the Bible, of the great poverty and afflictions of the best of men. Though he was no great scholar, he had sense enough to observe, that a time of public prosperity was not always a time of public virtue; and he thought that what was true of a whole nation might be true of one man. So the more he prospered the more he prayed that prosperity might not corrupt his heart. And when he saw
lately

lately signs of public distress coming on, he was not half so much frightened as some others were, because he thought it might do us good in the long run; and he was in hopes that a little poverty might bring on a little penitence. The great grace he laboured after was that of a cheerful submission. He used to say, that if the Lord's Prayer had only contained those four little words THY WILL BE DONE, it would be worth more than the biggest book in the world without them.

Dr. Shepherd, the worthy vicar, (with whom the farmer's wife had formerly lived as housekeeper) was very fond of taking a walk with him about his grounds, and he used to say, that he learnt as much from the farmer as the farmer did from him. If the doctor happened to observe, I am afraid these long rains will spoil this fine piece of oats, the farmer would answer, But then, sir, think how good it is for the grass. If the doctor feared the wheat would be but indifferent, the farmer was sure the rye would turn out well. When grass failed, he did not doubt but turnips would be plenty. Even for floods and inundations he would find out some way to justify Providence. 'Tis better, said he, to have our lands a little overflowed, than that the springs should be dried up, and our cattle faint for lack of water. When the drought came, he thanked GOD that the season would be healthy; and high winds, which frightened others, he said served to clear the air. Whoever, or whatever was wrong,

wrong, he was always sure that Providence was in the right. And he used to say, that a man with ever so small an income, if he had but frugality and temperance, and cut off all vain desires, and cast his care upon God, was richer than a lord who was tormented by vanity and covetousness. When he saw others in the wrong, he did not, however, abuse them for it, but took care to avoid the same fault. He had sense and spirit enough to break through many old, but very bad customs of his neighbours. If a thing is wrong in itself, (said he one day to farmer Hodges) a whole parish doing it can't make it right. And as to it's being an old custom, why, if it be a good one I like it the better for being old, because it has had the stamp of ages, and the sanction of experience on it's worth. But if it be old as well as bad, that is another reason for my trying to put an end to it, that we may not mislead our children as our fathers have misled us.

THE ROOF-RAISING.

Some years after he was settled, he built a large new barn. All the workmen were looking forward to the usual holiday of roof-raising. On this occasion it is a custom to give a dinner to the workmen, with so much liquor after it that they got so drunk, that they not only lost the remaining half-day's work, but they were not always able to work the following day.

Mrs.

Mrs. White provided a plentiful dinner for roof-raising, and gave each man his mug of beer. After a hearty meal they began to grow clamorous for more drink. The farmer said, My lads, I don't grudge you a few gallons of ale merely for the sake of saving my liquor, though that is some consideration, especially in these dear times, but I never will, knowingly, help any man to make a beast of himself. I am resolved to break through a bad custom. You are now well refreshed. If you will go cheerfully to your work, you will half a day's pay to take on Saturday night more than you would if this afternoon were wasted in drunkenness. For this your families will be the better: whereas, were I to give you more liquor when you have already had enough, I should help to rob them of their bread. But I wish to shew you, that I have your good at heart full as much as my own profit. If you will now go to work, I will give you all another mug at night when you leave off. Thus your time will be saved, your families helped, and my ale will not go to make reasonable creatures worse than brute beasts.

Here he stopped. You are in the right on't, Master, said Tom the thatcher; you are a hearty man, Farmer, said John Plane the carpenter. Come along boys, said Tim Brick the mason; so they all went merrily to work, fortified with a good dinner. There was only one drunken surly fellow, who refused, that was Dick Guzzle the smith. Dick never works above two or three days

days in the week, and spends the others at the Red Lion. He swore, that if the farmer did not let him have as much liquor as he liked at Roof-Raising, he would not strike another stroke, but would leave the job unfinished, and he might get hands where he could. Farmer White took him at his word, and paid him off directly: glad enough to get rid of such a sot, whom he had only employed from pity to a large and almost starving family. When the men came for their mug in the evening, the farmer brought out the remains of the cold gammon; they made a hearty supper, and thanked him for having broke through a foolish custom, which was afterwards much left off in that parish, though Dick would not come into it, and lost most of his work in consequence.

Farmer White's labourers were often complaining, that things were so dear that they could not buy a bit of meat. He knew it was partly true, but not intirely, for it was before these very hard times that their complaints began. One morning he stept out to see how an outhouse which he was thatching went on. He was surprised to find the work at a stand. He walked over to the thatcher's house. Tom, said he, I desire that piece of work may be finished directly. If a shower comes my grain will be spoiled. Indeed, Master, I shan't work to-day, nor to-morrow neither, said Tom. You forget that 'tis Easter Monday, and to-morrow is Easter Tuesday. And so on Wednesday I shall thatch away,

away, master. But 'tis hard if a poor man, who works all the year, may not enjoy these few holidays, which come but once a year.

Tom, said the farmer, when these days were first put into our prayer-book, the good men who ordained them to be kept, little thought that the time would come when *holy-day* should mean *drunken-day*. How much dost think now I shall pay thee for this piece of thatch? Why you know, master, you have let it to me by the great. I think between this and to morrow night, as the weather is so fine, I could clear about four shillings, after I have paid my boy; but thatching does not come often, and other work is not so profitable. Very well, Tom; and how much now do you think you may spend in these two holidays? Why, master, if the ale is pleasant, and the company merry, I do not expect to get off for less than three shillings. Tom, can you do pounds, shillings, and pence? I can make a little score, master, behind the kitchen door, with a bit of chalk, which is as much as I want. Well, Tom, add the four shillings you would have earned to the three you intend to spend, what does that make? Let me see! three and four make seven. Seven shillings, master. Tom, you often tell me the times are so bad that you can never buy a bit of meat. Now here is the cost of two joints at once; to say nothing of the sin of wasting time and getting drunk. I never once thought of that, said Tom. Now Tom, said the farmer, if I were you, I would step over to butcher Jobbins's, buy a shoulder of mutton, which being left from Saturday's market you will get a little cheaper. This I would make my wife bake in a deep dish full of potatoes. I would then go to work, and when the dinner was ready I would go and enjoy it with my wife and children; you need not give the mutton to the brats; the potatoes will have all the gravy, and be very savory for them. Aye, but I've got no beer, master, the times are so hard that a poor man can't afford to brew a drop of drink now as we used to do.

Times are bad, and malt is very dear, Tom, and yet both don't prevent you from spending seven shillings in keeping holiday. Now send for a quart of ale, as it is to be a feast; and you will even then be four shillings richer than if you had gone to the publick house. I would have you put by these four shillings, till I could add a couple to them; with this I would get a bushel of malt, and my wife should brew it, and you may take a pint of your own beer at home of a night, which will do you more good than a gallon at the Red Lion. I have a great mind to take your advice, master, but I shall be made such fun of at the Lion! they will so laugh at me if I don't go! Let those laugh that win, Tom. But, master, I have got a friend to meet me there. Then ask your friend to come and eat a bit of your cold mutton at night, and here is six-pence for another pot, if you will promise to brew a small cask of your own. Thank you, master,

master, and so I will; and I won't go to the Lion. Come, boy, bring the helm, and fetch the ladder. And so Tom was upon the roof in a twinkling.

THE SHEEP SHEARING.

Dr. Shepherd happened to say to Farmer White one day, that there was nothing he disliked more than the manner in which sheep-shearing and harvest-home were kept by some in his parish.—What, said the good doctor, just when we are blest with a prosperous gathering in of these natural riches of our land, the fleece of our flocks; when our barns are crowned with plenty, and we have, through the divine blessing on our honest labour, reaped the fruits of the earth in due season; is that very time to be set apart for ribaldry, and riot, and drunkenness? Do we thank God for his mercies, by making ourselves unworthy and unfit to enjoy them? When he crowns the year with his goodness, shall we affront him by our impiety?

I thank you for the hint, sir, said the farmer. I am resolved to rejoice though, and others shall rejoice with me: and we will have a merry night on't.

So Mrs. White dressed a very plentiful supper of meat and pudding; and spread out two tables. The farmer sat at the head of one, consisting of some of his neighbours, and all his work-people. At the other sat his wife, with two long benches on each side of her. On these sat all the old and infirm poor, especially those who lived in the workhouse, and had no day of festivity to look forward to in the whole year but this. On the grass, in the little court, sat the children of his labourers, and of the other poor, whose employment it had been to gather flowers, and dress and adorn the horns of the ram; for the farmer did not wish to put an end to any old custom, if it was innocent. His own children stood by the table, and he gave them plenty of pudding, which they carried to the children of the poor, with a little draught of cider to every one. The farmer, who never sat down without begging a blessing on his meal, did it with suitable solemnity on the present joyful occasion.

This feast, though orderly and decent, was yet hearty and chearful. Dr. Shepherd dropped in with a good deal of company he had at his house, and they were much pleased. When the doctor saw how the aged and the infirm poor were enjoying themselves, he was much moved; he shook the farmer by the hand, and said, " But thou, when thou makest a feast, call the blind, and the lame, and the halt; they cannot recompense thee, but thou shalt be recompensed at the resurrection of the just."

Sir, said the farmer, 'tis no great matter of expence; I kill a sheep of my own; potatoes are as plenty as blackberries, with people who have a little forethought. I save much more cider in the course of a year by never allowing any carousing

rousing in my kitchen, or drunkenness in my fields, than would supply many such feasts as these, so that I shall be never the poorer at Christmas. It is cheaper to make people happy, sir, than to make them drunk. The doctor and the ladies condescended to walk from one table to the other, and heard many merry stories, but not one profane word, or one indecent song; so that he was not forced to the painful necessity either of reproving them, or leaving them in anger. When all was over, they sung the sixty-fifth psalm, and the ladies all joined in it, and when they got home to the vicarage to tea, they declared they liked it better than any concert.

THE HARD WINTER.

In the famous cold winter of the present year 1795, it was edifying to see how patiently farmer White bore that long and severe frost. Many of his sheep were frozen to death, but he thanked God that he had still many left. He continued to find in-door work that his men might not be out of employ. The season being so bad, which some others pleaded as an excuse for turning off their workmen, he thought a fresh reason for keeping them. Mrs. White was so considerate, that just at that time she lessened the number of her hogs, that she might have more whey and skim-milk to assist poor families. Nay, I have known her live on boiled meat for a long while together,

together, in a sickly season, because the pot-liquor made such a supply of broth for the sick poor. As the spring came on, and things grew worse, she never had a cake, a pye, or a pudding in her house; notwithstanding she used to have plenty of these good things, and will again, I hope, when the present scarcity is over; though she says she never will use such white flour again, even if it should come down to five shillings a bushel.

All the parish now began to murmur. Farmer Jones was sure the frost had killed the wheat. Farmer Wilson said the rye would never come up. Brown, the maltster, insisted the barley was dead at the root. Butcher Jobbins said beef would be a shilling a pound. All declared there would not be a hop to brew with. The orchards were all blighted; there would not be apples enough to make a pye; and as to hay there would be none to be had for love nor money.—I'll tell you what, said farmer White, the season is dreadful; the crops are unpromising just now; but 'tis too early to judge. Don't let us make things worse than they are. We ought to comfort the poor, and you are driving them to despair. Don't you know how much God was displeased with the murmurs of his chosen people? And yet, when they were tired of manna he sent them quails; but all did not do. Nothing satisfies grumblers. We have a promise on our side, that " there shall be seed-time and harvest-time to the end." Let us then hope for a good day, but provide against an evil one. Let us rather

prevent

prevent the evil before it is come upon us, than sink under it when it comes. Grumbling cannot help us; activity can. Let us set about planting potatoes in every nook and corner, in case the corn *should* fail, which, however, I don't believe will be the case. Let us mend our management before we are driven to it by actual want. And if we allow our honest labourers to plant a few potatoes for their families in the headlands of our ploughed fields, or other waste bits of ground, it will do us no harm, and be a great help to them. The way to lighten the load of any public calamity is not to murmur at it, but put a hand to lessen it.

The farmer had many temptations to send his corn at an extravagant price to *a certain sea-port town*, but as he knew that it was intended to export it against law, he would not be tempted to encourage unlawful gain; so he threshed out a small mow at a time, and sold it to the neighbouring poor far below the market-price. He served his own workmen first. This was the same to them as if he had raised their wages, and even better, as it was a benefit of which their families were sure to partake. If the poor in the next parish were more distressed than his own, he sold to them at the same rate. For, said he, there is no distinction of parishes in heaven, and though charity begins at home, yet it ought not to end there.

He had been used in good times now and then to catch a hare or a partridge, as he was qualified;

qualified; but he now resolved to give up that pleasure. So he parted from a couple of spaniels he had; for he said he could not bear that his dogs should be eating the meat, or the milk, which so many men, women, and children wanted.

THE WHITE LOAF.

ONE day, it was about the middle of last July, when things seemed to be at the dearest, and the Rulers of the land had agreed to set the example of eating nothing but coarse bread, Dr. Shepherd read, before sermon in the church, their public declaration, which the magistrates of the county sent him, and which they had also signed themselves. Mrs. White, of course, was at church, and commended it mightily. Next morning the doctor took a walk over to the farmer's, in order to settle further plans for the relief of the parish. He was much surprized to meet Mrs. White's little maid Sally with a very small white loaf, which she had been buying at a shop. He said nothing to the girl, as he never thought it right to expose the faults of a mistress to her servant; but walked on, resolving to give Mrs. White a severe lecture for the first time in his life. He soon changed his mind, for on going into the kitchen, the first person he saw was Tom the thatcher, who had had a sad fall from a ladder; his arm, which was slipped out of his sleeve, was swelled in a frightful manner. Mrs. White

White was standing at the dresser making the little white loaf into a poultice, which she laid upon the swelling in a large clean old linen cloth.

I ask your pardon, my good Sarah, said the doctor; I ought not, however appearances were against you, to have suspected that so humble and prudent a woman as you are, would be led either to indulge any daintiness of your own, or to fly in the face of your betters, by eating white bread while they are eating brown. Whenever I come here, I see it is not needful to be rich in order to be charitable. A bountiful rich man would have sent Tom to a surgeon, who would have done no more for him than you have done; for in those inflammations the most skilful surgeon could only apply a poultice. Your kindness in dressing the wound yourself, will, I doubt not, perform the cure at the expence of that three-penny loaf and a little hog's lard. And I will take care that Tom shall have a good supply of rice from the subscription.—And he shan't want for skim-milk, said Mrs. White; and was he the best lord in the land, in the state he is in, a dish of good rice milk would be better for him than the richest meat.

THE PARISH MEETING.

On the tenth of August, the vestry held another meeting, to consult on the best method of further assisting the poor. The prospect of abundant crops now cheered every heart. Farmer White, who had a mind to be a little jocular with his desponding neighbours, said, Well, neighbour Jones, all the wheat was killed, I suppose; the barley is all dead at the root.—Farmer Jones looked sheepish, and said, to be sure the crops had turned out better than he thought.—Then, said Dr. Shepherd, let us learn to trust Providence another time; let our experience of his past goodness strengthen our faith.

Among other things, they agreed to subscribe for a large quantity of rice, which was to be sold out to the poor at a very low price, and Mrs. White was so kind as to undertake the trouble of selling it. After their day's work was over, all who wished to buy at these reduced rates, were ordered to come to the farm on the Tuesday evening. Dr. Shepherd dropped in at the same time, and when Mrs. White had done weighing her rice, the doctor spoke as follows:

My honest friends, it has pleased God for some wise end, to visit this land with a scarcity, to which we have been but little accustomed. There are some idle evil-minded people, who are on the watch for public distresses; not that they may humble themselves under the mighty hand of God (which is the true use to be made of all troubles) but that they may benefit themselves by disturbing the public peace. These people, by riot and drunkenness, double the evil which they pretend to cure. Riot will complete our misfortunes, while peace, industry, and good management, will go near to cure them. Bread, to be sure, is uncommonly dear. Among the various ways of making it cheaper, one is to reduce the quality of it, another to lessen the quantity we consume. If we cannot get enough of coarse wheaten bread, let us make it of other grain. Or let us mix one half of potatoes, and one half of wheat. This last is what I eat in my own family; it is pleasant and wholesome. Our blessed Saviour ate barley bread, you know, as we are told in the last month's Sunday Reading of the Cheap Repository*, which I hope you have all heard; as I desired the master of the Sunday-school to read it just after evening-service, when I know many of the parents are apt to call in at the school. This is a good custom, and one of those little books shall be often read at that time.

My good women, I truly feel for you at this time of scarcity; and I am going to shew my good-will, as much by my advice as my subscription. It is my duty, as your friend and minister, to tell you, that one half of your present hardships is owing to BAD MANAGEMENT. I often meet your children without shoes and stockings, with great luncheons of the very whitest bread, and that three times a day. Half that quantity, and still less if it were coarse, put into a dish of good onion or leek porridge, would make them an excellent breakfast. Many too,

---

* See Cheap Repository, Tract on the Scarcity, printed for T. Evans, Long-lane, West Smithfield, London.

of the very pooreſt of you, eat your bread hot from the oven; this makes the difference of one loaf in five; I aſſure you 'tis what I cannot afford to do. Come, Mrs. White, you muſt aſſiſt me a little. I am not very knowing in theſe matters myſelf; but I know that the rich would be twice as charitable as they are, if the poor made a better uſe of their bounty. Mrs. White, do give theſe poor women a little advice how to make their pittance go further than it now does. When you lived with me, you were famous for making us nice cheap diſhes, and I dare ſay you are not leſs notable now you manage for yourſelf.

Indeed, neighbours, ſaid Mrs. White, what the good doctor ſays is very true. A halfpenny worth of oatmeal, or groats, with a leek or onion, out of your own garden, which coſts nothing, a bit of ſalt, and a little coarſe bread, will breakfaſt your whole family. It is a great miſtake at any time to think a bit of meat is ſo ruinous, and a great load of bread ſo cheap. A poor man gets ſeven or eight ſhillings a week; if he is careful he brings it home. I dare not ſay how much of this goes for tea in the afternoon, now ſugar and butter are ſo dear, becauſe I ſhould have you all upon me; but I will ſay, that too much of this little goes even for bread, from a miſtaken notion that it is the hardeſt fare. This, at all times, but particularly juſt now, is bad management. Dry peas, to be ſure, have been very dear lately; but now they are plenty enough.

enough. I am certain then, that if a shilling or two of the seven or eight was laid out for a bit of coarse beef, a sheep's head, or any such thing, it would be well bestowed. I would throw a couple of pound of this into the pot, with two or three handfuls of grey peas, an onion, and a little pepper. Then I would throw in cabbage, or turnip, and carrot; or any garden stuff that was most plenty; let it stew two or three hours, and it will make a dish fit for his Majesty. The working men should have the meat; the children don't want it; the soup will be thick and substantial, and requires no bread.

RICE MILK.

You who can get skim milk, as all our workmen can, have a great advantage. A quart of this, and a quarter of a pound of the rice you have just bought, a little bit of all-spice, and brown sugar, will make a dainty and cheap dish.

Bless your heart! muttered Amy Grumble, who looked as dirty as a cinder-wench, with her face and fingers all daubed with snuff; rice milk, indeed! it is very nice to be sure for those who can dress it, but we have not a bit of coal; rice is of no use to us without firing; and yet, said the Doctor, I see your tea-kettle boiling twice every day, as I pass by the poor-house, and fresh butter at eleven-pence a pound on your shelf. O' dear, sir, cried Amy, a few sticks serve to boil the tea-kettle. And a few more, said the Doctor, will boil the rice milk, and give twice the nourishment at a quarter of the expence.

RICE PUDDING.

Pray, *Sarah*, said the Doctor, how did you use to make that pudding my children were so fond of? And I remember, when it was cold, we used to have it in the parlour for supper. Nothing more easy, said Mrs. White. I put half a pound of rice, two quarts of skim milk, and two ounces of brown suggar. Well, said the Doctor, and how many will this dine? Seven or eight, sir. Very well, and what will it cost? Why, sir, it did not cost you so much, because we baked it at home, and I used our own milk; but it will not cost above seven-pence to those who pay for both. Here, too, bread is saved.

Pray, Sarah, let me put in a word, said farmer White. I advise my men to raise each a large bed of parsnips. They are very nourishing, and very profitable. Six-penny worth of seed, well sowed, and trod in, will produce more meals than four sacks of potatoes; and what is material to you who have so little ground, it will not require more than an eighth part of the ground which the four sacks will take. Parsnips are very good the second day warmed in the frying-pan, and a little rasher of pork, or bacon, will give them a nice flavour.

Dr. Shepherd now said, As a proof of the nourishing quality of parsnips, I was reading in a history a history book this very day, that the American Indians make a great part of their bread of parsnips, though Indian corn is so famous: it will make a little variety too.

A CHEAP STEW.

I remember, said Mrs. White, a cheap dish, so nice that it makes my mouth water. I peel some raw potatoes, slice them thin, put the slices into a deep frying-pan, or pot, with a little water, an onion, and a bit of pepper. Then I get a bone or two of a breast of mutton, or a little strip of salt pork, and put it into it. Cover it down close, keep in the steam, and let it stew for an hour.

You really get me an appetite, Mrs. White, by your dainty receipts, said the Doctor. I am resolved to have this dish at my own table. I could tell you another very good dish, and still cheaper, answered she. Come, let us have it, cried the Doctor. I shall write all down as soon as I get home, and I will favour any body with a copy of these receipts who will call at my house. And I will do more, Sir, said Mrs. White, for I will put any of these women in the way how to dress it the first time, if they are at a loss. But this is my dish:

Take two or three pickled herrings, put them into a stone jar, fill it up with potatoes, and a little water, and let it bake in the oven till it is done. I would give one hint more, added she; I have taken to use nothing but potatoe starch;

and though I say it, that should not say it, nobody's linen in a common way looks better than ours.

The Doctor now said, I am sorry for one hardship which many poor people labour under, I mean the difficulty of getting a little milk. I wish all farmer's wives were as considerate as you are, Mrs. White. A little milk is a great comfort to the poor, especially when their children are sick; and I have known it answer to the seller as well as to the buyer, to keep a cow or two on purpose to sell it out by the quart, instead of making butter and cheese.

Sir, said farmer White, I beg leave to say a word to the men, if you please, for all your advice goes to the women. If you will drink less gin you may get more meat. If you abstain from the ale-house, you may, many of you, get a little one-way beer at home. Aye, that we can farmer, said poor Tom, the thatcher, who was now got well. Easter Monday for that—I say no more. A word to the wife. The farmer smiled, and went on. The number of public houses in many a parish brings on more hunger and rags than all the taxes in it, heavy as they are. All the other evils put together hardly make up the sum of that one. We are now raising a fresh subscription for you. This will be our rule of giving. We will not give to sots, gamblers, and sabbath-breakers. Those who do not set their young children to work on week-days, and send them to school on Sundays, deserve little favour.

favour. No man should keep a dog till he has more food than his family wants. If he feeds them at home, they rob his children; if he starves them, they rob his neighbours. We have heard in a neighbouring city, that some people carried back the subscription loaves because they were too coarse; but we hope better things of you. Here Betty Plane begged, with all humility, to put in a word. Certainly, said the Doctor, we will listen to all modest complaints, and try to redress them. You are pleased to say, sir, said she, that we might find much comfort from buying coarse bits of beef. And so we might, but you do not know, sir, that we could seldom get them, even when we had the money, and times were so bad. How so, Betty? Sir, when we go to butcher Jobbins, for a bit of shin, or any other lean piece, his answer is, You can't have it to-day. The cook at the great house has bespoke it for gravy, or the Doctor's maid, (begging your pardon, sir,) has just ordered it for soup. Now, sir, if such kind gentlefolks were aware, that this gravy and soup, not only consume a great deal of meat, which, to be sure, those have a right to do who can pay for it; but that it takes away those coarse pieces which the poor would buy, if they bought at all, I am sure they would not do it. For, indeed, the rich have been very kind, and I don't know what we should have done without them.

I thank

I thank you for the hint Betty, said the Doctor, and I assure you I will have no more gravy soup. My garden will supply me with soups, that are both wholesomer and better; and I will answer for my lady at the great house, that she will do the same. I hope this will become a general rule, and then we shall expect that butchers will favour you in the prices of the coarse pieces, if *we* who are rich buy nothing but the prime. In our gifts we shall prefer, as the farmer has told you, those who keep steadily to their work: such as come to the vestry for a loaf, and do not come to church for the sermon, we shall mark, and prefer those who come constantly whether there are any gifts or not. But there is one rule from which we never will depart. Those who have been seen aiding, or abetting any riot, any attack on butchers, bakers, wheat mows, mills, or millers, we will not relieve; but with the quiet, contented, hard-working man, I will share my last morsel of bread. I shall only add, though it has pleased God to send us this visitation as a punishment, yet we may convert this short trial into a lasting blessing, if we all turn over a new leaf. Prosperity had made most of us careless. The thoughtless profusion of some of the rich could only be exceeded by the idleness, and bad management, of some of the poor. Let us now at last, adopt that good old maxim, *every one mend one*. And may God add his blessing!

The people now chearfully departed with their rice, resolving, as many of them as could get milk, to put one of Mrs. White's receipts in practice that very night; and a rare supper they had.

I hope soon to give a good account how this parish improved in ease and comfort, by their improvement in frugality and good management.

Z.

THE COTTAGE COOK,

OR

Mrs. JONES's CHEAP DISHES,

SHEWING THE WAY TO DO MUCH GOOD
WITH LITTLE MONEY.

MRS. JONES was a great merchant's lady. She was liberal to the poor, in giving them money; but as she was too much taken up with the world, she did not spare so much of her time and thoughts about doing good as she ought, so that her money was often ill bestowed. In the late troubles, Mr. Jones, who had lived in a grand manner, failed, and he took his misfortunes so much to heart that he fell sick and died. Mrs. Jones retired on a very narrow income to the small village of Weston, where she seldom went out except to church. Though a pious woman, she was too apt to indulge her sorrow; and though she did not neglect to read and pray, yet she gave up a great part of her time to melancholy thoughts, and grew quite inactive.

She

She well knew how sinful it would be for her to seek a cure for her grief in worldly pleasures, which is a way many people take under afflictions; but she was not aware how wrong it was to weep away that time which might have been better spent in drying the tears of others.

It was happy for her, that Mr. Simpson, the vicar of Weston, was a pious man. One Sunday he happened to preach on the good Samaritan. It was a charity sermon, and there was a collection at the door. He called on Mrs. Jones after church, and found her in tears. She told him she had been much moved by his discourse, and she wept because she had so little to give to the plate; for though she felt very keenly for the poor in these dear times, yet she could not assist them. Indeed, Sir, added she, I never so much regretted the loss of my fortune, as this afternoon, when you bade us *go and do likewise*. You do not, replied Mr. Simpson, enter into the spirit of our Saviour's parable, if you think you cannot *go and do likewise* without being rich. In the case of the Samaritan, you may observe, that charity was afforded more by kindness, and care, and medicine, than by money. You, madam, were as much concerned in my sermon as Sir John with his great estate; and, to speak plainly, I have been sometimes surprised that you should not put yourself in the way of being more useful.

Sir, said Mrs. Jones, I am grown shy of the poor since I have nothing to give them. Nothing! madam,

madam, replied the clergyman, do you call your time, your talents, your kind offices, nothing? I will venture to say that you might do more good than the richest man in the parish could do by merely giving his money. Instead of sitting here, brooding over your misfortunes, which are past remedy, bestir yourself to find out ways of doing much good with little money; or even without any money at all. You have lately studied œconomy for yourself. Instruct your poor neighbours in that important art. They want it almost as much as they want money. You have influence with the few rich persons in the parish; exert that influence. Betty, my house-keeper, shall assist you in any thing in which she can be useful. Try this for one year, and if you then tell me that you should have better shewn your love to God and man, and been a happier woman had you continued gloomy and inactive, I shall be much surprised, and shall consent to your resuming your present way of life.

The sermon and this discourse made so deep an impression on Mrs. Jones, that she formed a new plan of life, and set about it at once, as every body does who is in earnest. Her chief aim was the happiness of her poor neighbours in the next world; but she was also very desirous to promote their present comfort. The plans she pursued with a view to the latter object shall be explained in this little book. Mrs. Jones was much respected by all the rich persons in Weston, who had known her in her prosperity. Sir John was thoughtless, lavish, and indolent. The Squire was over-frugal, but active, sober, and not ill-natured. Sir John loved pleasure, the Squire loved money. Sir John was one of those popular sort of people who get much praise and yet do little good; who subscribe with equal readiness to a cricket match, or a charity school; who take it for granted that the poor are to be indulged with bell-ringing and bon-fires, and to be made drunk at Christmas; this Sir John called being kind to them; but he thought it was folly to teach them, and madness to think of reforming them. He was, however, always ready to give his guinea; but I question whether he would have given up his hunting and his gaming to have cured every grievance in the land. On the other hand, the Squire would assist Mrs. Jones in any of her plans if it cost him nothing; so she shewed her good sense by never asking Sir John for advice, or the Squire for subscriptions, and by this prudence gained the full support of both.

Mrs. Jones resolved to spend two or three days in a week in getting acquainted with the state of the parish, and she took care never to walk out without a few little good books in her pocket to give away. This, though a cheap, is a most important act of charity; it has various uses; it furnishes the poor with knowledge, which they have no other way of obtaining; and it is the best introduction for any useful conversation
which

which the giver of the book may wish to introduce.

She found that among the numerous wants she met with, no small share was owing to bad management, or to imposition: she was struck with the small size of the loaves. Wheat was now not very dear, and she was sure a good deal of blame rested with the baker. She sent for a shilling loaf to the next great town where the mayor often sent to the bakers' shops to see that the bread was proper weight. She weighed her town loaf against her country loaf, and found the latter two pounds lighter than it ought to be. This was not the sort of grievance to carry to Sir John; but luckily the Squire was also a magistrate, and it was quite in his way. He told her he could remedy the evil if some one would lodge an information against the baker.

THE INFORMER.

She dropt in on the blacksmith. He was at dinner. She enquired if his bread was good. Aye, good enough, mistress, for you see it is as white as your cap, if we had but more of it. Here's a six-penny loaf, you might take it for a penny roll! He then heartily cursed Crib, the baker, and said, he ought to be hanged. Mrs. Jones now told him what she had done, how she had detected the fraud, and assured him the evil should be redressed on the morrow, provided he would appear and inform. I inform! said he, with a shocking oath, hang an informer! I scorn the office. You are nice in the wrong place, friend, replied Mrs. Jones, for you don't scorn to abuse the baker, nor to be in a passion, nor to swear, though you scorn to redress a public injury, and to increase your children's bread. Let me tell you, there is nothing in which you ignorant people mistake more than in your notions about *informers*. Informing is a lawful way of obtaining redress; and though it is a mischievous and a hateful thing to go to a justice about every trifling matter, yet laying an information on important occasions, without malice, or bitterness of any kind, is what no honest man ought to be ashamed of. The shame is to commit the offence, not to inform against it. I, for my part, should perhaps do right if I not only informed against Crib, for making light bread, but against you for swearing at him. Well, but madam, said the smith, a little softened, don't you think it a sin and a shame to turn Informer? So far from it, when a man's motives are good, said Mrs. Jones, that in such clear cases as the present, I think it a duty and a virtue. If it is right that there should be laws, it must be right that they should be put in execution; but how can this be, if people will not inform the magistrates when they see the laws broken? *An informer by trade* is commonly a knave; a rash, malicious, or passionate informer is a fire-brand; but honest and prudent informers are almost as useful members of society as the judges of the land. If you continue in your present mind on this subject,

do

do not you think that you will be anfwerable for the crimes you might have prevented by informing, and be a fort of accomplice of the villains who commit them?

Well, madam, faid the fmith, I now fee plainly enough that there is no fhame in turning informer when my caufe is good. And your motive right, always mind that, faid Mrs. Jones, Next day the fmith attended, Crib was fined in the ufual penalty, his light bread was taken from him and given to the poor. The juftices refolved henceforward to infpect the bakers in their diftrict; and all of them, except Crib, and fuch as Crib, were glad of it, for honefty never dreads a trial. Thus had Mrs. Jones the comfort of feeing how ufeful people may be without expence; for if fhe could have given the poor fifty pounds, fhe would not have done them fo great, or fo lafting a benefit; and the true light in which fhe had put the bufinefs of *informing* was of no fmall ufe.

There were two fhops in the parifh, but Mrs. Sparks at the Crofs, had not half fo much cuftom as Wills, at the Sugar Loaf, though fhe fold her goods a penny in a fhilling cheaper, and all agreed that they were much better. Mrs. Jones afked Mrs. Sparks the reafon. Madam, faid the fhopkeeper, Mr. Wills will give longer truft. Befides this, his wife keeps fhop on a Sunday morning while I am at church. Mrs. Jones now reminded Mr. Simpfon to read the King's

Proclamation

Proclamation against vice and immorality next Sunday, at church, and prevailed on the Squire to fine any one who should keep open shop on a Sunday. She also put the people in mind that a shopkeeper, who would sell on a Sunday, would be more likely to cheat them all the week, than one who went to church.

She also laboured hard to convince them how much they would lessen their distress, if they would contrive to deal with Mrs. Sparks for ready money, rather than with Wills on long credit; those who listened to her found their circumstances far more comfortable at the year's end, while the rest, tempted, like some of their betters, by the pleasure of putting off the evil day of payment, like them at last found themselves plunged in debt and distress. She took care to make a good use of such instances in her conversation with the poor, and, by perseverance, she at length brought them so much to her way of thinking, that Wills found it to be his interest to alter his plan, and sell his goods on as good terms and as short credit as Mrs. Sparks sold hers. This compleated Mrs. Jones's success, and she had the satisfaction of having put a stop to three or four great evils in the parish of Weston, without spending a shilling in doing it.

Patty Smart and Jenny Rose were thought to be the two best managers in the parish. They both told Mrs. Jones, that the poor would get the coarse pieces of meat cheaper, if the gentlefolks did not buy them for soups and gravy.

Mrs.

Mrs. Jones thought there was reason in this: so away she went to Sir John, the Squire, the Surgeon, the Attorney, and the Steward, the only persons in the parish who could afford to buy costly things. She told them, that if they would all be so good as to buy only prime pieces, which they could very well afford, the coarse and cheap joints would come more within the reach of the poor. Most of the gentry readily consented. Sir John cared not what his meat cost him, but told Mrs. Jones, in his gay way, that he would eat any thing, or give any thing, so that she would not tease him with long stories about the poor. The Squire said, he should prefer vegetable soups, because they were cheaper, and the Doctor preferred them because they were wholsomer. The Steward chose to imitate the Squire; and the Attorney found it would be quite ungenteel to stand out. So gravy soups became very unfashionable in the parish of Weston; and I am sure if rich people did but think a little on this subject, they would become as unfashionable in many other places.

When wheat grew cheaper, Mrs. Jones was earnest with the poor women to bake large brown loaves at home, instead of buying small white ones at the shop. Mrs. Betty had told her, that baking at home would be one step towards restoring the good old management. Only Betty Smart and Jenny Rose baked at home in the whole parish, and who lived so well as they did? Yet the general objection seemed reasonable.

They could not bake without yeast, which often could not be had, as no one brewed except the great folks and the public houses. Mrs. Jones found, however, that Patty and Jenny contrived to brew as well as to bake. She sent for these women, knowing that from them she could get truth and reason. How comes it, said she to them, that you two are the only poor women in the parish who can afford to brew a small cask of beer? Your husbands have not better wages than other men. True, madam, said Patty, but they never set foot in a public house. I will tell you the truth. When I first married, our John went to the Checquers every night, and I had my tea and fresh butter twice a-day at home. This slop, which consumed a deal of sugar, began to *rake* my stomach sadly, as I had neither meat nor milk; at last, (I am ashamed to own it) I began to take a drop of gin to quiet the pain, till in time I looked for my gin as regularly as for my tea. At last the gin, the alehouse, and the tea, began to make us both sick and poor, and I had like to have died with my first child. Parson Simpson then talked so finely to us on the subject of improper indulgences that we resolved, by the grace of God, to turn over a new leaf, and I promised John, if he would give up the Checquers, I would break the gin bottle, and never drink tea in the afternoon, except on Sundays, when he was at home with me. We have kept our word, and both our eating and drinking, our health, and our con-

P sciences

sciences are better for it. Though meat is sadly dear, we can buy two pounds of fresh meat for less than one pound of fresh butter, and it gives five times the nourishment. And dear as malt is, I contrive to keep a drop of drink in the house for John, and John will make me drink half a pint with him every evening, and a pint a-day when I am a nurse.

As one good deed as well as one bad one brings on another, this conversation set Mrs. Jones on enquiring why so many ale-houses were allowed. She did not chuse to talk to Sir John on this subject, who would only have said, let them enjoy themselves poor fellows; if they get drunk now and then, they work hard. But those who have this false good-nature forget, that while the man is *enjoying himself*, as it is called, his wife and children are ragged and starving. True christian good-nature never indulges one at the cost of many, but is kind to all. The Squire, who was a friend to order, took up the matter. He consulted Mr. Simpson. The Lion, said he, is necessary. It stands by the road side: travellers must have a resting place. As to the Checquers and the Bell they do no good but much harm. Mr. Simpson had before made many attempts to get the Checquers put down; but, unluckily, it was Sir John's own house, and kept by his late butler. Not that Sir John valued the rent, but he had a false kindness which made him support the cause of an old servant, though he knew he kept a dif-
orderly

orderly house. The Squire, however, now took away the licence from the Lion. And a fray happening soon after at the Checquers, (which was near the church) in time of divine service, Sir John was obliged to suffer the house to be put down as a nuisance. You would not believe how many poor families were able to brew a little cask when the temptations of those alehouses were taken out of their way. Mrs. Jones, in her evening walks had the pleasure to see many an honest man drinking his wholesome cup of beer by his own fire-side, his rosy children playing about his knees, his clean chearful wife singing her youngest baby to sleep, rocking the cradle with her foot, while with her hands she was making a dumpling for her kind husband's supper. Some few, I am sorry to say, though I don't chuse to name names, still preferred getting drunk once a week at the Lion, and drinking water at other times.

The good women being now supplied with yeast from each other's brewings, would have baked, but two difficulties still remained. Many of them had no ovens, for since the new bad management had crept in, many cottages have been built without this convenience. Fuel also was scarce at Weston. Mrs. Jones advised the building a large parish oven. Sir John subscribed to be rid of her importunity, and the Squire because he thought every improvement in œconomy would reduce the poor rate. It was soon accomplished, and to this oven, at a certain hour, three times a week, the elder children carried their loaves which their mothers had made at home, and paid a halfpenny, or a penny, according to their size, for the baking.

Mrs. Jones found that no poor women in Weston could buy a little milk, as the farmers' wives did not care to rob their dairies. This was a great distress, especially when the children were sick. So Mrs. Jones advised Mrs. Sparks, at the Cross, to keep a couple of cows, and sell out the milk by halfpennyworths. She did so, and found, that though this plan gave her some additional trouble, she got full as much by it as if she had made cheese and butter. She also sold rice at a cheap rate, so that with the help of the milk, and the public oven, a fine rice pudding was to be had for a trifle.

The girls' school, in the parish, was fallen into neglect, for though many would be subscribers, yet no one would look after it. I wish this was the case at Weston only; many schools have come to nothing, and many parishes are quite destitute of schools, because too many gentry neglect to make it a part of the duty of their grown-up daughters to inspect the instruction of the poor. It was not in Mr. Simpson's way to see if girls were taught to work. This is ladies business. Mrs. Jones consulted her counsellor, Mrs. Betty, and they went every Friday to the school, where they invited mothers as well as daughters to come, and learn to cut out to the best advantage. Mrs. Jones had not
been

been bred to thefe things, but by means of Mrs. Cowper's excellent cutting-out-book, fhe foon became miftrefs of the whole art. She not only had the girls taught to make and mend, but to wafh and iron too*. She alfo allowed the mother, or eldeft daughter of every family, to come once a week, and learn how to drefs *one cheap difh.* One Friday, which was cooking day, who fhould pafs by but the Squire, with his gun and dogs. He looked into the fchool for the firft time. Well, madam, faid he, what good are you doing here? What are your girls learning and earning? Where are your manufactures? Where is your fpinning and your carding? Sir, faid fhe, this is a fmall parifh, and you know ours is not a manufacturing county; fo that when thefe girls are women, they will not be much employed in fpinning. However, we teach them a little of it, and ftill more of knitting, that they may be able to get up a fmall piece of houfehold linen once a year, and provide the family with ftockings, by employing the odds and ends of their time in thefe ways. But there is a manufacture which I am carrying on, and I know of none within my own reach which is fo valuable. What can that be? faid the Squire. *To make good wives for working men,* faid fhe. Is not mine an excellent ftaple commodity? I am

---

* How Mrs. Jones managed her Sunday Schools, and alfo her method of religious inftruction on week days, may be fhewn hereafter.

teaching these girls the art of industry and good management. It is little encouragement to an honest man to work hard all the week, if his wages are wasted by a slattern at home. Most of these girls will probably become wives to the poor, or servants to the rich; to such the common arts of life are of great value; now as there is little opportunity for learning these at the school-house, I intend to propose that such gentry as have sober servants, shall allow one of these girls to come and work in their families one day in a week, when the house-keeper, the cook, the house-maid, or the laundry-maid, shall be required to instruct them in their several departments. This I conceive to be the best way of training good servants. What have you got on the fire, madam? said the Squire; for your pot really smells as savory, as if Sir John's French cook had filled it. Sir, replied Mrs. Jones, I have lately got acquainted with Mrs. White, who has given us an account of her cheap dishes, and nice cookery, in one of the Cheap Repository little books*. Mrs. Betty and I have made all her dishes, and very good they are, and we have got several others of our own. Every Friday we come here and dress one. These good women see how it is done, and learn to dress it at their own houses. I take home part for my own dinner, and what is left I give to each in turn. I

---

* See "The Way to Plenty," sold by T. Evans, Long Lane, West Smithfield. Price 1½.

hope

hope I have opened their eyes on a sad mistake they had got into, *that we think any thing is good enough for the poor.* Now I do *not* think any thing good enough for the poor which is not clean, wholesome, and palatable, and what I myself would not chearfully eat if my circumstances required it.

Pray, Mrs. Betty, said the 'squire, oblige me with a bason of your soup. The squire found it so good after his walk, that he was almost sorry he had promised to buy no more legs of beef, and declared, that not one sheep's head should ever go to his kennel again. He begged his cook might have the receipt, and Mrs. Jones wrote it out for her. She has also been so obliging as to favour me with a copy of all her receipts. And as I hate all monopoly, and see no reason why such cheap, nourishing, and savoury dishes should be confined to the parish of Weston, I print them, that all other parishes may have the same advantage. Not only the poor, but all persons with small incomes may be glad of them.—Well, madam, said Mr. Simpson, who came in soon after, which is best, to sit down and cry over our misfortunes, or to bestir ourselves to do our duty to the world?— Sir, replied Mrs. Jones, I thank you for the useful lesson you have given me. You have taught me that our time and talents are to be employed with zeal in God's service, if we wish for his favour here or hereafter; and that one great employment of them, which he requires, is the promotion of the prefent, and much more the future happinefs of all around us. You have taught me that much good may be done with little money; and that the heart, the head, and the hands are of fome ufe as well as the purfe.

May all who read this account of Mrs. Jones, *go and do likewife!*

RECEIPT I.

Two pounds of beef, four onions, ten turnips, half a pound of rice, a large handful of parfley, thyme, and favoury; fome pepper and falt; eight quarts of water. Cut the beef in flices, and after it has boiled fome time, cut it ftill fmaller. The whole fhould boil gently about two hours, on a flow fire. If fuel be fcarce, it may be ftewed all night in an oven, and warmed up next day. You may add oatmeal and potatoes.

RECEIPT II.

Take half a pound of beef, mutton, or pork, cut it into fmall pieces; half a pint of peafe, four fliced turnips, fix potatoes cut very fmall, two onions; put to them feven pints of water. Let the whole boil gently over a very flow fire two hours and a half. Then thicken it with a quarter of a pound of oatmeal. After the thickening is put in, boil it a quarter of an hour, stirring

stirring it all the time; then season it with salt and pepper.

RECEIPT III.

Take two pounds of salt beef, or pork, cut it into very small bits, and put it into a pot with six quarts of water, letting it boil on a slow fire for three quarters of an hour; then put a few carrots, parsnips, or turnips, all cut small; or a few potatoes sliced; a cabbage, and a couple of cresses. Thicken the whole with a pint of oatmeal. All these to be well seasoned with salt and pepper.

SOUPS.

The following soups Mrs. Sparks sold every Saturday in small quantities, a pint of the soup with a bit of the meat warmed up on Sunday, made a dinner for a grown person.

An ox cheek, two pecks of potatoes, a quarter of a peck of onions, one ounce of pepper, half a pound of salt, boiled altogether in ninety pints of water till reduced to sixty; any garden-stuff may be thrown in.

FRIENDLY HINTS.

The difference between eating bread new and stale, is one loaf in five.

If you turn your meat into broth it will go much farther than if you roast or bake it.

If you have a garden make the most of it. A bit of leek, or an onion, makes all dishes savoury at small expence.

If the money spent on fresh butter were spent on meat, poor families would be much better fed than they are.

If the money spent on tea were spent on home-brewed beer, the wife would be better fed, the husband better pleased, and both would be healthier.

Keep a little Scotch barley, rice, dry pease, and oatmeal in the house. They are all cheap, and don't spoil. Keep also pepper and ginger.

Pay your debts, serve God, and love your neighbour.

THE SUNDAY SCHOOL.

I Promised, in the Cottage Cook, to give some account of the manner in which Mrs. Jones set up her school. She did not much fear being able to raise the money, but money is of little use, unless some persons of sense and piety can be found to direct these institutions. Not that I would discourage those who set them up, even in the most ordinary manner, and from mere views of worldly policy. It is something gained to rescue children from idling away their Sabbath

Sabbath in the fields or the streets. It is no small thing to keep them from those tricks to which a day of leisure tempts the idle and the ignorant. It is something for them to be taught to read; it is much to be taught to read the Bible, and much, indeed, to be carried regularly to church. But all this is not enough. To bring these institutions to answer their highest end, can only be effected by God's blessing on the best directed means, the choice of able teachers, and a diligent attention in some pious gentry to visit and inspect the schools.

ON RECOMMENDATIONS.

Mrs. Jones had one talent that eminently qualified her to do good, namely, judgment; this, even in the gay part of her life, had kept her from many mistakes; but though she had sometimes been deceived herself, she was very careful not to deceive others, in recommending people to fill any office for which they were unfit, either through selfishness or false kindness. She used to say, there is always some one appropriate quality which every person must possess, in order to fit them for any particular employment. Even in this quality, said she to Mr. Simpson, the clergyman, I do not expect perfection; but if they are destitute of this, whatever good qualities they may possess besides, though they may do for some other employment, they will not do for this. If I want a pair of shoes, I go to a shoemaker;

maker; I do not go to a man of another trade, however ingenious he may be, to afk him if he cannot *contrive* to make me a pair of fhoes. When I lived in London, I learned to be much on my guard as to recommendations. I found people often wanted to impofe on me fome one who was a burthen to themfelves. Once I remember, when I undertook to get a matron for an hofpital, half my acquaintance had fome one to offer me. Mrs. Gibfon fent me an old cook, whom fhe herfelf had difcharged for wafting her own provifions, yet fhe had the confcience to recommend this woman to take care of the provifions of a large community. Mrs Grey fent me a difcarded houfekeeper, whofe conftitution had been ruined by fitting up with Mrs. Grey's gouty hufband, but who fhe yet thought might do well enough to undergo the fatigue of taking care of an hundred poor fick people. A third friend fent me a woman who had no merit but that of being very poor, and it would be charity to provide for her. The truth is, the lady was obliged to allow her a fmall penfion till fhe could get her off her own hands by turning her on thofe of others.

It is very true, madam, faid Mr. Simpfon, the right way is always to prefer the good of the many to the good of one; if, indeed, it can be called doing good to any one to place them in a ftation in which they muft feel unhappy, by not knowing how to difcharge the duties of it. I will tell you how I manage. If the perfons recommended

mended are objects of charity, I privately subscribe to their wants; I pity and help them, but I never promote them to a station for which they are unfit, as I should by so doing hurt a whole community to help a distressed individual.

Thus Mrs. Jones resolved, that the first step towards setting up her school should be to provide a suitable mistress. The vestry were so earnest in recommending one woman, that she thought it worth looking into. On enquiry, she found it was a scheme to take a large family off the parish; they never considered that a very ignorant woman, with a family of young children, was not fit for a school; all they considered was, that the profits of the school might enable her to live without parish pay. Mrs. Jones refused another, though she could read well, and was decent in her conduct, because she used to send her children to the shop on Sundays. And she objected to a third, a very sensible woman, because she was suspected of making an outward profession of religion a cloak for immoral conduct. Mrs. Jones knew she must not be too nice neither, she knew she must put up with many faults at last. I know, said she to Mr. Simpson, the imperfection of every thing that is human. As the mistress will have much to bear with from the children, so I expect to have something to bear with in the mistress; and she and I must submit to our respective trials, by thinking how much God has to bear with in us all. But there are

are three things which a mistress must not be without, *good sense, activity,* and *piety.* Without the first she will mislead others; without the second she will neglect them; and without the third, though she may civilize, yet she will never christianize them.

Mr. Simpson said, he really knew but of one person in the parish who was fully likely to answer her purpose: this, continued he, is no other than my housekeeper, Mrs. Betty Crew. It will, indeed, be a great loss to me to part from her; and to her it will be a far more fatiguing life than that which she at present leads. But ought I to put my own personal comfort, or ought Betty to put her own ease and quiet, in competition with the good of above an hundred children? This will appear still more important, if we consider the good done, not as a *fruit* but *seed*; if we take into the account how many yet unborn may become Christians, in consequence of our making these children Christians. For how can we calculate the number which may be hereafter trained for heaven, by those very children we are going to teach, when they themselves shall become parents, and you and I are dead and forgotten? To be sure, by parting from Betty, my peas-soup will not be quite so well flavoured, nor my linen so neatly got up; but the day is fast approaching when all this will signify but little; but it will not signify a little whether one hundred immortal souls were the better from my making this petty sacrifice. Betty Crew is a

real

real Christian, has excellent sense, and had a good education from my mother. She has also had a little sort of training for the business, for when the poor children come to the parsonage for the broth on a Saturday evening, Betty is used to appoint them all to come at the same time, and after she has filled their pitchers, she ranges them round her in the garden, and examines them in their catechism. She is just and fair in dealing out the broth and beef, not making my favour to the parents depend on the skill of their children. But her own old caps, and ribbons, and cast off cloaths, are bestowed as little rewards on the best scholars. So that taking the time she spends in working for them, and the things she gives them, there is many a lady who does not exceed Betty in acts of charity; this I mention to confirm your notion, that it is not necessary to be rich in order to do good; a religious upper servant has great opportunities of this sort, if the master is disposed to encourage her.

My readers, I trust, need not be informed, that this is that very Mrs. Betty Crew who assisted Mrs. Jones in teaching poor women to cut out linen and dress cheap dishes, as related in the Cottage Cook. Mrs. Jones in the following week, got together as many of the mothers as she could, and spoke to them as follows:

MRS. JONES'S EXHORTATION.

My good women, on Sunday next I propose to open a school for the instruction of your children.

dren. Those among you, who know what it is to be able to read your Bible, will, I doubt not, rejoice that the same blessing is held out to your children. You who are *not* able yourselves to read what your Saviour has done and suffered for you, ought to be doubly anxious that your children should reap a blessing which you have lost. Would not that mother be thought an unnatural monster who should stand by and snatch out of her child's mouth the bread which a kind friend had just put into it? But such a mother would be merciful compared with her who should rob her children of the opportunity of learning to read the word of God when it is held out to them. Remember, that if you slight the present offer, or if, after having sent your children a few times, you should afterwards keep them at home under vain pretences, you will have to answer for it at the day of judgment. Let not your poor children, *then*, have cause to say, My fond mother was my worst enemy. I might have been bred up in the fear of the Lord, and she opposed it for the sake of giving me a little paltry pleasure.—For an idle holiday, I am now brought to the gates of hell! My dear women, which of you could bear to see your darling child condemned to everlasting destruction? Which of you could bear to hear him accuse you as the cause of it? Is there any mother here present, who will venture to say,—I will doom the child I bore to sin and hell, rather than put them or myself to a little present pain,

by

by curtailing their evil inclinations? I will let them spend the Sabbath in ignorance and idleness, instead of rescuing them from vanity and sin, by sending them to school? Let that mother, who values her child's pleasure more than his soul, now walk away, while I set down in my list the names of all those who wish to bring their young ones up in the way that leads to eternal life, instead of indulging them in the pleasures of sin, which are but for a moment.

When Mrs. Jones had done speaking, most of the women thanked her for her good advice, and hoped that God would give them grace to follow it; promising to send their children constantly. Others, who were not so well-disposed, were yet afraid to refuse, after the sin of so doing had been so plainly set before them. The worst of the women had kept away from this meeting, resolving to set their faces against the school. Most of them who were present, as soon as they got home, set about providing their children with what little decent apparel they could raise. Many a willing mother lent her tall daughter her hat, best cap, and white handkerchief, and many a grateful father spared his linen waistcoat and bettermost hat, to induce his grown up son to attend; for it was a rule with which Mrs. Jones began, that she would not receive the younger children out of any family who did not send their elder ones. Too many made excuses that their shoes were old, or their hat worn out. But Mrs. Jones told them not to bring any excuses to her which they could not bring to the day of judgment; and among those excuses she would hardly admit any except accidents, sickness, or attendance on sick parents, or young children.

SUBSCRIPTIONS.

Mrs. Jones was very desirous of getting the help and countenance of the farmers and tradespeople, whose duty and interest she thought it was to support a plan calculated to improve the virtue and happiness of the parish. Most of them subscribed, and promised to see that their workmen sent their children. She met with little opposition till she called on farmer Hoskins. She told him, as he was the richest farmer in the parish, she came to him for a handsome subscription. Subscription! said he; it is nothing but subscriptions, I think; a man had need be made of money.—Farmer, said Mrs. Jones, God has blessed you with abundant prosperity, and he expects you should be liberal in proportion to your great ability.—I do not know what you mean by blessing, said he; I have been up early and late, lived hard while I had little; and now when I thought I had got forward in the world, what with tythes and subscriptions it all goes, I think.—Mr. Hoskins, said Mrs. Jones, this is but an ungrateful return for all your blessings.— You are again at your blessings, said the farmer, but let every one work as hard as I have done, and I dare say he will do as well. It is to my own

own induſtry I owe what I have. My crops have been good, becauſe I minded my ploughing and ſowing.—O, farmer! cried Mrs. Jones, you forget whoſe ſuns and ſhowers make your crops to grow; but I do not come to preach, but to beg.—Well, madam, what is it now? Flannel or French? or weavers, or a new church, or large bread, or cheap rice? or what other new whim-wham for getting the money out of one's pocket?—I am going to eſtabliſh a Sunday ſchool, farmer; and I come to you as one of the principal inhabitants of the pariſh, hoping your example will ſpur on the reſt to give.—Why, then, ſaid the farmer, as one of the principal inhabitants of the pariſh, I will give nothing; hoping it will ſpur on the reſt to refuſe. Of all the fooliſh inventions, and new-fangled devices to ruin the country, that of teaching the poor to read is the very worſt.—And I, farmer, think that to teach good principles to the lower claſſes, is the moſt likely way to ſave the country. Now, in order to this, we muſt teach them to read.— Not with my conſent, nor my money, ſaid the farmer; for I know it always does more harm than good.—So it may, ſaid Mrs. Jones, if you only teach them to read, and then turn them adrift to find out books for themſelves *. There is

---

* It was this conſideration chiefly, which ſtimulated the conductors of the Cheap Repoſitory to ſend forth that variety of little books ſo peculiarly ſuited to the young. They conſidered, that by means of Sunday Schools, multitudes were

is a proneness in the heart to evil, which it is our duty to oppose, and which I see you are promoting. Only look round your own kitchen, I am ashamed to see it hung round with loose songs and ballads. I grant, indeed, it would be better for your men and maids, and even your daughters, not to be able to read at all than to read such stuff as this. But if, when they ask for bread, you will give them a stone, nay worse, a serpent, your's is the blame. Then taking up a penny book which had a very loose title, she went on—I do not wonder, if you who read such books as these, think it safer that people should not read at all. The farmer grinned, and said, It is hard if a man of my substance may not divert myself; when a bit of fun costs only a penny, and a man can spare that penny, there is no harm done. When it is very hot, or very wet, and I come in to rest, and have drank my mug of cider, I like to take up a bit of a jest book, or a comical story, to make me laugh.—O, Mr. Hoskins, replied Mrs. Jones, when you come in to rest from a burning sun or shower, do you never think of him whose sun it is that is ripening your corn? or whose shower is filling the year, or causing the grass to grow? I could tell you of some books which would strengthen such thoughts, whereas such as you read only

were now taught to read, who would be exposed to be corrupted by all the ribaldry and profaneness of loose songs, and vicious stories; and that it was a bounden duty to counteract such temptations.

serve to put them out of your head. Mrs. Jones having taken pains to let Mr. Hoskins know, that all the genteel and wealthy people had subscribed, he at last said, Why, as to the matter of that, I do not value a crown; only I think it might be better bestowed, and I am afraid my own workmen will fly in my face if once they are made scholars, and that they will think themselves too good to work.—Now you talk soberly and give your reasons, said Mrs. Jones; weak as they are, they deserve an answer. Do you think that either man, woman, or child, ever did his duty the worse, only because he knew it the better?—No, perhaps not.—Now, the whole extent of learning which we intend to give the poor, is only to enable them to read the Bible, a book which brings to us the glad tidings of salvation, in which every duty is explained, every doctrine brought into practice, and the highest truths made level to the meanest understanding. The knowledge of that book, and its practical influence on the heart, is the best security you can have, both for the industry and obedience of your servants. Now can you think any man will be the worse servant for being a good Christian?—Perhaps not.—Are not the duties of children, of servants, and the poor, expressly set forth in the Bible?—Yes.—Do you think any duties are likely to be so well performed from any human motives, such as fear, or prudence, as from these religious motives, which are backed with the sanction of rewards and

and punishments, of heaven or hell? Even upon your own principles of worldly policy, do you think a poor man is not less likely to steal a sheep or a horse, who was taught, when a boy, that it was a sin to rob a hen-roost or an orchard, than one who has been bred in ignorance? Will your property be secured so effectually by the stocks on the green, as by teaching the boys in the school, that *for all these things God will bring them into judgment?* Is a poor fellow who can read his Bible, so likely to sleep or to drink away his few hours of leisure, as one who *cannot* read? He may, and he often does, make a bad use of his reading, but I doubt he would have been as bad without it. And the hours spent in learning to read, will always have been among the most harmless ones of his life.

Well, madam, said the farmer, if you do not think that religion will spoil my young servants, I do not care if you do put me down for half a guinea. What has farmer Dobson given?—Half a guinea, said Mrs. Jones. Well, cried the farmer, it shall never be said I did not give more than he, who is only a renter. Dobson give half a guinea? Why, he wears his coat as thread-bare as a labourer.—Perhaps, replied Mrs. Jones, that is one reason why he gives so much. Well, put me down a guinea, cried the farmer; as scarce as guineas are just now, I'll never be put upon the same footing with Dobson neither. Yes, and you must exert yourself besides, in insisting that your workmen send their children, and

and often look into the school yourself to see if they are there, and reward or discourage them accordingly, added Mrs. Jones. The most zealous teachers will flag in their exertions, if they are not animated and supported by the wealthy; and your poor youth will soon despise religious instruction as a thing forced upon them, if it be not made pleasant by the encouraging presence, kind words, and little gratuities, from their betters.

Here Mrs. Jones took her leave; the farmer insisted on waiting on her to the door. When they got into the yard, they spied Mr. Simpson, who was standing near a little group of females, consisting of the farmer's two young daughters, and a couple of rosy dairy-maids, an old blind fiddler, and a woman who led him. The woman had laid a basket on the ground, out of which she was dealing some songs to the girls, who were kneeling round it, and eagerly picking out such whose titles suited their tastes. On seeing the clergyman come up, the fiddler's companion (for I am sorry to say she was not his wife) pushed some of the songs to the bottom of the basket, turned round to the company, and in a whining tone, asked, if they would please to buy a godly book. Mr. Simpson saw through the hypocrisy at once, and instead of making any answer, took out of one of the girl's hands, a song which the woman had not been able to snatch away. He was shocked and grieved to see that these young girls were about to read, to

sing

sing, and to learn by heart such ribaldry as he was ashamed even to cast his eyes on. He turned about to the girl, and gravely, but mildly said, Young woman, what do you think should be done to a person who should be found carrying a box of poison round the country, and leaving a little at every house? The girls all agreed, that such a person ought to be hanged. That he should, said the farmer, if I was upon the jury, and quartered too. The fiddler and his woman were of the same opinion; declaring, *they* would not do such a wicked thing for the world, for if they were poor they were honest. Mr. Simpson, turning to the other girl, said, Which is of most value the soul or the body?—The soul, sir, said the girl.—Why so? said he.—Because, sir, I have heard you say in the pulpit, the soul is to last for ever.—Then, cried Mr. Simpson, in a stern voice, turning to the fiddler's woman, are you not ashamed to sell poison for that part which is to last for ever? poison for the soul?— Poison! said the terrified girl, throwing down the book, and shuddering as people do who are afraid they have touched something infectious. Poison! echoed the farmer's daughters, recollecting with horror the ratsbane which Lion, the old house dog, had got at the day before, and after eating which she had seen him drop down dead in convulsions. Yes, said Mr. Simpson to the woman, I do again repeat, the souls of these innocent girls will be poisoned and may be

eternally

eternally ruined, by this vile trash which you carry about.

I now see, said Mrs. Jones to the farmer, the reason why you think learning to read does more harm than good. It is indeed far better that they should never know how to tell a letter, unless you keep such trash as this out of their way, and provide them with what is good, or at least what is harmless. Still this is not the fault of reading, but the abuse of it. Wine is still a good cordial, though it is too often abused to the purpose of drunkenness.

The farmer said that neither of his maids could read their horn-book, though he owned he often heard them singing that song which the parson had thought so bad, but for his part it made him as merry as a nightingale.

Yes, said Mrs. Jones, as a proof that it is not merely being able to read which does the mischief, I have often heard as I have been crossing a hay-field, young girls singing such indecent ribaldry as has driven me out of the field, though I well knew they could not read a line of what they were singing, but had caught it from others. So you see you may as well say the memory is a wicked talent because some people misapply it, as to say that reading is dangerous because some folks abuse it.

While they were talking, the fiddler and his woman were trying to steal away unobserved, but Mr. Simpson stopped them, and sternly said, woman I shall have some farther talk with you.

I am

I am a magistrate as well as a minister, and if I know it, I will no more allow a wicked book to be sold in my parish than a dose of poison. The girls threw away all their songs, thanked Mr. Simpson, begged Mrs. Jones would take them into her school after they had done milking in the evenings, that they might learn to read only what was proper. They promised they would never more deal with any but sober, honest hawkers, such as sell good little books, Christmas carols, and harmless songs, and desired the fiddler's woman never to call there again.

This little incident afterwards confirmed Mrs. Jones in a plan she had before some thoughts of putting in practice. This was, after her school had been established a few months, to invite all the well-disposed grown-up youth of the parish to meet her at the school an hour or two on a Sunday evening, after the necessary business of the dairy, and of serving the cattle was over. Both Mrs. Jones and her agent had the talent of making this time pass so agreeably by their manner of explaining scripture, and of impressing the heart by serious and affectionate discourse, that in a short time the evening school was nearly filled with a second company, after the younger ones were dismissed. In time, not only the servants, but the sons and daughters of the most substantial people in the parish attended. At length many of the parents, pleased with the improvement so visible in the young people, got a habit of dropping in, that they might learn

learn how to instruct their own families. And it was observed that as the school filled, not only the fives-court, and public house were thinned, but even Sunday gossiping and tea-visiting declined. Even Farmer Hoskins, who was at first angry with his maids for leaving off those *merry* songs, (as he called them), was so pleased by the manner in which the psalms were sung at the school, that he promised Mrs. Jones to make her a present of half a sheep towards her first May-day feast. Of this feast some account shall be given hereafter; and the reader may expect some further account of the Sunday School next month in the History of Hester Wilmot.

Z.

THE HISTORY OF HESTER WILMOT;

OR, THE

SECOND PART OF THE SUNDAY SCHOOL.

HESTER WILMOT was born in the parish of Weston, of parents who maintained themselves by their labour; they were both of them ungodly, it is no wonder therefore they were unhappy. They lived badly together, and how could they do otherwise, for their tempers were very different, and they had no religion to smooth down this difference, or to teach them that they ought to bear with each others faults. Rebecca Wilmot was a proof that people may have some right qualities, and yet be but bad characters, and utterly destitute of religion. She was clean, notable, and industrious. Now I know some folks fancy that the poor who have these qualities need have no other, but this is a sad mistake, as I am sure every page in the Bible would shew; and it is a pity people do not consult it oftener. They direct their plowing and sowing by the Almanack, why will they not consult the Bible for the direction of their hearts and lives? Rebecca was of a violent ungovernable temper; and that very neatness which is in itself so pleasing, in her became a sin, for her affection to her husband and children was quite lost in an over-anxious desire to have her house reckoned the nicest in the parish. Rebecca was also a proof that a poor woman may be as vain as a rich one, for it was not so much the comfort of neatness, as the praise of neatness, which she coveted. A spot on her hearth, or a bit of rust on a brass candlestick would throw her into a violent passion. Now it is very right to keep the hearth clean and the candlestick bright, but it is very wrong so to set one's affections on a hearth, or a candlestick, as to make oneself unhappy if any trifling accident happens to them: and if Rebecca had been as careful to keep her heart without spot, or her life without blemish, as she was to keep her fire-irons free from either, she would have been held up in this history, not as a warning, but a pattern, and in that case her nicety would have come in for a part of the praise. It was no fault in Rebecca but a merit, that her oak table was so bright you could almost see to put your cap on in it; but it was no merit but a fault, that when John, her husband, laid down his cup of beer upon it so as to leave a mark, she would fly out into so terrible a passion that all the children were forced to run to corners; now poor John having no corner to run to, ran to the ale-house, till

that

that which was at first a refuge, too soon became a pleasure.

Rebecca never wished her children to learn to read, because she said it would only serve to make them lazy, and she herself had done very well without it. She would keep poor Hester from church to stone the space under the chairs in fine patterns and whim-whams. I don't pretend to say there was any harm in this little decoration, it looks pretty enough, and it is better to let the children do that than do nothing. But still these are not things to set one's heart upon, and besides Rebecca only did it as a trap for praise; for she was sulky and disappointed if any ladies happened to call in and did not seem delighted with the flowers which she used to draw with a burnt stick on the white-wash of the chimney corners. Besides, all this finery was often done on a Sunday, and there is a great deal of harm in doing right things at a wrong time, or in wasting much time on things which are of no real use, or in doing any thing at all out of vanity. Now I beg that no lazy slattern of a wife will go and take any comfort in her dirt from what is here said against Rebecca's nicety; for I believe, that for one who makes her husband unhappy through neatness, twenty do so by dirt and laziness. All excesses are wrong, but the excess of a good quality is not so common as the excess of a bad one.

John Wilmot was not an ill-natured man, but he had no fixed principle. Instead of setting himself to cure his wife's faults by mild reproof and a good example, he was driven by them into still greater faults himself. It is a common case with people who have no religion when any cross accident befals them, instead of trying to make the best of a bad matter, instead of considering their trouble as a trial sent from God to purify them, or instead of considering the faults of others as a punishment for their own sins, what do they do but either sink down at once into despair, or else run for comfort into evil courses. Drinking is the common remedy for sorrow, if that can be called a remedy, the end of which is to destroy soul and body. John now began to spend all his leisure hours at the Bell. He used to be fond of his children, but when he could not come home in quiet and play with the little ones, while his wife dressed him a bit of hot supper, he grew in time not to come home at all. He who has once taken to drink can seldom be said to be guilty of one sin only; John's heart became hardened. His affection for his family was lost in self-indulgence. Patience and submission on the part of his wife might have won much upon a man of John's temper, but instead of trying to reclaim him, his wife seemed rather to delight in putting him as much in the wrong as she could, that she might be justified in her constant abuse of him. I doubt whether she would have been as much pleased with his reformation as she was with always talking of his faults, though I know it

was

was the opinion of the neighbours, that if she had taken as much pains to reform her husband by reforming her own temper, as she did to abuse him and expose him, her endeavours might have been blessed with success. Good christians, who are trying to subdue their own faults, can hardly believe that the ungodly have a sort of savage satisfaction in trying, by indulgence of their own evil tempers, to lessen the happiness of those with whom they have to do. Need we look any farther for a proof of our own corrupt nature, when we see mankind delight in sins which have neither the temptation of profit or pleasure, such as plaguing, vexing, or abusing each other.

Hester was the eldest of their five children, she was a sharp sensible girl; but at fourteen years old she could not tell a letter, nor had she ever been taught to bow her knee to him who made her, for John's, or rather Rebecca's house, had seldom the name of God pronounced in it, except to be blasphemed.

It was just about this time, if I mistake not, that Mrs. Jones set up her Sunday School, of which Mrs. Betty Crew was appointed mistress, as was related last month. Mrs. Jones finding that none of the Wilmots were sent to school, took a walk to Rebecca's house, and civilly told her she called to let her know that a school was opened, to which she desired her to send her children on the Sunday following, especially her eldest daughter Hester. Well, said Rebecca, and what will you give her if I do? Give her!

her! replied Mrs. Jones, that is rather a rude question, and asked in a rude manner: however, as a soft answer turneth away wrath, I assure you that I will give her the best of learning; I will teach her to *fear God and keep his commandments*. I would rather you would teach her to fear me, and to keep my house clean, said this wicked woman. She shan't come, however, unless you will pay her for it. Pay her for it! said the lady, will it not be reward enough that she will be taught to read the word of God without any expence to you? For though many gifts both of books and cloathing will be given the children, yet you are not to consider these gifts so much in the light of payment as an expression of goodwill in your benefactors. I say, interrupted Rebecca, that Hester shan't go to school. Religion is of no use that I know of but to make people hate their own flesh and blood; and I see no good in learning but to make folks proud, and lazy, and dirty. I cannot tell a letter myself, and, though I say it, that should not say it, there is not a notabler woman in the parish. Pray, said Mrs. Jones mildly, do you think that young people will disobey their parents the more for being taught to fear God? I don't think any thing about it, said Rebecca, I shan't let her come, and there's the long and short of the matter. Hester has other fish to fry; but you may have some of these little ones if you will? No, said Mrs. Jones, I will not; I have not set up a nursery but a school. I am not at all this

expence

expence to take crying babes out of the mother's way, but to instruct reasonable beings in the way to eternal life; and it ought to be a rule in all schools not to take the troublesome *young* children unless the mother will try to spare the *elder* ones, who are capable of learning. But, said Rebecca, I have a young child which Hester must nurse while I dress dinner. And she must iron the rags, and scour the irons, and dig the potatoes, and fetch the water to boil them. As to nursing the child, that is indeed a necessary duty, and Hester ought to stay at home part of the day to enable you to go to church; and families should relieve each other in this way, but as to all the rest they are no reasons at all, for the irons need not be scoured so often, and the rags should be ironed, and the potatoes dug, and the water fetched on the Saturday, and I can tell you that neither your minister here, nor your judge hereafter, will accept of any such excuses.

All this while Hester staid behind, pale and trembling, lest her unkind mother should carry her point. She looked up at Mrs. Jones with so much love and gratitude as to win her affection, and this good lady went on trying to soften this harsh mother. At last Rebecca condescended to say, well, I don't know but I may let her come now and then when I can spare her, provided I find you make it worth her while. All this time she had never asked Mrs. Jones to sit down, nor had once bid her young children be quiet, though they were crying and squalling the whole time. Rebecca fancied this rudeness was the only way she had of shewing she thought herself as good as her guest, but Mrs. Jones never lost her temper. The moment she went out of the house, Rebecca called out loud enough for her to hear, and ordered Hester to get the stone and a bit of sand to scrub out the prints of that dirty woman's shoes. Hester in high spirits chearfully obeyed, and rubbed out the stains so neatly, that her mother could not help lamenting that so handy a girl was going to be spoiled by being taught godliness, and learning, and such nonsense.

Mrs. Jones, who knew the world, told her agent, Mrs. Crew, that her grand difficulty would arise not so much from the children as the parents. These, said she, are apt to fall into that sad mistake, that because their children are poor and have little of this world's goods, the mothers must make it up to them in false indulgence. The children of the gentry are much more reproved and corrected for their faults, and bred up in far stricter discipline. He was a King who said, *chasten thy son, and let not thy rod spare for his crying.* But do not lose your patience, the more vicious the children are, you must remember the more they stand in need of your instruction. When they are bad, comfort yourself with thinking, how much worse they would have been but for you; and what a burthen they would become to society if these evil tempers were to receive no check. The great
thing

thing which enabled Mrs. Crew to teach well, was, the deep infight she had got into the corruption of human nature. And I doubt if any one can make a thoroughly good teacher of religion and morals who wants this master-key to the heart. Others indeed may teach knowledge, decency, and good manners; but those, however valuable, are not Christianity. Mrs. Crew, who knew that out of the heart proceed lying, theft, and all that train of evils which begin to break out even in young children, applied her labours to correct this root of evil. But though a diligent, she was an humble teacher, well knowing that unless the grace of God blessed her labours, she should but labour in vain.

Hester Wilmot never failed to attend the school, whenever her perverse mother would give her leave, and her delight in learning was so great, that she would work early and late to gain a little time for her book. As she had a quick capacity, she learned soon to spell and read, and Mrs. Crew observing her diligence, used to lend her a book to carry home, that she might pick up a little at odd times. It would be well if teachers would make this distinction. To give, or lend books to those who take no delight in them is an useless expence; while it is kind and right to assist well-disposed young people with every help of this sort. Those who love books seldom hurt them, while the slothful, who hate learning, will wear out a book more in a week than the diligent will do in a year.

year. Hester's way was to read over one question in her catechism, or one verse in her hymn-book, by fire-light before she went to bed; this she thought over in the night; and when she was dressing herself in the morning she was glad to find she always knew a little more than she had done the morning before. It is not to be believed how much those people will be found to have gained at the end of the year, who are accustomed to work up all the little odd ends and remnants of leisure; who value time even more than money; and who are convinced that minutes are no more to be wasted than pence. Nay, he who finds he has wasted a shilling may by diligence hope to fetch it up again; but no repentance, or industry, can ever bring back one wasted hour. My good young reader, if ever *you* are tempted to waste an hour, go and ask a dying man what he would give for that hour which you are throwing away, and according as he answers, so do you act.

As her mother hated the sight of a book, Hester was forced to learn out of sight: it was no disobedience to do this, as long as she wasted no part of that time which it was her duty to spend in useful labour. She would have thought it a sin to have left her work for her book; but she did not think it wrong to steal time from her sleep, and to be learning an hour before the rest of the family were awake. Hester would not neglect the washing-tub, or the spinning-wheel, even to get on with her catechism; but she
thought

thought it fair to think over her questions, while she was washing and spinning. In a few months she was able to read fluently in St. John's gospel, which is the easiest. But Mrs. Crew did not think it enough that her children could read a chapter, she would make them understand it also. It is in a good degree owing to the want of religious knowledge in teachers, that there is so little religion in the world. Unless the Bible is laid open to the understanding, children may read from Genesis to the Revelation, without any other improvement than barely learning how to pronounce the words. Mrs. Crew found there was but one way to compel their attention; this was by obliging them to return back again to her the sense of what she had read to them, and this they might do in their own words, if they could not remember the words of scripture. Those who had weak capacities would, to be sure, do this but very imperfectly; but even the weakest, if they were willing, would retain something. She so managed, that *saying the Catechism* was not merely an act of the memory, but of the understanding; for she had observed formerly, that those who had learned the Catechism in the common formal way, when they were children, had never understood it when they became men and women, and it remained in the memory without having made any impression on the mind. Thus this fine summary of the christian religion is considered as little more than a form of words, the being able to repeat which is a qualification for

being

being confirmed by the bishop, instead of being considered as really containing those grounds of christian faith and practice, by which they are to be confirmed christians.

Mrs. Crew used to say to Mrs. Jones, Those who teach the poor must indeed give line upon line, precept upon precept, here a little and there a little, as they can receive it. So that teaching must be a great grievance to those who do not really make it a *labour of love.* I see so much levity, obstinacy, and ignorance, that it keeps my own forbearance in continual exercise, so that I trust that I am getting good myself while I am doing good to others. No one, Madam, can know till they try, that after they have asked a poor untaught child the same question nineteen times, they must not lose their temper, but go on and ask it the twentieth. Now and then, when I am tempted to be impatient, I correct myself, by thinking over that active proof which our blessed Saviour requires of our love to him when he says, " *Feed my lambs.* "

Hester Wilmot had never been bred to go to church, for her father and mother had never thought of going themselves, unless at a christening in their own family, or at a funeral of their neighbours, both of which they considered merely as opportunities for good eating and drinking, and not as offices of religion.

As poor Hester had no comfort at home, it was the less wonder she delighted in her school, her Bible, and church, for so great is God's goodness, that he is pleased to make religion a peculiar comfort to those who have no other comfort. The God whose name she had seldom heard but when it was *taken in vain*, was now revealed to her as a God of infinite power, justice, and holiness. What she read in her Bible, and what she felt in her own heart, convinced her she was a sinner; and her catechism said the same. She was much distressed one day on thinking over this promise which she had just made, (in answer to the question which fell to her lot), " To renounce the devil and all his works, the pomps and vanities of this wicked world, and all the sinful lusts of the flesh." I say she was distressed on finding that these were not merely certain words which she was bound to repeat; but certain conditions which she was bound to perform. She was sadly puzzled to know how this was to be done, till she met with these words in her Bible: *My grace is sufficient for thee.* But still she was at a loss to know how this grace was to be obtained. Happily Mr. Simpson preached on the next Sunday from this text, " *Ask and ye shall have,*" &c. In this sermon was explained to her the nature, the duty, and the efficacy of prayer. After this she opened her heart to Mrs. Crew, who taught her the great doctrines of Scripture, in a serious, but plain way. Hester's own heart led her to assent to that humbling doctrine of the catechism, that " *We are by nature born in sin;*" and truly glad was she

to

to be relieved by hearing of "*That spiritual grace by which we have a new birth unto righteousness.*" Thus her mind was no sooner humbled by one part, than it gained comfort from another. On the other hand, while she was rejoicing in "*A lively hope in God's mercy through Christ,*" her mistress put her in mind that, that was the only *true* repentance, "*By which we forsake sin.*" Thus the catechism explained by a pious teacher was found to contain "*All the articles of the christian faith.*"

Mrs. Jones greatly disapproved the practice of turning away the scholars because they were grown up. Young people, said she, want to be warned at sixteen more than they did at six, and they are commonly turned adrift at the very age when they want most instruction; when dangers and temptations most beset them. They are exposed to more evil by the leisure of a Sunday evening than by the business of a whole week: but then religion must be made pleasant, and instruction must be carried on in a kind, and agreeable, and familiar way. If they once dislike the teacher they will soon get to dislike what is taught, so that a master or mistress is in some measure answerable for the future piety of young persons, inasmuch as that piety depends on their manner of making religion pleasant as well as profitable. To attend Mrs. Jones's evening instructions was soon thought not a task but a holiday. In a few months

months it was reckoned a disadvantage to the character of any young person in the parish to know they did not attend the evening school. At first, indeed, many of them came only with a view to learn to sing psalms; but, by the blessing of God, they grew fond of instruction, and some of them became truly pious. Mrs. Jones spoke to them one Sunday evening as follows:—My dear young women, I rejoice at your improvement; but I rejoice with trembling. I have known young people set out well, who afterwards fell off. The heart is deceitful. Many like religious knowledge, who do not like the strictness of a religious life. I must therefore watch whether those who are diligent at church and school are diligent in their daily walk. Whether those who say they believe in God, really obey him. Whether they who profess to love Christ keep his commandments. Those who hear themselves commended for early piety, may learn to rest satisfied with the praise of man. People may get a knack at religious phrases without being religious; they may even get to frequent places of worship as an amusement, in order to meet their friends, and may learn to delight in a sort of *spiritual gossip*, while religion has no power in their hearts. But I hope better things of you, and things that accompany salvation, though I thus speak.

What became of Hester Wilmot, with some account of Mrs. Jones's May-day feast for her school, my readers shall be told next month.

Z.

PART II.

THE NEW GOWN.

HESTER WILMOT, I am sorry to observe, had been by nature peevish, and lazy; she would, when a child, now and then slight her work, and when her mother was very unreasonable she was too apt to return her a saucy answer, but when she became acquainted with her own heart, and with the scriptures, these evil tempers were, in a good measure, subdued, for she now learnt to imitate, not her violent mother, but *him who was meek and lowly.* When she was scolded for doing ill, she prayed for grace to do better; and the only answer she made to her mother's charge, " that religion only served to make people lazy," was to strive to do twice as much work, in order to prove, that it really made them diligent. The only thing in which she ventured to disobey her mother was, that when she ordered her to do week days work on a Sunday, Hester cried, and said, she did not dare disobey God, but to show that she did not wish to save her own labour, she would do a double portion of work on the Saturday night, and rise two hours earlier on the Monday morning.

Once,

Once, when she had worked very hard, her mother told her she would treat her with a holiday the following sabbath, and take her a fine walk to eat cakes and drink ale, at Weston fair, which, though it was professed to be kept on the Monday, yet, to the disgrace of the village, always began on the Sunday evening*. Rebecca, who would on no account have wasted the Monday, which was a working day, in idleness and pleasure, thought she had a very good right to enjoy herself at the fair on the Sunday evening, as well as to take her children. Hester earnestly begged to be left at home, and her mother, in a rage, went without her. A wet walk, and more ale than she was used to drink, gave Rebecca a dangerous fever; during this illness, Hester, who would not follow her to a scene of dissolute mirth, attended her night and day, and denied herself necessaries that her sick mother might have comforts. And though she secretly prayed to God that this sickness might change her mother's heart, yet she never once reproached her, or put her in mind, that it was caught by indulging in a sinful pleasure. Another Sunday

* This practice is too common. Those fairs which profess to be kept on Monday, commonly begin on the Sunday. It is much to be wished that magistrates would put a stop to it, as Mr. Simpson did at Weston, at the request of Mrs. Jones. There is another great evil worth the notice of Justices. In many villages, during the fair, ale is sold at private houses, which have no licence, to the great injury of sobriety and good morals.

night her father told Hester, he thought she had now been at school long enough for him to have a little good of her learning, so he desired she would stay at home and read to him. Hester cheerfully ran and fetched her Testament. But John fell a laughing, called her a fool, and said, it would be time enough to read the Testament to him when he was going to die, but at present he must have something merry. So saying, he gave her a song-book which he had picked up at the Bell. Hester having cast her eyes over it, refused to read it, saying, she did not dare offend God by reading what would hurt her own soul. John called her a canting hypocrite, and said, he would put the Testament in the fire, for that there was not a more merry girl than she was before she became religious. Her mother for once took her part, not because she thought her daughter in the right, but because she was glad of any pretence to shew her husband was in the wrong, though she herself would have abused Hester for the same thing if John had taken her part. John with a shocking oath, abused them both, and went off in a violent passion. Hester, instead of saying one undutiful word against her father, took up a Psalter in order to teach her little sisters, but Rebecca was so provoked at her for not joining her in her abuse of her husband, that she changed her humour, said John was in the right, and Hester a perverse hypocrite, who only made religion a pretence for being undutiful to her parents. Hester bore all in silence and committed her cause to him "who judgeth righteously." It would have been a great comfort to her if she had dared to go to Mrs. Crew, and to have joined in the religious exercises of the evening at school. But her mother refused to let her, saying, it would only harden her heart in mischief. Hester said not a word, but after having put the little ones to bed, and heard them say their prayers out of sight, she went and sat down in her own little loft, and said to herself, it would be pleasant to me to have taught my little sisters to read, I thought it was my duty, for David has said, "Come ye children, hearken unto me, I will teach you the fear of the Lord." It would have been still more pleasant to have passed the evening at school, because I am still ignorant, and fitter to learn than to teach; but I cannot do either without flying in the face of my mother; God sees fit to night to change my pleasant duties into a painful trial. I give up my will, and I submit to the will of my father; but when he orders me to commit a known sin, then I dare not do it, because, in so doing, I must disobey my father which is in heaven. Now it so fell out, that this dispute happened on the very Sunday next before Mrs. Jones's yearly feast. On May-day all the school attended her to church, each in a stuff gown of their own earning, and a cap and white apron of her giving. After church there was an examination made into the learning and behaviour of the scholars; those who were most perfect in their chapters, and who

brought

brought the best character for industry, humility, and sobriety, received a Bible, or some other good book.

Now Hester had been a whole year hoarding up her little savings, in order to be ready with a new gown on the May-day feast. She had never got less than two shillings a week by her spinning, besides working for the family, and earning a trifle by odd jobs. This money she faithfully carried to her mother every Saturday night, keeping back, by consent, only two-pence a week towards the gown. The sum was compleat, the pattern had long been settled, and Hester had only on the Monday morning to go to the shop, pay her money, and bring home her gown to be made. Her mother happened to go out that morning early to iron in a gentleman's family, where she usually staid a day or two, and Hester was busy putting the house in order before she went to the shop.

On that very Monday there was to be a meeting at the Bell, of all the idle fellows in the parish, John Wilmot of course was to be there. Indeed he had accepted a challenge of the Blacksmith to a batch at all-fours. The Blacksmith was flush of money, John thought himself the best player; and that he might make sure of winning, he resolved to keep himself sober, which he knew was more than the other would do. John was so used to go upon tick for ale, that he got to the door of the Bell before he recollected that he could not keep his word with the gambler

without

without money, and he had not a penny in his pocket, so he sullenly turned homewards. He dared not apply to his wife, as he knew he should be more likely to get a scratched face than a six-pence from her; but he knew that Hester had received two shillings for her last week's spinning on Saturday, and perhaps she might not yet have given it to her mother. Of the hoarded sum he knew nothing. He asked her if she could lend him half a crown, and he would pay her next day. Hester, pleased to see him in good-humour, after what had passed the night before, ran up and fetched down her little box, and, in the joy of her heart that he now desired something she could comply with, without wounding her conscience, cheerfully poured out her whole little stock upon the table. John was in raptures at the sight of three half crowns and a six-pence, and eagerly seized it, box and all, together with a few hoarded halfpence at the bottom, though he had only asked to borrow half a crown. None but one whose heart was hardened by a long course of drunkenness could have taken away the whole, and for such a purpose. He told her she should certainly have it again next morning, and, indeed, intended to pay it, not doubting but he should double the sum. But John over-rated his own skill, or luck, for he lost every farthing to the Blacksmith, and sneaked home before midnight, and quietly walked up to-bed. He was quite sober, which Hester thought a good sign. Next morning she asked him,

him, in a very humble way, for the money, which she said she would not have done, but that if the gown was not bought directly it would not be ready in time for the feast. John's conscience had troubled him a little for what he had done, for when he was not drunk he was not ill-natured, and he stammered out a broken excuse, but owned he had lost the money, and had not a farthing left. The moment Hester saw him mild and kind, her heart was softened, and she begged him not to vex; adding, that she would be contented never to have a new gown as long as she lived, if she could have the comfort of always seeing him come home as sober as he was last night. For Hester did not know that he had refrained from getting drunk, only that he might gamble with a better chance of success, and that when a gamester keeps himself sober, it is not that he may practise a virtue, but that he may commit a worse crime. I am, indeed, sorry for what I have done, said he, you cannot go to the feast, and what will Madam Jones say? Yes, but I can, said Hester, for God looks not at the gown, but at the heart, and I am sure he sees mine full of gratitude at hearing you talk so kindly; and if I thought my dear father would change his present evil courses, I should be the happiest girl at the feast to-morrow. John walked away mournfully, and said to himself, surely there must be something in religion, since it can thus change the heart. Hester was a pert girl, and now she is as mild as a lamb. She was

an

an indolent girl, and now she is up with the lark. She was a vain girl, and would do any thing for a new ribbon; and now she is contented to go in rags to a feast at which every one else will have a new gown. She deprived herself of her gown to give me the money, and yet this very girl, so dutiful in some things, would submit to be turned out of doors, rather than read a loose book at my command, or break the Sabbath. I do not understand this, there must be some mystery in it. All this he said as he was going to work. In the evening he did not go to the Bell; whether it was owing to his new thoughts, or to his not having a penny in his pocket, I will not take upon me positively to say, but I believe it was a little of one, and a little of the other.

As the pattern of the intended gown had long been settled in the family, and as Hester had the money by her, it was looked on as good as bought, so that she was trusted to get it brought home, and made in her mother's absence. Indeed, so little did Rebecca care about the school, that she would not have cared any thing about the gown, if her vanity had not made her wish that her daughter should be the best drest of any girl at the feast. Being from home, as was said before, she knew nothing of the disappointment. On May-day morning, Hester, instead of keeping from the feast, because she had not a new gown, or meanly inventing any excuse, dressed herself out as neatly as she could in her poor old things, and went to join the school in order to go to church. Whether Hester had formerly indulged a little pride of heart, and talked of this gown rather too much, I am not quite sure; certain it is, there was a great hue and cry made at seeing Hester Wilmot, the neatest girl, the most industrious girl in the school, come to the May-day feast in an old stuff gown, when every other girl was so creditably drest. Indeed, I am sorry to say, there were two or three much too smart for their station, and who had dizened themselves out in very improper finery, which Mrs. Jones made them take off before her. I mean this feast, said she, as a reward of industry and piety, and not as a trial of skill who can be finest, and outvie the rest in show. If I do not take care, my feast will become an encouragement, not to virtue, but to vanity. I am so great a friend to decency of apparel that I even like to see you deny your appetites that you may be able to come decently dressed to the house of God. To encourage you to do this, I like to set apart this one day of innocent pleasure, against which you may be preparing all the year, by laying aside something every week towards buying a gown out of your little savings. But, let me tell you, that meekness and an humble spirit is of more value in the sight of God and good men, than the gayest cotton gown, or the brightest pink ribbon in the parish.

Mrs. Jones, for all this, was as much surprised as the rest, at Hester's mean garb: but such is the power of a good character, that she gave her
credit

credit for a right intention, especially as she knew the unhappy state of her family. For it was Mrs. Jones's way (and it is not a bad way) always to wait, and enquire into the truth, before she condemned any body of good character, though appearances were against them. As we cannot judge of people's motives, said she, we may, from ignorance, often condemn their best actions, and approve of their worst. It will be always time enough to judge unfavourably, and let us give others credit as long as we can, and then we, in our turn, may expect a favourable judgment from others, and remember who has said, "judge not, that ye be not judged." Hester was no more proud of what she had done for her father, than she was humbled by the meanness of her garb, and though Betty Stiles, one of the girls, whose finery had been taken away, sneered at her, Hester never offered to clear herself, by exposing her father, though she thought it right secretly to inform Mrs. Jones of what had past. When the examination of the girls began, Betty Stiles was asked some questions on the fourth and fifth commandments, which she answered very well. Hester was asked nearly the same questions, and, though she answered them no better than Betty had done, they were all surprised to see Mrs. Jones rise up, and give a handsome Bible to Hester, while she gave nothing to Betty. This girl cried out rather pertly, Madam, it is very hard that I have no book, I was as perfect as Hester. I have often told

told you, said Mrs. Jones, that religion is not a thing of the tongue but of the heart. That girl gives me the best proof that she has learned the fourth commandment to good purpose, who persists in keeping holy the Sabbath-day, though commanded to break it by a parent whom she loves. And that girl best proves that she keeps the fifth, who gives up her own comfort, and cloathing, and credit, " to honour and obey her father and mother," even though they are not such as she could wish. Betty Stiles, though she could answer the questions so readily, went abroad last Sunday, when she should have been at school, and refused to nurse her sick mother, when she could not help herself. Is this having learnt these two commandments to any good purpose?

Farmer Hoskins, who stood by, whispered to Mrs. Jones, Well, Madam, now you have convinced even me of the benefit of religious instruction, now I see there is a meaning to it. I thought it was in at one ear and out at the other, and that a song was as well as a psalm; but now I have found the proof of the pudding is in the eating. I see your scholars must *do* what they *hear*, and *obey* what they *learn*. Why, at this rate, they will all be the better servants for being really godly, and so I will add a pudding to next year's feast.

The pleasure Hester felt in receiving a new Bible, made her forget that she had on an old gown. She walked to church in a thankful frame;

frame; but how great was her joy, when she saw, among a number of working men, her own father going into church! As she past by him, she cast on him a look of so much joy and affection, that it brought tears into his eyes, especially when he compared her mean dress with that of the other girls, and thought who had been the cause of it. John, who had not been at church for some years, was deeply struck with the service. The confession with which it opens went to his heart. He felt, for the first time, that he was "a miserable sinner, and that there was no health in him." He now felt compunction for sin in general, though it was only his ill-behaviour to his daughter which had brought him to church. The sermon was such as served to strengthen the impression which the prayers had made, and when it was over, instead of joining the ringers (for the belfry was the only part of the church John liked, because it usually led to the alehouse) he quietly walked back to his work. It was, indeed, the best day's work he ever made. He could not get out of his head the whole day the first words he heard at church: "When the wicked man turneth away from his wickedness, and doth that which is lawful and right, he shall save his soul alive." At night, instead of going to the Bell, he went home, intending to ask Hester to forgive him; but as soon as he got to the door, he heard Rebecca rating his daughter for having brought such a disgrace on the family as to be seen in that old rag of a gown, and infifted on knowing what fhe had done with the money. Hefter tried to keep the fecret, but her mother declared fhe would turn her out of doors, if fhe did not tell the truth. Hefter was at laft forced to confefs fhe had given it to her father. Unfortunately for poor John, it was at this very moment he opened the door. The mother now divided her fury between her guilty hufband and her innocent child, till from words fhe fell to blows. John defended his daughter, and received fome of the ftrokes intended for the poor girl. This turbulent fcene partly put John's good refolutions to flight, though the patience of Hefter did him almoft as much good as the fermon he had heard. At length the poor girl efcaped up ftairs, not a little bruifed, and a fcene of much violence paffed between John and Rebecca. She declared fhe would not fit down to fupper with fuch a brute, and fet off to a neighbour's houfe, that fhe might have the pleafure of abufing him the longer. John, whofe mind was much difturbed, went up ftairs without his fupper. As he was paffing by Hefter's little room he heard her voice, and as he concluded fhe was venting bitter complaints againft her unnatural parents, he ftopped to liften, refolving to go in and comfort her. He ftopped at the door, for, by the light of the moon, he faw her kneeling by her bedfide, and praying fo earneftly that fhe did not hear him. As he made fure fhe could be praying for nothing but his death, what was his furprife to hear these words, "O Lord, have mercy upon my dear father and mother, teach me to love them, to pray for them, and do them good; make me more dutiful and more patient, that, adoring the doctrine of God, my Saviour, I may recommend his holy religion, and my dear parents may be brought to love and fear thee, through Jesus Christ."

Poor John, who would never have been hardhearted if he had not been a drunkard, could not stand this, he fell down on his knees, embraced his child, and begged her to teach him how to pray. He prayed himself as well as he could, and though he did not know what words to use, yet his heart was melted; he owned he was a sinner, and begged Hester to fetch the prayerbook, and read over the confession with which he had been so struck at church. This was the pleasantest order she had ever obeyed. Seeing him deeply affected with a sense of sin, she pointed out to him the Saviour of sinners; and in this manner she past some hours with her father, which were the happiest of her life; such a night was worth a hundred cotton, or even silk gowns. In the course of the week Hester read over the confession, and some other prayers, to her father so often that he got them by heart, and repeated them while he was at work. She next taught him the fifty-first Psalm. And at length he took courage to kneel down and pray before he went to bed. From that time he bore his wife's ill-humour much better than he had ever done, and, as he knew her to be neat, and notable, and saving, he began to think, that if her temper was not quite so bad, his home might still become as pleasant a place to him as ever the Bell had been: but unless she became more tractable he did not know what to do with his long evenings after the little ones were in bed, for he began, once more, to delight in playing with them. Hester proposed that she should teach him to read an hour every night, and he consented. Rebecca began to storm, from the mere trick she had got of storming; but finding that he now brought home all his earnings, and that she got both his money and his company (for she had once loved him) she began to reconcile herself to this new way of life. In a few months John could read a psalm; in learning to read it he also got it by heart, and this proved a little store for private devotion, and while he was mowing he could call to mind a text to cheer his labour. He now went constantly to church, and often dropped in at the school on a Sunday evening to hear their prayers. He expressed so much pleasure at this, that one day Hester ventured to ask him if they should set up family prayer at home? John said he should like it mightily, but as he could not yet read quite well enough, he desired Hester to try to get a proper book and begin next Sunday night. Hester had bought, of a pious hawker, for three half-pence

pence*, the Book of Prayers, printed for the Cheap Repository.

When Hester read the exhortation at the beginning of this little book, her mother, who sat in the corner, and pretended to be asleep, was so much struck that she could not find a word to say against it. For a few nights, indeed, she continued to sit still, or pretended to rock the young child while her husband and daughter were kneeling at their prayers. She expected John would have scolded her for this, and so perverse was her temper, that she was disappointed at his finding no fault with her. Seeing at last that he was very patient, and that though he prayed fervently himself he suffered her to do as she liked, she lost the spirit of opposition for want of something to provoke it. As her pride began to be subdued, some little disposition to piety was awakened in her heart. By degrees she slid down on her knees, though at first it was behind the cradle, or the clock, or in some corner, where she thought they would not see her. Hester rejoiced even in this outward change in her mother, and prayed that God would at last be pleased to touch her heart as he had done that of her father.

As John now spent no idle money, he had saved up a trifle by working over-hours; this he

---

* These prayers may be had also divided into two parts, one fit for private persons, the other for families, price one halfpenny.

kindly offered to Hester to make up for the loss of her gown. Instead of accepting it, Hester told him, that as she herself was young and healthy, she should soon be able to clothe herself out of her own savings, and begged him to make her mother a present of this gown, which he did. It had been a maxim of Rebecca, that it was better not to go to Church at all than go in an old gown. She had, however, so far conquered this evil notion, that she had lately gone pretty often. This kindness of the gown touched her not a little, and the first Sunday she put it on, Mr. Simpson happened to preach from this text, "God resisteth the proud, but giveth grace to the humble." This sermon so affected Rebecca that she never once thought she had her new gown on, till she came to take it off when she went to bed, and that very night, instead of skulking behind, she knelt down by her husband.

There was one thing sunk deep in Rebecca's mind; she had observed, that since her husband had grown religious he had been so careful not to give her any offence, that he was become scrupulously clean; took off his dirty shoes before he sat down, and was very cautious not to spill a drop of beer on her shining table. Now it was rather remarkable, that as John grew more neat Rebecca grew more indifferent to neatness. But both these changes arose from the same cause, the growth of religion in their hearts. John grew cleanly from the fear of giving pain to his wife,

while

while Rebecca grew indifferent from having discovered the sin and folly of an over anxious care about trifles. When the heart is once given up to God, such vanities die of themselves.

Hester continues to grow in grace, and in knowledge. Last Christmas-day she was appointed an under teacher in the school, and many people think that some years hence, if any thing should happen to Mrs. Crew, Hester may be promoted to be head mistress.

Z.

THE BEGGARLY BOY.

A PARABLE.

ONCE on a time a poor beggarly boy, who used to carry matches about the streets, was met by a very rich and worthy Gentleman, who, observing his hollow eyes, his sallow looks, and his bent body, as well as the extreme filth with which he was covered, was touched with such compassion for the lad, that he was disposed to render him some effectual relief; and accordingly the gentleman dropt a hint, that he had a mind to do something considerable for him. The boy, never expecting any such goodness as this, and indeed not listening very attentively, did not at first understand what was said; upon which the gentleman spoke more plainly to him, asking him whether he had a mind to have his dirty rags exchanged for a new livery coat and some clean linen? for, said he, if you have a mind to it I will take you into my service; and, in that case, I shall fit you out afresh, and I shall take care
also

also that your health is looked after, and when you have served me faithfully for a few years, which you may do very comfortably to yourself, I will even set you up in life. The lad, after this, could not help understanding the offer; but he seemed as far as ever from accepting it, for he was now quite unwilling to believe the gentleman; and he shewed, by his manner, that he would have been better pleased to have sold a halfpennyworth of matches in his usual way, carrying off the halfpenny in his hand, than to have had all the fine promises which the best and richest man in the world could make to him.

This kind gentleman, however, persisting in his inclination to do the lad a service, proceeded next to reason with him: he advised him, for his own sake, to listen a little more to what was said, and then remarked to him how ill he looked, which the boy, though very dangerously sick, was not sensible of himself; and represented to him the difference between leading the wretched sort of life he did, and getting into a regular and comfortable service. Nay, he went so far as even to beg and entreat him, at the same time observing that he had no objection to the lad's satisfying himself that the person who addressed him was no cheat or impostor; and, in proof of it, he told him his name, informed him how he might learn all particulars of his character, and gave him a direction to his place of abode. In short, he condescended to say every thing that could, in such a case, be supposed necessary

to

to give a poor boy confidence and encouragement. In the course of the conversation I should have observed, that the gentleman, as a proof of his generosity, threw down a shilling, which the lad picked up, with very little gratitude in his countenance, but with no small conceit at his own quickness and cleverness in seizing hold of it; after which, he grew as proud as could be of having got possession of the piece of money, not considering at all that it was a mere present, and that he had not given the gentleman a single match for it out of his basket.

I am persuaded my readers will, by this time, be aware that this was a lad who had a very mean and low mind; otherwise, he would undoubtedly have been overjoyed at such an opportunity of getting above his present base condition; besides which, I should remark, that he had been a long time living among a set of rogues and vagabonds, who being one of them nearly as bad as another, and having seldom seen among them any persons of a different character, had learnt to fancy themselves a very creditable sort of people, and, when they got together, were just as proud, in their way, as if they had been the greatest Lords and Dukes in the kingdom. At night the lad went home, and slept among these old companions, in a vile unwholesome room, where, though each would affect now and then to be merry and gay, yet, in fact, they were all of them dying by inches, and, in the judgment of any rational or feeling man, who might condescend to put in his
head

head among them, they undoubtedly were altogether in as sorrowful and wretched a plight as can well be imagined.

In short, then, with grief and pain do I speak it, this poor beggarly boy entirely neglected the prodigious offer which had been made to him: he returned to his former company, continued in his petty trade, and dragged on the little remainder of his life in the old way, just as if nothing had happened.

I now propose, by means of this story, which is a mere allegory or parable, to expose the conduct of those persons, who are unwilling to comply with the gracious invitations of our Saviour, in his Gospel; for he is that kind and willing friend (with reverence be it spoken) who offers to take us mean and needy creatures into his service, and we, if we turn away, and refuse the offer, may be likened to this foolish beggarly boy, having nothing better to plead, as I think I shall be able to shew, than one or other of those very excuses, which, when put in his mouth, have appeared so absurd and monstrous.

Let us see whether there is not some general likeness between the two cases. I will begin by supposing our Saviour, in his Gospel, to address himself to a man who is quite thoughtless and unbelieving. Now such persons are commonly much more wicked than they imagine, for by following their natural inclinations, and taking no thought to their ways, they permit a thousand evil dispositions to grow upon them; the consequence

quence of this is, that when the Gospel first meets with such persons, it finds them quite covered over with wickedness, as this boy was with dirt; though, like him, they are unconscious of it. It commonly finds them also eagerly engaged in some poor pursuit of this life, as this boy was in selling matches.

I would next observe, that, in general, when the vast and unspeakable offers of the Gospel are first mentioned in the ears of such a person as I have been describing, his mind is so ill prepared for the subject, and his thoughts are apt to be so completely turned another way, that he probably does not understand, nor even listen to what is said to him; just like this boy, who, when he was first spoken to, refused to listen to the gentleman, and continued to think of nothing but his common traffic.

But let us next suppose the man to have the Gospel more clearly explained to him; he is now invited to put off his sins, which have been represented by the filth and dirt, to enter into the service, and put on as it were, the livery of Christ; as his acknowledged servant, and after spending the short period of his life on earth in a state of comfortable and willing obedience to his Deliverer and Redeemer, he is then told to expect that he shall be raised to Heaven, and that he shall be made happy for ever and ever. How astonishing is this proposal! What then is the next difficulty? It is this; that the worldly man will not believe the truth of the promise

which

which is held out to him: like the offer to this beggarly boy, it seems too good to be true, or rather, it is too vast to be conceived by him. Why should this great gentleman trouble himself to think of me, or to do so much to serve me, said the foolish boy in the fable. "Why should the great God stoop so low to me, or think of sending his Son from Heaven to save me?" says the fool who disbelieves the Bible. The boy, therefore, turned again to his old way, notwithstanding the offer he had met with; and the worldly man is for doing the same, though he has heard of the invitation of the Gospel; for he wants faith to trust in God, as the other did to trust the gentleman his benefactor; and he therefore esteems the smallest of the good things of this life, the merest halfpenny in hand, to be more than eternal happiness in expectation.

But let us see how the Gospel condescends even to our infirmity. The kind gentleman was represented as reasoning with this dull and distrustful lad, informing him also of the steps which he ought to take, as the means of satisfying his doubts, and of getting possession, at length, of the blessing. He appealed also to the lad's own experience of the hardships of his present condition, warning him also of his future danger, and assuring him, at the same time, of the mild nature of that service to which he was invited; and after answering every objection, the gentleman condescended even to implore and intreat this poor miserable fellow, that, for his own sake,

sake, he would not remain inattentive to the offer.

So is it with the Gospel: it stoops, as it were, to all our weaknesses and infirmities; it calls to us at the first, with an inviting voice, to come forward and approach it; for we are not expected to receive every truth at once; still less are we required to believe without evidence: for, in the proposals of the Gospel, every thing is fair, as well as plain and practicable. It does not ask us, for instance, to effect any thing without sufficient means for it, to make bricks without straw, to strive without hope of success, or to do what is impossible for us: on the contrary, we are asked only to shew a willing mind, and to use those plain and simple means which the Gospel itself sets before us: as for example; we are called upon to read the scriptures, to attend upon the preaching of the Gospel, and whatever may be the other religious advantages, either of good books, or Christian friends, which are put in our way, we are required to make an honest and diligent use of them, than which nothing surely can be more just and reasonable; and then, because after all we are so weak and helpless, we are only told the more particularly to pray to God for his grace to assist us.

Again; how does the Gospel also appeal to our experience, as the gentleman did to the beggarly boy's experience of the misery of his condition? Have we never smarted, in consequence of those sins which we have fallen into through

through our neglect of the Gospel? Have we never found ourselves afflicted, destitute, and even miserable for the want of it? Have we never known an hour when the merciful help and protection of an heavenly Father would have proved a comfort and a blessing to us? Yet how can we expect to enjoy this protection in the time of our necessity, if, instead of entering into his family, we choose, like this helpless and inconsiderate boy, to place ourselves at a distance? Hear then how the Gospel calls to us to cast ourselves on the care of our Redeemer: "Come unto me (says Christ) all ye that are weary and heavy laden, and I will give you rest; take my yoke upon you, for my yoke is easy, and my burthen is light, and ye shall find rest unto your souls." How does our Saviour also, in the same manner as was said of the benevolent man in the parable, turn suppliant, as it were, to the sinner. "Ye will not come unto me, that ye might have life." "Why will ye die, O house of Israel." "We, therefore, (says the Apostle) as ambassadors for Christ, beseech you in Christ's stead, be ye reconciled to God." Thus then, if after all the encouragements of the Gospel, we still turn away from it, and resolve to do without it, all the miserable consequences which will follow must be laid at our own door; and whenever the day of our extremity shall come, we shall be forced to own, that we are left, like this boy, entirely without excuse.

It has been remarked in the story, that the same gentleman who made this great offer to the beggarly boy, threw him down a shilling in token of his liberality, for which the lad never thought of thanking him, but merely grew proud upon it, as well as conceited of his own cleverness in catching hold of the piece. What a very mean spirit was this! and yet is not this the very spirit in which worldly-minded men receive the temporal blessings thrown down to them by their heavenly Father? If a little worldly wealth is cast by a bounteous Providence into their lap, they immediately grow haughty in consequence of it; and, like this boy, they take to themselves credit for the ability they have shewn in the manner of getting possession of it: many men, for instance, if they get a good crop, or a good year's trade, are as full of themselves, and as thoughtless of him who is the giver of it, as this boy was; nor are they at all encouraged by God's providential goodness to look up to Him for the further blessings of the Gospel.

Reader, if thou art thus vain of any of thine earthly goods, thou mayest behold thy likeness in this part of the character of the boy!

We come now more particularly to speak of the causes which lead men to act the strange part they do, in rejecting the Gospel. I doubt not that this foolish lad might find a thousand plausible reasons, in his own mind, by which he might disguise from himself the folly and absurdity

surdity of his conduct. He might say, as it has been already hinted, I do not choose to venture on all this change in my way of life. I am afraid of giving myself up so entirely to the gentleman. Poor, foolish fellow! what then, hadst thou any thing to lose by the change?— Could such a lad as thou wast be meaner, dirtier, or poorer than thou wast already? In like manner we may say to every sinner who raises a like objection; what then art thou fearful of becoming wickeder than thou art, by entering into the service of Christ? Is it that thy conscience pricks thee in proportion as thou drawest nearer to him? Art thou afraid on this account to make the venture?

Or the lad might say, perhaps, as the sinner is apt to say, I have lived hitherto in my present way of life, and why should I not go on in it? which is but saying, in other words, I have lived hitherto in dirt, or I have lived hitherto in sin, and why may I not live on in it? than which there cannot be a more miserable reason, though, I fear, there is hardly a more common one.

But let us, as I said, lay open the true cause. We have already observed, that this boy had long dwelt in the company of a sad set of vagabonds, who being very numerous, and one of them as bad as another, contrived to keep each other in countenance, so as to pass, forsooth, for very decent people. This is exactly the case with the multitude of wicked and worldly-minded people; they live in great flocks together, they see none but those who are much like themselves, and they have no more idea of a truly Christian life, than this boy had of the sort of life led in the family of this great gentleman; so that when the Gospel calls to them to repent, and change their course, and enter into the service of Christ, they see no need for it, they are as good as their neighbours, and having no other rule of judging except this, they pronounce themselves to be well enough already. But I would wish such persons to reflect on the error of this boy, and to recollect, that many a coat which seems clean enough to a poor man, appears very dirty in the eyes of a delicate gentleman, and that, in like manner, many a life which a worldly person thinks innocent, appears to be a very wicked one in the eyes of a Christian.

The grand cause of all, however, which makes men reject the Gospel, is one which must be traced still further. It was remarked of this boy, that he had no heart for the sort of benefit which was offered him, for that he had a very mean and low mind: he had therefore not merely fallen into bad company, but he had chosen it: he was not only used to dirt, but he really loved it; he had no delight in cleanliness, for his taste, unhappily, lay quite the other way.

Now this, when it is considered, will serve to explain very clearly the several circumstances in his conduct, and it will also account very sufficiently for his entire refusal of the offer. His rudeness in not attending to the gentleman when he first called

called to him, as well as his continual absence of mind afterwards, his difficulty in believing any thing that could be said to him, his false reasoning upon it, his seeming dullness and ingratitude, and insensibility, as well as the bad choice which he made of his company, may all be traced, directly or indirectly, to this principal cause, that the lad was a poor low-lived fellow, that loved to grovel in the dirt, and had no kind of heart or inclination to get into a good service.

And need we fear to remark, that in this also the likeness holds, and that we have here especially, the exact picture of the irreligious person?

It is often pleaded, by those who would defend the characters of irreligious people, that one man, for instance, happens merely to be rather inattentive to the Gospel; that another is unfortunately drawn out of the way of it by what is thought an innocent attention to his worldly business; a third gravely tells you that he finds a difficulty in believing it; a fourth contrives some way or other to pervert it, so as to get no good from it, and seem to have a strange twist in his head whenever he reasons upon it; a fifth is said to be a man who is without those warm feelings which are supposed to distinguish those who affectionately embrace it; and of a seventh, perhaps, it is said by some simple good-natured relation, or acquaintance, that the man has a good heart indeed, but that unluckily he has fallen into bad company; but let it be remembered, that just thus it might be pleaded, that this beggarly boy was by turns inattentive and wrong-headed, and dull of feeling, as well as used to bad company. These excuses, if allowed in the one instance, should be allowed equally in the other. The true root of the matter in each case lies deeper. The irreligious man, like the boy in the parable, has, in the worst sense of the words, a base and low mind: like him, he has no heart for the great things that are offered him; he has no heart for the favour of God, for the honour of living in his service, for the comforts of the Gospel in this world, or for the gift of eternal life. Like the beggarly boy, he may say what he will, but he is of an earthly, grovelling spirit, and the true explanation of the whole matter is, that as the one is inclined to dirt, so the other has a leaning to the side of sin. Do you think that if this beggarly boy had loved cleanliness, and abominated every degree of dirt, he would have remained as he was? No; undoubtedly he would have caught at the opportunity offered him; and he would, as it were, at all hazards, have run after the gentleman: so if a man longs to be freed from sin, if he wishes above all things to cleanse his ways, to purify himself even as God is pure, and to become holy as God is holy, do you think he will not catch at the Gospel? undoubtedly he will do so. Yes; for it will be suited in every part of it to the state of his mind, and to all his wants and wishes; and therefore why should he not receive it? He will feel his way, indeed, but he will by degrees heartily embrace every doctrine of it. This, then, is the man who will accept God for his father, Christ for his Saviour, the Holy Spirit for his Sanctifier and Comforter; the Scriptures will be his Guide; the World will be no more to him than the place of his pilgrimage; his fellow Christians will be viewed by him as his fellow travellers, and Heaven will be his home, where he hopes to be joined to the Spirits of Just Men made perfect, and to dwell in the presence of his Maker, and of his Saviour, for ever and ever.

And now, Reader, if thou art one who hast hitherto been a stranger to religion, and hast gone thy dull and daily round without any thought of the matter, for once thou hast been met, methinks, on thy way, like this beggarly boy, by a voice of exhortation. Even in this little tale, the offer of the Gospel, perhaps rather unexpectedly, hath been held out to thee, or some hint at least may have been given, by which, if thou wilt attend to it, thou shalt assuredly find in the end that thy whole condition shall be altered: and yet, perhaps, like this beggarly boy, thou art now returning for the remainder of this very day to thy old habits, just as if thou hadst not read this story. Some business calls thee, or some pleasure waits thee, so farewel to all thought of the Gospel, for thou must be gone.—But, methinks, as thou departest, thy heart should approve of this beggarly boy, should admire his wisdom, and praise the turn of his spirit, for if thou goest away condemning him, thou condemnest thyself also.—Oh! no: his case is too bad to be defended; for he, who, in a worldly sense, *refuses a good offer*, is set down for a fool, by common consent of all men. But, ah! how few will be persuaded to use the same reasoning in religion, which they apply to all their worldly matters! How few will see with the same eyes, and try by the same rule, their temporal, and their eternal interests! So true is that saying of the Scriptures, " that the children of this world are wiser in their generation than the children of light."

THE
PILGRIMS.
AN ALLEGORY.

———

METHOUGHT I was once upon a time travelling through a certain land which was very full of people, but, what was rather odd, not one of all this multitude was at home; they were all bound to a far distant country. Though it was permitted by the Lord of the land that these Pilgrims might associate together for their present mutual comfort and convenience; and each was not only allowed, but commanded to do the others all the services he could upon their journey, yet it was decreed, that every individual traveller must enter the far country singly. There was a great gulf at the end of the journey which every one must pass alone, and at his own risk, and the friendship of the whole united world could be of no use in shooting that gulf. The exact time when each was to pass was not known to any; this the Lord always kept a close secret out of kindness, yet still they were as sure that the time must come, and that at no very great distance, as if they had been informed of the very moment. Now, as they knew they were always liable to be called away at an hour's notice, one would have thought they would have been chiefly employed in packing up, and preparing, and getting every thing in order. Not they indeed. It was almost the only thing which they did not think about.

Now I only appeal to you, my readers, if any of you are setting out upon a little common journey, if it is only to London or York, is not all your leisure time employed in settling your business at home, and packing up every little necessary for your expedition? And does not the fear of neglecting any thing you ought to remember, or may have occasion for, haunt your mind, and sometimes even intrude upon you unseasonably? And when you are actually on your journey, especially if you have never been to that place before, or are likely to remain there, don't you begin to think a little about the pleasures and the employments of the place, and to wish to know a little what sort of a city London or York is? Don't you wonder what is doing there, and whether you are properly qualified for the business, or the company you expect to be engaged in? Do you never look at the map, or consult Brookes's Gazetteer? And don't you try to
pick

pick up from your fellow-passengers in the stage-coach any little information you can get? And though you may be obliged, out of civility, to converse with them on common subjects, yet do not your secret thoughts still run upon London or York, its business, or its pleasures? And above all, if you are likely to set out early, are you not afraid of over-sleeping, and does not that fear keep you upon the watch, so that you are commonly up and ready before the porter comes to summon you? Reader! if this be your case, how surprised will you be to hear that the travellers to the far country have not half your prudence, though bound on a journey of infinitely more importance, to a land where nothing can be sent after them, and which when they are once settled, all errors are irretrievable.

I observed that these pilgrims, instead of being upon the watch, lest they should be ordered off unprepared; instead of laying up any provision, or even making memorandums of what they would be likely to want, spent most of their time in crowds, either in the way of traffic or diversion. At first, when I saw them so much engaged in conversing with each other, I thought it a good sign, and listened attentively to their talk, not doubting but the chief turn of it would be about the climate, or treasures, or society they should probably meet with in the far country. I supposed they might be also discussing about the best and safest road to it, and that each was availing himself of the knowledge of his neighbour, on a subject of equal importance to all. I listened to every party, but in scarcely any did I hear one word about the land to which they were bound, though it was their home, the place where their whole interest, expectation, and inheritance lay; to which also great part of their friends were gone before, and whither they were sure all the rest would follow. Instead of this, their whole talk was about the business, or the pleasures, or the fashions, of the strange country which they were merely passing through, and in which they had not one foot of land which they were sure of calling their own for the next quarter of an hour. What little estate they had was *personal* and not real, and that was a mortgaged, life-hold tenement of clay, not properly their own, but only lent to them on a short uncertain lease, of which threescore years and ten was considered as the longest period, and very few indeed lived in it to the end of the term; for this was always at the *will of the Lord*, part of whose prerogative it was, that he could take away the lease at pleasure, knock down the stoutest tenant at a single blow, and turn out the poor shivering, helpless tenant naked, to that far country for which he had made no provision. Sometimes, in order to quicken the Pilgrim in his preparation, the Lord would break down the tenement by slow degrees, sometimes he would let it tumble by its own natural decay, for as it was only built to last a certain term, it would sometimes grow so uncomfortable by increasing dilapidations even before the

ordinary

ordinary lease was out, that the lodging was hardly worth keeping, though the tenant could seldom be persuaded to think so, but fondly clung to it to the last. First the thatch on the top of the tenement changed colour, then it fell off and left the roof bare; then "the grinders ceased because they were few;" then the windows became so darkened that the owner could scarcely see through them; then one prop fell away, then another, then the uprights became bent, and the whole fabric trembled and tottered, with every other symptom of a falling house. On some occasions the Lord ordered his messengers, of which he had a great variety, to batter, injure, deface, and almost demolish the frail building even while it seemed new and strong; this was what the landlord called *giving warning*; but many a tenant would not take warning, and was so fond of staying where he was, even under all these inconveniences, that at last he was cast out by ejectment, not being prevailed on to leave his dwelling in a proper manner, though one would have thought the fear of being turned out would have whetted his diligence in preparing for *a better and a more enduring inheritance*. For though the people were only tenants at will in these crazy tenements, yet through the goodness of the same Lord, they were assured that he never turned them out of these habitations before he had on his part provided for them a better, so that there was not such another landlord in the world; and though their present dwelling was but frail, being only slightly run up to serve the occasion, yet they might hold their future possession by a most certain tenure, the word of the Lord himself, which was entered in a covenant, or title-deed, consisting of many sheets, and because a great many good things were given away in this deed, a book was made of which every soul might get a copy. This indeed had not always been the case, because, till a few ages back, there had been a sort of monopoly in the case, and "the wise and prudent," that is, the cunning and fraudful, had hid these things from the "babes and sucklings," that is, from the low and ignorant, and many frauds had been practised, and the poor had been cheated of their right; so that not being allowed to read and judge for themselves, they had been sadly imposed upon; but all these tricks had been put an end to more than two hundred years when I passed through the country, and the meanest man who could read might then have a copy, so that he might see himself what he had to trust to, and even those who could not read, might hear it read once or twice every week, at least, without pay, by learned men whose business it was. But it surprised me to see how few comparatively made use of these vast advantages. Of those who *had* a copy, many laid it carelessly by, expressed a *general* belief in the truth of the title-deed, a *general* satisfaction that they should come in for a share of the inheritance, a *general* good opinion of the Lord whose word it was, and a *general* disposition to take his promise upon trust; always, however intending, at a *convenient season*, to inquire farther into the matter, but this convenient season seldom came, and this neglect of theirs was construed into a forfeiture of the inheritance.

At the end of this country lay the vast gulf mentioned before; it was shadowed over by a broad and thick cloud, which prevented the pilgrims from seeing in a distinct manner what was doing behind it, yet such beams of brightness now and then darted through the cloud as enabled those who used a telescope provided for that purpose, to see *the substance of things hoped for*; but it was not every one who could make use of this telescope; no eye indeed was *naturally* disposed to it; but an earnest desire of getting a glimpse of the invisible realities, gave such a strength and steadiness to the eye, as enabled it to discern many things which could not be seen by the natural sight. Above the cloud was this inscription, *The things which are seen are temporal, but the things which are not seen are eternal.* Of these last many glorious descriptions had been given, but as those splendors were at a distance, and as the pilgrims in general did not care to use the telescope, these distant glances made little impression. The glorious inheritance which lay beyond the cloud, was called, *The things above*, while a multitude of trifling objects, which appeared contemptibly small when looked at through the telescope, were called,

The things below. Now as we know it is nearness which gives size and bulk to any object, it was not wonderful that these ill-judging pilgrims were more struck with these baubles and trifles, which, by lying close at hand, were visible and tempting to the naked eye, and which made up the sum of *The things below,* than with the remote glories of *The things above:* but this was chiefly owing to their not making use of the telescope, through which, if you examined thoroughly *The things below,* they seemed to shrink almost down to nothing, while *The things above* appeared the more beautiful and vast, the more the telescope was used. But the surprising part of the story was this, not that the pilgrims were captivated at first sight with *The things below,* for that was natural enough, but that when they had tried them all over and over, and found themselves deceived and disappointed in almost every one of them, it did not at all lessen their fondness, and they grasped at them again with the same eagerness as before. There were some gay fruits which looked alluring, but on being opened instead of a kernel they were found to contain rottenness, and those which seemed the fullest often proved on trial to be quite hollow and empty. Those which were most tempting to the eye were often found to be wormwood to the taste, or poison to the stomach, and many flowers that seemed most bright and gay had a worm gnawing at the root.

Among

Among the chief attractions of *The things below* were certain little lumps of yellow clay, on which almost every eye and every heart was fixed. When I saw the variety of uses to which this clay could be converted, and the respect which was shewn to those who could scrape together the greatest number of pieces, I did not much wonder at the general desire to pick up some of them. But when I beheld the anxiety, the wakefulness, the competitions, the contrivances, the tricks, the frauds, the scuffling, the pushing, the turmoiling, the kicking, the shoving, the cheating, the circumvention, the envy, the malignity, which was excited by a desire to possess this article; when I saw the general scramble among those who had little to get much, and of those who had much to get more, then I could not help applying to these people a Proverb in use among us, *that gold may be bought too dear.* Though I saw that there were various sorts of baubles which engaged the hearts of different travellers, such as an ell of red or blue ribbon, for which some were content to forfeit their future inheritance, committing the sin of Esau without his temptation of hunger; yet the yellow clay I found was the grand object for which most hands scrambled and most souls were risked. One thing was extraordinary, that the nearer these people were to being turned out of their tenement, the fonder they grew of these pieces of clay, so that I naturally concluded they meant to take the clay with them to the far country; but I soon

I soon learnt this clay was not current there, the Lord having declared to these pilgrims, that as *they had brought nothing into this world, they could carry nothing out.*

I inquired of the different people who were raising the various heaps of clay, some of a larger, some of a smaller size, why they discovered such unremitting anxiety, and for whom? Some whose piles were immense, told me they were heaping up for their children; this I thought very right, till on casting my eyes round, I observed many of the children of these very people had large heaps of their own. Others told me it was for their grand-children; but on enquiry, I found these were not yet born, and in many cases there was little chance that they ever would. The truth, on a close examination, proved to be, that the true genuine heapers really heaped for themselves; that it was in fact neither for friend or child, but to gratify an inordinate appetite of their own. Nor was I much surprised after this to see these yellow hoards at length *canker, and the rust of them become a witness against the hoarders, and eat their flesh as it were fire.*

Many, however, who had set out with a high heap of their father's raising, before they had got one third of their journey had scarcely a single piece left. As I was wondering what had caused these enormous piles to vanish in so short a time, I spied scattered up and down the country all sorts of odd inventions, for some or other of which the vain possessors of the great heaps of clay had trucked and bartered them away in fewer hours than their ancestors had spent years in getting them together. O what a strange unaccountable medley it was! and what was ridiculous enough, I observed that the greatest quantity of the clay was always exchanged for things that were of no use that I could discover, owing I suppose to my ignorance of the manners of that country.

In one place I saw large heaps exhausted in order to set two idle pampered horses a running; but the worst part of the joke was, the horses did not run to fetch or carry any thing, but merely to let the gazers see which could run fastest. Now this gift of swiftness, exercised to no one useful purpose, was only one out of many instances, I observed, of talents used to no end. In another place I saw whole piles of the clay spent to maintain long ranges of buildings full of dogs, on provisions which would have nicely fattened some thousands of pilgrims who sadly wanted fattening, and whose ragged tenements were out at elbows, for want of a little help to repair them. Some of the piles were regularly pulled down once in seven years in order to corrupt certain needy pilgrims to belie their consciences. Others were spent in playing with white stiff bits of paper painted over with red and black spots, in which I thought there must be some conjuring, because the very touch of these painted pasteboards made the heaps fly from one to to another, and back again to the same, in a way that natural causes could not account for. There was another proof that there must be some magic in this business, which was that if a pasteboard with red spots fell into a hand which wanted a black one, the person changed colour, his eyes flashed fire, and he discovered other symptoms of madness, which shewed there was some witchcraft in the case. These clean little pasteboards, as harmless as they looked, had the wonderful power of pulling down the highest piles in less time than all the other causes put together. I observed that many small piles were given in exchange for an enchanted liquor, which when the purchaser had drank to a little excess, he lost all power of managing the rest of his heap without losing the love of it.

Now I found it was the opinion of sober pilgrims, that either hoarding the clay, or trucking it for any such purposes as the above, was thought exactly the same offence in the eyes of the Lord, and it was expected that when they should come under his more immediate jurisdiction in the far country, the penalty annexed to hoarding and squandering would be nearly the same. While I examined the countenances of the owners of the heaps, I observed that those who I well knew never intended to make any use at all of their heap, were far more terrified at the thought of losing it, or of being torn from it, than those were who were employing it in the most useful manner. Those who best knew what to do with it, set their hearts

hearts leaft upon it, and were always moft willing to leave it. But fuch riddles were common in this odd country.

Now I wondered why thefe Pilgrims, who were naturally made erect with an eye formed to look up to *The things above*, yet had their eyes almoft conftantly bent in the other direction riveted to the earth, and faftened *on things below*, juft like thofe animals who walk on all four. I was told they had not always been fubject to this weaknefs of fight and pronenefs to earth: That they had originally been upright and beautiful, having been created after the image of the Lord, who was himfelf the perfection of beauty; that he had, at firft, placed them in a far fuperior fituation, which he had given them in perpetuity; but that their firft anceftors fell from it through pride and careleffnefs; that upon this the freehold was taken away, they loft their original ftrength, brightnefs, and beauty, and were driven out into this ftrange country; where however they had every opportunity given them of recovering their health, and the Lord's favour and likenefs; for they were become fo disfigured, and were grown fo unlike him, that you would hardly believe they were his own children, though, in fome, the refemblance was become again vifible. The Lord, however, was fo merciful, that inftead of giving them up to the dreadful confequences of their own folly, as he might have done without any impeachment of his juftice, that he gave them immediate comfort,

and

and promised them, that in due time, his own Son should come down and restore them to the future inheritance which he should purchase for them. And now it was that in order to keep up their spirits, after they had lost their estate through the folly of their ancestors, that he began to give them a part of their former Title Deed. He continued to send them portions of it from time to time by different faithful servants, whom, however, these ungrateful people generally used ill, and some of whom they murdered. But for all this the Lord, was so very forgiving, that he at length sent these mutineers a Proclamation of full and free pardon by his Son, who, though they used him in a more cruel manner than they had done any of his servants, yet after having *finished the work his Father had given him to do*, went back into the far country to prepare a place for all them who believe in him; and there he still lives, begging and pleading for those unkind people whom he still loves and forgives, and will restore to the purchased inheritance on the easy terms of their being heartily sorry for what they have done, thoroughly desirous of pardon, and convinced that *He is able and willing to save to the utmost all them that come unto him.*

I saw, indeed, that many old offenders appeared to be sorry for what they had done; that is, they did not like to be punished for it. They were willing enough to be delivered from the penalty of their sin, but they did not heartily wish to be delivered from the power of it.

Many declared, in the most public manner, once every week, that they were very sorry they had done amiss, *that they had erred and strayed like lost sheep*; but it was not enough to *declare* their sorrow ever so often if they gave no other sign of their penitence. For there was so little truth in them, that the Lord required other proofs of their sincerity beside their own word, for they often lied with their lips and dissembled with their tongue. But those who professed to be penitents were neither allowed to raise heaps of clay, by circumventing their neighbours, or to keep great piles lying by them useless; nor must they barter them for any of those idle vanities which reduced the heaps on a sudden: for I found that among the grand articles of future reckoning, the use they had made of the heaps would be a principal one.

I was sorry to observe many of the fairer part of these Pilgrims spend too much of their heaps in adorning and beautifying their tenements of clay, in painting, white-washing, and enamelling them. All those tricks, however, did not preserve them from decay, and when they grew old, they even looked worse for all this cost and varnish. Some, however, acted a more sensible part, and spent no more upon their mouldering tenements than just to keep them whole and clean, and in good repair, which is what every tenant ought to do; and I observed that those who were moderate in the care of their own tenements, were most attentive to repair and warm

the

the ragged tenements of others. But none did this with much zeal or acceptance, but those who had acquired a habit of overlooking the *things below*, and who also by the constant use of the Telescope, had got their natural weak and dim sight so strengthened, as to be able to discern pretty distinctly the nature of the *things above*. The habit of fixing their eyes on these glories, made all the shining trifles which compose the mass of *things below* at last appear in their own diminutive littleness. For it was in this case particularly true, that things are only big or little by comparison; and there was no other way of making the *things below* appear as small as they really were, but by comparing them by means of the Telescope with the *things above*. But I observed that the false judgment of the Pilgrims ever kept pace with their wrong practices, for those who kept their eyes fastened on the *things below*, were reckoned wise in their generation, while the few who looked forward to the future glories, were accounted by the bustlers, or heapers, to be either fools or mad.

Well—most of these Pilgrims went on in adorning their tenements, adding to their heaps, grasping the *things below* as if they would never let them go, shutting their eyes instead of using their Telescope, and neglecting their Title Deed, as if it was the Parchment of another man's estate and not their own; till one after another each felt his tenement tumbling about his ears.— Oh! then what a busy, bustling, anxious, terrifying,

ing, distracting moment was that! What a deal of business was to be done, and what a strange time was this to do it in! Now to see the confusion and dismay, occasioned by having left every thing to the last minute. First some one was sent for to make over the yellow heaps to another, which the heaper now found would be of no use to himself in shooting the gulf; a transfer which ought to have been made while the tenement was sound. Then there was a consultation between two or three masons at once, perhaps to try to patch up the walls, and strengthen the props, and stop the decays of the tumbling tenement; but not till the masons were forced to declare it was past repairing, (a truth they were rather too apt to keep back) did the tenant seriously think it was time to pack up, prepare, and be gone. Then what sending for the wise men who professed to explain the Title Deed! And oh, what remorse that they had neglected to examine it till their senses were too confused for so weighty a business! What reproaches, or what exhortations to others to look better after their own affairs! Even to the wisest of the inhabitants the falling of their tenements was a solemn thing; solemn, but not surprising; they had long been packing up and preparing; they praised their Lord's goodness that they had been suffered to stay so long; many acknowledged the mercy of their frequent warnings, and confessed that those very dilapidations which had made the house uncomfortable had been a blessing, as it had set
them

them on diligent preparation for their future inheritance, had made them more earnest in examining their title to it, and had set them on such a frequent application to the Telescope, that *The things above* had seemed every day to approach nearer and nearer. These desired not to be *uncloathed but to be cloathed upon, for they knew that if their frail Tabernacle was dissolved, they had an house not made with hands, eternal in the heavens.*

Z.

THE
Servant-Man turned Soldier;

OR,

The Fair Weather Christian.

A PARABLE.

WILLIAM was a lively young servant, who lived in a *great but very irregular family*. His place was, on the whole, agreeable to him, and suited to his gay thoughtless temper. He found a plentiful table and a good cellar. There was, indeed, a good deal of work to be done, though it was performed with much disorder and confusion. The family in the main were not unkind to him, though they often contradicted and crossed him, especially when things went ill with themselves. This, William never much liked, for he was always fond of having his own way. There was a merry, or rather a noisy and riotous servants' hall; for disorder and quarrels are indeed

deed

deed the usual effects of plenty and unrestrained indulgence. The men were smart but idle, the maids were showy, but licentious, and all did pretty much as they liked for a time, but the time was commonly short. The wages were reckoned high, but they were seldom paid, and it was even said by sober people, that the master was insolvent, and never fulfilled any of his flattering engagements, or his most positive promises; but still, notwithstanding his real poverty, things went on with just the same thoughtlessness and splendor, and neither masters or servants looked beyond the jollity of the present hour.

In this unruly family there was little church going, and still less praying at home. They pretended, it is true, in a general way, to believe in the Bible, but it was only an outward profession, few of them read it at all, and even of those who did read it still fewer were governed by its laws. There was indeed a Bible lying on the table in the great hall, which was kept for the purpose of administering an oath, but was seldom used on any other occasion; and some of the heads of the family were of opinion that this was its only real use, as it might serve to keep the lower parts of it in order.

William, who was fond of novelty and pleasure, was apt to be negligent of the duties of the house. He used to stay out on his errands, and one of his favourite amusements was going to the parade to see the soldiers exercise. He saw with envy how smartly they were dressed; listened with

with rapture to the music, and fancied that a soldier had nothing to do but to walk to and fro in a certain regular order, to go through a little easy exercise; in short, to live without fighting, fatigue, or danger.

O, said he, whenever he was affronted at home, what a fine thing it must be to be a soldier! to be so well dressed, to have nothing to do but to move to the pleasant sound of fife and drum, and to have so many people come to look at one, and admire one! *O it must be a fine thing to be a soldier!*

Yet when the vexation of the moment was over, he found so much ease and diversion in his master's house, so suited to his low taste and sensual appetites, that he thought no more of the matter. He forgot the glories of a soldier, and eagerly returned to all the mean gratifications of the kitchen. His evil habits were but little attended to by those with whom he lived; his faults, among which were lying and swearing, were not often corrected by the family, who had little objection to those sins, which only offended God and did not much affect their own interest or property. And except that William was obliged to work rather more than he liked, he found little, while he was young and healthy, that was very disagreeable in this service. So he went on, still thinking however, when things went a little cross, what a fine thing it was to be a soldier! At last one day as he was waiting at dinner, he had the misfortune to let fall a china dish,

dish, and broke it all to pieces. It was a curious dish, much valued by the family as they pretended; this family were indeed apt to set a false fantastic value on things, and not to estimate them by their real worth. The heads of the family, who had generally been rather patient and good-humoured with William, as I said before, for those vices, which though offensive to God did not touch their own pocket, now flew out into a violent passion with him, called him a thousand hard names, and even threatened to horse-whip him for his shameful negligence.

William, in a great fright, for he was a sad coward at bottom, ran directly out of the house to avoid the threatened punishment, and happening just at that very time to pass by the parade where the soldiers chanced to be then exercising, his resolution was taken in a moment. He instantly determined to be no more a slave, as he called it; he would return no more to be subject to the humours of a tyrannical family; no, he was resolved to be free, or at least, if he must serve, he would serve no master but the King.

William, who had now and then happened to hear from the accidental talk of the soldiers, that those who served the *great family* he had lived with, were slaves to their tyranny and vices, had also heard in the same casual manner, that the service of the *King* was *perfect freedom*. Now he had taken it into his head to hope that this might be a freedom to do evil, or at least to do nothing,

nothing, so he thought it was the only place in the world to suit him.

A fine likely young fellow as William was, had no great difficulty to get enlisted. The few forms were soon settled, he received the bounty-money as eagerly as it was offered, took the oaths of allegiance, and was joined to the regiment, and heartily welcomed by his new comrades. He was the happiest fellow alive. All was smooth and calm. The day happened to be very fine, and therefore William always reckoned upon a fine day. The scene was gay and lively, the music cheerful; he found the exercise very easy, and he thought there was little more expected from him.

He soon began to flourish away in his talk; and when he met with any one of his old fellow servants, he fell a prating about marches and counter-marches, and blockades, and battles, and sieges, and blood, and death, and triumphs, and victories, all at random, for these were words and phrases he had picked up without at all understanding what he said. He had no knowledge, and therefore he had no modesty; he had no experience, and therefore he had no fears.

All seemed to go on swimmingly, for he had had as yet no trial. He began to think with triumph what a mean life he had escaped from in the old quarrelsome family, and what a happy, honourable life he should have in the army. *O there was no life like the life of a soldier.*

In a short time, however, war broke out, his regiment was one of the first which was called out to actual and hard service. As William was the most raw of all the recruits he was the first to murmur at the difficulties and hardships, the cold and hunger, the fatigue and danger, of being a soldier. O what watchings, and perils, and trials, and hardships, and difficulties, he now thought attended a military life! Surely, said he, I could never have suspected all this misery when I used to see the men on the parade in our town.

He now found, when it was too late, that all the field-days he used to attend, all the evolutions and exercises which he had observed the soldiers to go through in the calm times of peace and safety, were only meant to fit, train, and qualify them, for the actual service which they were now sent out to perform by the command of the *King*.

The truth is, William often complained when there was no real hardship to complain of; for the common troubles of life fell out pretty much alike to the *great family* which William had left, and to the soldiers in the *King's army*. But the spirit of obedience, discipline, and self-denial of the latter seemed hardships to one of William's loose turn of mind. When he began to murmur some good old soldier clapped him on the back, saying, " cheer up lad, it is a kingdom you are to strive for, if we faint not, henceforth there is laid up for us a great reward, we have the *King's* word for it, man." William observed that to
those

those who truly believed this, their labours were as nothing, but he himself did not at the bottom believe it; and it was observed of all the soldiers who failed, the true cause was, that they did not really believe the *King's* promise. He was surprised to see that those soldiers, who used to bluster, and boast, and deride the assaults of the enemy, now began to fall away; while such as had faithfully obeyed the *King's* orders, and believed in his *word*, were sustained in the hour of trial. Those who had trusted in their own strength all fainted on the slightest attack, while those who had put on the *armour of the King's* providing, *the sword*, and *the shield*, and *the helmet*, and *the breast-plate*, and whose *feet were shod* according to order, now " endured hardship as good soldiers, and were enabled to fight the good fight."

An engagement was expected immediately. The men were ordered to prepare for battle. While the rest of the corps were so preparing, William's whole thoughts were bent on contriving how he might desert. But alas! he was watched on all sides, he could not possibly devise any means to escape. The danger increased every moment, the battle came on. William, who had been so sure and confident before he entered, flinched in the moment of trial, while his more quiet and less boastful comrades prepared boldly to do their duty. William looked about on all sides, and saw that there was no eye upon him, for he did not know that the *King's* eye was always every where at once. He at last thought he spied a chance of escaping, not from the enemy, but from his own army. While he was endeavouring to escape, a ball from the opposite camp took off his leg. As he fell, the first words which broke from him were; Alas! while I was in my duty I was preserved, but in the very act of deserting I am wounded. He lay expecting every moment to be trampled to death, but as soon as the confusion was a little over, he was taken off the field by some of his own party, laid in a place of safety, and left to himself, after his wound was dressed.

The skirmish, for it proved nothing more, was soon over. The greater part of the regiment escaped in safety, while the few who fell, rejoiced that they fell in their duty. William, in the mean time, suffered cruelly both in mind and body. To the pains of a wounded soldier, he added the disgrace of a coward, and the infamy of a deserter. O, cried he, why was I such a fool as to leave the *great family* I lived in, where there was meat and drink enough and to spare, only on account of a little quarrel? I might have made up that with them as we had done our former quarrels. Why did I leave a life of ease and pleasure, where I had only a little rub now and then, for a life of daily discipline and constant danger? Why did I turn soldier? O, what a miserable animal is a soldier!

As he was sitting in this weak and disabled condition, uttering the above complaints, he observed

served a venerable old officer, with thin grey locks on his head, and on his face deep wrinkles engraved by time, and many an honest scar inflicted by war. William had heard this old officer highly commended for his extraordinary courage and conduct in battle, and in peace he used to see him cool and collected; devoutly employed in reading and praying in the interval of more active duties. He could not help comparing this officer with himself. I, said he, flinched and drew back, and would even have deserted in the moment of peril, and now in return, I have no consolation in the hour of repose and safety. I would not fight then, I cannot pray now. O why would I ever think of being a soldier? He then began afresh to weep and lament, and he groaned so loud that he drew the notice of the officer who came up to him, kindly sat down by him, took him by the hand, and inquired with as much affection as if he had been his brother, what was the matter with him, and what particular distress, more than the common fortune of war, it was which drew from him such bitter groans? I know something of surgery, added he, let me examine your wound, and assist you with such little comforts as I can.

William at once saw the difference between the soldiers in the *King's* army, and the people in the *great family*; the latter commonly withdrew their kindness in sickness and trouble, when it was most wanted, and this was just the very time when the others came forward to assist. He told the officer his little history, the manner of his living in the *great family*, the trifling cause of his quarrelling with it, and the slight ground of his entering into the *King's* service. Sir, said he, I quarrelled with the family, and I thought I was at once fit for the army: I did not know the qualifications it required. I had not reckoned on discipline, and hardships, and self-denial. I liked well enough to sing a loyal song, or drink the King's health, but I find I do not relish working and fighting for him, though I rashly promised even to lay down my life for his service if called upon, when I took the bounty money and the oath of allegiance. In short, sir, I find that I long for the ease and sloth, the merriment and the feasting of my old service; I find I cannot be a soldier, and, to speak truth, I was in the very act of deserting when I was stopped short by the cannon ball. So that I feel the guilt of deserting, and the misery of having lost my leg into the bargain.

The officer thus replied, your state is that of every worldly, irreligious man. The *great family* you served is a just picture of the WORLD. The wages the world promises to those who are willing to do its work are high, but the payment is attended with much disappointment; nay, the world, like your great family, is in itself insolvent, and in its very nature incapable of making good the large promises, and of paying the high rewards, which it holds out to tempt its credulous followers. The ungodly world, like your family, cares little for church, and still less for prayers; and considers the Bible rather as an instrument to make an oath binding, in order to keep the vulgar in obedience, than as containing in itself a perfect rule of faith and practice, and as a title-deed to heaven. The generality of men love the world as you did your service, while it smiles upon them, and gives them easy work, and plenty of meat and drink; but as soon as it begins to cross and contradict them, they get out of humour with it, just as you did with your service. They then think its drudgery hard, its rewards low. They find out that it is high in its expectations from them, and slack in its payments to them. And they begin to fancy (because they do not hear religious people murmur as they do) that there must be some happiness in religion. The world, which takes no account of their deeper sins, at length brings them into discredit for some act of imprudence, just as your family overlooked your lying and swearing, but threatened to drub you for breaking a china dish; such is the judgment of the world, it patiently bears with those who only break the laws of God, but severely punishes the smallest negligence by which its own property is injured. The world sooner pardons the breaking ten commandments of God, than even a china dish of its own.

After some cross or opposition, worldly men, as I said before, begin to think how much content and cheerfulness they remember to have seen in religious people. They, therefore, begin to fancy that religion must be an easy and delightful, as well as a good thing. They have heard that "her ways are ways of pleasantness, and all her paths are peace;" and they persuade themselves, that by this is meant worldly pleasantness and sensual peace. They resolve at length to try it, to turn their back upon the world, to engage in the service of God, and turn christians; just as you resolved to leave your old service, to enter into the service of the King, and turn soldier. But as you quitted your place in a passion, so they leave the world in a huff. They do not count the cost. They do not calculate upon the darling sins, the habitual pleasures, the ease and vanities which they undertake, by their new engagements, to renounce, any more than you counted what indulgences you were going to give up when you quitted the luxuries and idleness of your place to enlist in the soldier's warfare. They have, as I said, seen christians cheerful, and they mistook the ground of their cheerfulness; they fancied it arose not because, through grace, they had conquered difficulties, but because they had no difficulties in their passage. They fancied that religion found the road smooth, whereas it only helps the sufferer to bear with a rough road without complaint. They do not know that these Christians are of good cheer, not because the world is free from tribulation, but because Christ, their captain,

has

has "overcome the world." But the irreligious man, who has only seen the outside of a Christian in his worldly intercourse, knows little of his secret conflicts, his trials, his self-denials, his warfare with the world without, and with his own corrupt desires within.

The irreligious man quarrels with the world, on some such occasion as you did with your place. He now puts on the outward forms and ceremonies of religion, and assumes the badges of Christianity, just as you were struck with the shows of a field day; just as you were pleased with the music and the marching, and put on the cockade and the red coat. All seems smooth for a little while. He goes through the outward exercises of a Christian, a degree of credit attends his new profession, but he never suspects there is either difficulty or discipline attending it; he fancies religion is a thing for talking about, and not a thing to engage the heart and the life. He never suspects that all the psalm-singing he joins in, and the sermons he hears, and the other means he is using, are only as the exercises and the evolutions of the soldiers, to fit and prepare him for actual service; and that these means are no more religion itself, than the exercises and evolutions of your parade were real warfare.

At length some trial arises. This nominal Christian is called to differ from the world in some great point; something happens which may strike at his comfort, or his credit, or security. This cools his zeal for religion, just as the view of an engagement cooled your courage as a soldier. He finds he was only *angry* with the world, he was not *tired* of it he was out of humour with the world, not because he had seen through its vanity and emptiness, but because the world was out of humour with him. He finds that it is an easy thing to be a fair-weather Christian, bold where there is nothing to be done, and confident where there is nothing to be feared. Difficulties unmask him to others; temptations unmask him to himself; he discovers, that though he is a high professor, he is no Christian; just as you found out that your red coat, and your cockade, your shoulder-knot, and your musket, did not prevent you from being a coward.

Your misery in the military life, like that of the nominal Christian, arose from your love of ease, your cowardice, and your self-ignorance. You rushed into a new way of life, without trying after one qualification for it. A total change of heart and temper were necessary for your new calling. With new views and new principles the soldier's life would have been not only easy but delightful to you. But while, with a new profession, you retained your old nature, it is no wonder if all discipline seemed intolerable to you.

The true Christian, like the brave soldier, is supported under dangers by a strong faith that the fruits of that victory for which he fights will be safety, peace, and glory. But, alas! the pleasures

pleasures of this world are present and visible; the kingdom and the crown for which he strives are remote; because they are distant, he is apt to think them uncertain. He is therefore apt to fail, because nothing short of a lively faith can outweigh the present temptation, and teach him to prefer the future joys of conquest to the present pleasures of sloth.

Whether William went back to his old service, or was received again into the army, may be known hereafter.

Z.

THE
SORROWS OF YAMBA;

OR, THE

Negro Woman's Lamentation.

To the Tune of *Hosier's Ghost*.

IN St. Lucie's distant isle,
  Still with Afric's love I burn;
Parted many a thousand mile,
  Never, never to return.

Come, kind death! and give me rest;
  Yamba has no friend but thee;
Thou canst ease my throbbing breast,
  Thou canst set the Prisoner free.

Down my cheeks the tears are dripping,
  Broken is my heart with grief;
Mangled my poor flesh with whipping,
  Come, kind Death! and bring relief.

Born on Afric's golden coast,
  Once I was as blest as you;
Parents tender I could boast,
  Husband dear, and children too.

Whity

Whity man he came from far,
   Sailing o'er the briny flood;
Who, with help of British Tar,
   Buys up human flesh and blood.

With the baby at my breast
   (Other two were sleeping by)
In my hut I sat at rest,
   With no thought of danger nigh.

From the bush at even-tide,
   Rush'd the fierce man-stealing crew;
Seiz'd the children by my side,
   Seiz'd the wretched Yamba too.

Then for love of filthy gold,
   Strait they bore me to the sea,
Cramm'd me down a Slave-ship's hold,
   Where were hundreds stow'd like me.

Naked on the platform lying,
   Now we cross the tumbling wave;
Shrieking, sickening, fainting, dying;
   Deed of shame for Britons brave!

At the savage Captain's beck,
   Now, like brutes, they make us prance;
Smack the cat about the deck,
   And in scorn they bid us dance.

Nauseous horse-beans they bring nigh,
   Sick and sad we cannot eat;
Cat must cure the fulks, they cry,
   Down their throats we'll force the meat.

I, in groaning pass'd the night,
　　And did roll my aching head;
At the break of morning light,
　　My poor child was cold and dead.

Happy, happy, there she lies;
　　Thou shalt feel the lash no more;
Thus full many a Negro dies,
　　Ere we reach the destin'd shore.

Thee, sweet infant, none shall sell;
　　Thou hast gain'd a wat'ry grave;
Clean escap'd the tyrants fell,
　　While thy mother lives a slave.

Driven like cattle to a fair,
　　See, they sell us, young and old;
Child from mother too they tear,
　　All for love of filthy gold.

I was sold to Massa hard;
　　Some have Massas kind and good;
And again my back was scarr'd,
　　Bad and stinted was my food.

Poor and wounded, faint and sick,
　　All expos'd to burning sky,
Massa bids me grass to pick,
　　And I now am near to die.

What, and if to death he send me,
　　Savage murder tho' it be,
British laws shall ne'er befriend me,
　　They protect not slaves like me.

Mourning

Mourning thus my wretched state
  (Ne'er may I forget the day)
Once in dusk of evening late,
  Far from home I dar'd to stray.

Dar'd, alas! with impious haste,
  Tow'rds the roaring sea to fly;
Death itself I long'd to taste,
  Long'd to cast me in and die.

There I met upon the Strand,
  English Missionary good;
He had Bible book in hand,
  Which poor me no understood.

Led by pity from afar,
  He had left his native ground;
Thus, if some inflict a scar,
  Others fly to cure the wound.

Strait he pull'd me from the shore,
  Bid me no self-murder do;
Talk'd of state when life is o'er,
  All from Bible good and true.

Then he led me to his cot,
  Sooth'd and pitied all my woe;
Told me 'twas the Christian's lot,
  Much to suffer here below.

Told me then of God's dear Son,
  (Strange and wond'rous is the story)
What sad wrong to him was done,
  Tho' he was the Lord of Glory.

Told me, too, like one who knew him,
  (Can such love as this be true?)
How he died for them that slew him,
  Died for wretched Yamba too.

Freely he his mercy proffer'd,
  And to Sinners he was sent!
E'en to Massa pardon's offer'd;
  O, if Massa would repent!

Wicked deed full many a time,
  Sinful Yamba too hath done;
But she wails to God her crime,
  But she trusts his only Son.

O, ye slaves whom Massas beat,
  Ye are stain'd with guilt within;
As ye hope for mercy sweet,
  So forgive your Massas' sin.

And with grief when sinking lo,
  Mark the Road that Yamba trod;
Think how all her pain and woe
  Brought the Captive home to God.

Now let Yamba, too, adore
  Gracious Heaven's mysterious plan;
Now I'll count my mercies o'er,
  Flowing thro' the guilt of man.

Now I'll bless my cruel capture,
  (Hence I've known a Saviour's name)
Till my grief is turn'd to rapture,
  And I half forget the blame.

But tho' here a Convert rare,
  Thanks her God for Grace divine;
Let not man the glory share;
  Sinner, still the guilt is thine.

Here an injured Slave forgives,
  There a host for vengeance cry;
Here a single Yamba lives,
  There a thousand droop and die.

Duly now baptiz'd am I,
  By good Missionary man:
Lord, my nature purify,
  As no outward water can!

All my former thoughts abhorr'd,
  Teach me now to pray and praise;
Joy and glory in my Lord,
  Trust and serve him all my days.

Worn, indeed, with grief and pain,
  Death I now will welcome in:
O, the heavenly prize to gain!
  O, to 'scape the power of Sin!

True of heart, and meek, and lowly,
  Pure and blameless let me grow!
Holy may I be, for holy,
  Is the place to which I go.

But, tho' death this hour may find me,
  Still with Afric's love I burn;
(There I've left a spouse behind me)
  Still to native land I turn.

And when Yamba sinks in death,
   This my latest prayer shall be,
While I yield my parting breath,
   O, that Afric might be free.

Cease, ye British sons of murder!
   Cease from forging Afric's chain;
Mock your Saviour's name no further,
   Cease your savage lust of gain.

Ye that boast " *Ye rule the waves,*"
   Bid no Slave-ship soil the sea;
Ye, that "*never will be slaves,*"
   Bid poor Afric's land be free.

Where ye gave to war its birth,
   Where your traders fix'd their den,
There go publish " *Peace on Earth,*"
   Go, proclaim " *good-will to men.*"

Where ye once have carried slaughter,
   Vice, and slavery, and sin;
Seiz'd on Husband, Wife, and Daughter,
   Let the Gospel enter in.

Thus, where Yamba's native home,
   Humble hut of rushes stood;
Oh, if there should chance to roam,
   Some dear Missionary good;

Thou in Afric's distant land,
   Still shalt see the man I love;
Join him to the Christian band,
   Guide his soul to realms above.

There no fiend again shall sever
   Those whom God hath join'd and blest:
There they dwell with him for ever,
   There " *the weary are at rest.*"

THE
SHOPKEEPER turned SAILOR;
OR, THE
Folly of going out of our Element.

A TALE I tell whose first beginning
May set some giddy folks a grinning;
But, only let it all unfold,
A sadder tale was never told.
    Some people, who for years before,
Had seldom pass'd their outer door,
For once determin'd to be gay,
And have one merry-making day.
Agreed, " a sailing we will go:"
Thus all was settled at a blow.
With hats and bonnets duly ty'd,
They bustle to the water-side;
And as the women stem the gale,
They seem already under sail:
Here, while we find them safe and sound,
A sailing only on dry ground,
We'll take occasion to declare
Who all these merry people were.

First, there was John; a Trader he
Clever and smart as you shall see;
High on the shelf, in nice array,
His various Wares and Patterns lay;
Call when you will the thing's at hand,
And John is ever at his stand.
I grant, indeed, his price was high,
But then his shew-glass caught the eye;
Besides, 'twas known and understood,
His things were all extremely good.
Walk in, and if you talk with John,
I warrant he will draw you on:
Not that he ventur'd on the sin,
Of taking any strangers in;
For John, dispute it he who can,
Was a plain, open, honest man;
You saw it written in his face;
And then he serv'd you with a grace:
With gentle air, and accent sweet,
Powder'd and dress'd so spruce and neat,
And most obliging in his speeches,
Unnumber'd ribbons down he reaches;
Presents before the Lady's view,
Each flow'ry edge, each beauteous hue,
Rolls and unrolls the slippery things,
And every finger has its wings;
Then waits, with rare command of face,
While Miss, in sad distressful case,
Puzzles, and frets, and doubts, between
A greenish blue, and blueish green.
At length each anxious mind is eas'd,
The bargain's struck, the Lady's pleas'd;

John

John humbly bows, then takes his flight
To write his bill as swift as light;
And ere the strangers march'd away,
He next as sweetly asks for pay.
Yet if there enter'd one he knew,
John always gave the credit due;
Welcom'd the friend with joyful looks,
Yet clapp'd the debt into his books:
And tho' he begg'd the bill might wait,
'Twas sent at Christmas sure as fate.

   At Christmas too (I tell his fame,
That traders all may do the same)
John calmly takes his books up stairs,
And balances his whole affairs;
Sees how his total credits stand,
And values all his stock in hand;
Then fairly puts on t'other side,
The debts he owes both far and wide;
The diff'rence is the sum he's worth,
'Tis all he has this year on earth;
Compares it with the year before,
" 'Tis less than then"—" O, no; 'tis more—"
" 'Tis vastly more," he says with glee,
" 'Tis right, 'tis right, my books agree!"

   But who, except a trader's self,
Can paint these joys of growing pelf!
Or rather, to correct my song,
Who paint the pleasures that belong
To honest industry and thrift,
While God is thank'd for every gift!
Ah! foolish John, so blest at home,
What need hadst thou so far to roam?

                                Could

Could thy new-fangled joys out-top
The hourly pleasures of thy shop;
Or if thy health an airing need,
And one grand holiday's decreed,
Couldst thou not go, to change the scene,
And take a turn upon the green?
Ah! foolish John, from what strange quarter
Could come this fancy for the water!
Well hast thou prosper'd while on shore,
There lab'ring nobly at the oar;
But if the wat'ry flood should ride thee,
Methinks some evil will betide thee:
And shouldst thou dare, when once afloat,
Thyself to *steer*, or row the boat,
The hour shall come—I see it nigh,
With my prophetic poet's eye,
When know, vain man, that thou shalt smart,
And all thy glory shall depart.
Then hear, ye Britons, while I preach,
This is the truth I mean to teach—
That he who in his shop is bright,
And skill'd to keep his reck'ning right,
Who steers in the good middle way,
And gets some custom, and some pay,
Marks when sad Bankrupt times prevail,
And carefully draws in his sail,
Keeps watch, has all his lanterns out,
And sees the dangers round about;
Pushes his trade with wind and oar,
And still gets forward more and more.
This trader, skill'd as he may be,
On shore a man of high degree,
May prove a very dunce at sea.

Ah! foolish John, no thoughts like these
Once enter'd to disturb his ease;
Onward he goes, and thinks it grand,
To quit the plain and simple land;
Leaves a good house of brick and mortar,
To try mere wood upon the water.

PART II.

'TWAS told you in a former lay,
How on a luckless evil day,
The trader John, a landsman brave,
Left the dry ground to try the wave.
    But here the Poet must rehearse,
In soft, and sweet, and tender verse,
How gentle Johnny had a wife,
The joy and solace of his life,
The sharer of his griefs and cares,
Privy to all his great affairs;
One who when ty'd in wedlock's noose
Had prov'd a helpmate fit for use;
One whom he married—not for whim—
But who could keep his house in trim;
No high-flown Miss, or belle, or beauty,
A simple girl that knew her duty;
Had well obey'd her father, mother,
And counsell'd well her younger brother;

Healthy when young, and rather stout;
Moral?—nay, more, she was devout:
And now a Christian quite at heart,
She carefully fulfils her part,
Well skill'd alike her house to guide,
And serve the shop at Johnny's side.
See now she works to help the trade,
And now instructs her under maid.
But 'tis her chief and special care,
Her husband's daily toil to spare;
When sick, or weary and opprest,
To ease the troubles of his breast,
To sooth his sorrows, calm his fears,
And help him thro' this vale of tears;
Remind him where his treasure lies,
And point to realms above the skies,
Where, when this shifting scene is o'er,
The faithful meet to part no more.
Now twenty summers, or above,
Have glided by and prov'd her love;
And tho' they may have marr'd her face,
Have ripen'd many a Christian grace:
Hence it may now be fairly guess'd,
Her latest days shall be her best.
John knows her worth, and now-a-days,
He grows quite eager in her praise;
For ev'ry calling friend is told,
" My wife is worth her weight in gold."

 To this blest couple there was born,
One daughter cheerful as the morn;
A maiden she of spotless fame,
E'en in her mirth quite clear from blame.

Train'd in Religion's "narrow way,"
Her mind untainted by a play,
She hates your giddy glitt'ring scenes,
Tho' long since enter'd on her teens;
Sees all things in a proper light,
And vice quite puts her in a fright;
Prompt and obedient from a child,
Obliging, humble, meek, and mild;
Still, before strangers, as a mouse;
Yet vastly useful in the house;
Toils for the shop, tho' seldom seen;
—Ah!— there she sits behind the screen:
There, like some flower both sweet and gay,
She shuns as yet the blaze of day;
(Well does her praise adorn my tale)
A new-blown lily of the vale.

Now should perchance some fool draw near,
And get to whisper in her ear,
Of plays, and balls, and fairs, and races,
Fine midnight routs, and public places,
And wonder how she can endure,
A life so useful, and so pure—
Extol her form, her piercing eyes,
And tell a hundred flatt'ring lies;
—While the sweet praise he thinks she sips,
The tortur'd maiden bites her lips;
Thinks his fine flatt'ry mere pretence,
And longs to tell him to talk sense;
Yet dreads to take the dunce in hand,
Lest he should still not understand.
But should he let his *vice* peep out,
The meek-ey'd girl can then turn stout;

For once ('tis said) in terms direct,
A spruce and saucy spark she check'd;
(She grew so solemn in her speeches,
The bucks give out that "Nancy preaches")
And once put on the sweetest air,
And begg'd a carman not to swear.
Thus while she spends her peaceful days,
Her parents' care she well repays;
Honours her father, loves her mother,
She'll prove, methinks, just such another;
And tho' scarce seen, except at church,
The men won't leave her in the lurch;
Some honest Christian man she'll strike,
No buck or blood—for like loves like.

 Next in my song, of equal fame,
Comes a good honest antient dame;
John's mother—with no fault but one—
I mean—she doated on her son;
For when her own dear spouse was gone,
Her whole affections fell to John;
'Twas then, the widow's age so great,
Her prospects small, her income strait,
That Johnny weighed the matter well,
And took her to his home to dwell:
No cost or trouble did he grudge,
For John had rightly learn'd to judge,
That people, once of little fame,
But now of high and mighty name,
Oft owe the glory of their station,
To the mere help of Education.
Quoth he—Were all men good and true,
Their wealth, methinks, might half be due

To some good dame, who now is found,
Quite thrust upon the mere back ground:
Besides (he added, half in tears)
A child is always in arrears,
In debt, alas! o'er head and ears.
 Oh, with what joy, what thanks and praise,
To the great length'ner of her days;
What feelings, not to be outdone,
Tow'rds her dear John, her only son,
Did the good parent take her station,
And kindly own the obligation!
And now his tenderness she pays,
By helping in a thousand ways.
Deck'd in her best, she comes in view,
And serves the shop from twelve to two;
Knows not each price, perhaps, quite pat,
Yet keeps the croud in civil chat,
Till John himself comes up to sell
A yard of lutestring, or an ell:
Next to the cook her aid she brings,
And does a hundred little things;
Loves her own self to lay the cloth,
To dress the sallad, skim the broth:
At shelling peas is quick and nimble,
Tho' now grown tardy with her thimble;
And always puts you quite at ease,
Walks out, and leaves you, if you please:
Plain as she seems, has much good sense,
And hence she never takes offence;
And all agree, for all are lenient,
The good old Lady's quite convenient.

Yet

Yet led me add, if things go wrong,
Madam soon shews her fears are strong;
And then she gives a certain spice
Of plain and downright good advice;
Talks in a most convincing tone,
Of what *she*'s seen, and what *she*'s known;
And in a way that vastly wins,
Will warn you of her own past sins:
Tranquil at eve, in elbow chair,
Tells what her former follies were;
Recounts her dangers, nice escapes,
Sad sufferings once, and aukward scrapes;
And while she paints her varied life,
Adds wisdom e'en to Johnny's wife:
John, warn'd of her, each matter weighs,
And Nancy trembles and obeys.

 Thus, some old seaman, once so brave,
And buffeted by wind and wave,
Of the rude seas too long the sport,
Enters at length some peaceful port;
Rejoices now no more to roam,
Yet acts as Pilot nearer home.

PART III.

LONG has the Muſe her tale delay'd,
Has ſtopp'd to talk of Johnny's trade;
Wife, daughter, mother too, of John,
And quite forgot to travel on.
Long has the Muſe with trembling fear,
View'd the ſad ſcene that now is near;
Hung back, indeed, from very fright,
And ſhrunk and ſtarted at the ſight.
As the tall ſteed, if he ſhould ſpy
Some unknown form of danger nigh,
Starts from his path, his eye-balls glare,
His feet fly prancing in the air,
Round on the ſpot, and round he wheels,
Upright upon his mere hind heels:
So have we ſtarted at the view
Of what our John is now to do,
Have gaily friſk'd it round and round,
Nor gain'd as yet an inch of ground.
   Come, gentle Muſe, the tale declare,
Sing how this bold advent'rous pair,
With mother brave, and willing daughter,
March'd to the borders of the water.
Sing how they trod the beech ſo ſteep,
Gaz'd at the wonders of the deep,
And ſtopt to view, as in a trance,
The awful ocean's vaſt expanſe;

                    Then

Then gaz'd at ev'ry paſsing boat,
Till they quite long'd to get on float.
The boatmen, as they croſs the Strand,
Spring from an alehouſe juſt at hand;
All on the party down they burſt,
And each is ſure that he was firſt.
Oh! how they preſs and fill the ground,
And puſh and elbow all around!
Each to a Lady makes his ſuit,
Till Nancy ſtarts, as at a brute:
While prudent Johnny, marching down,
Hires a ſnug boat for half a crown,
Of ſmaller ſize, but ſtiff and tight,
And having ſeen that all is right,
Rallies his daughter, claims his wife,
Burſts through the croud and ends the ſtrife.

 And now with ſelf-complacent grin,
The favour'd boatman hands them in;
But firſt he plants, as is his rule,
On the wave's edge his little ſtool,
And while he begs them to take care,
Preſents his elbow high in air.
All in they ſtept, all down they ſat;
All ſafe, all even, and all flat:
The boatman puſhes off the boat;
Was e'er ſuch treaſure all afloat!
And now amid the ſun's bright gleam,
See how they cut the ſilver ſtream!
See how the breeze begins to play!
See how it wafts them far away!

 Scarce had the party left the ſhore,
When Ruffman longs to ſpare his oar,

Points to the bench where lies a sail,
And begs to profit by the gale.
At first the boatman's words appal,
And all the female faces fall;
And madam bets ten thousand pound,
This instant we shall all be drown'd.
Mean time old Ruffman, with a sneer,
Forbids each vain and silly fear;
Talks of the seas that he hath cross'd,
Beaten, and blown, and tempest toss'd;
Tells of his dangers now no more,
While a green youth in days of yore,
Of feats perform'd by way of fun,
And boasts of matches he has won:
Then drops his tone, and quite allays
All the new fears he seem'd to raise;
Pleads his great care, asserts his skill,
Begs each dear Lady'll dread no ill;
For if he keeps the rope in hand,
The water's just as safe as land.

 Thus all objections down he beat,
And now the awful sail is set;
Ah! how they plough the whit'ning seas,
So fine, so glorious is the breeze;
How fresh and cooling too the air,
While the sail shades them from the glare;
The boatman, who a while before
Sat coatless, heated at the oar,
Now lolls his ease, observes the wind,
Steers with one careful hand behind;
While his right fist holds hard the sail,
Resists or humours well the gale;

        Then

Then half-appearing to turn back,
At once he stops and makes a tack;
Points at the distant land once more,
And seems to run you right ashore;
But ere he lets you quite touch ground,
Again he spins his vessel round,
And shifts across, with skill so nice,
The flutt'ring canvas in a trice;
Scuds o'er the spacious seas again;
Again he plows the mighty main;
Again the less'ning shore retires,
Woods, hills depart, and distant spires;
While the bright sun, yon clouds between,
Shines forth and gilds the glorious scene.

 The party, eas'd of all their fright,
Gaze round and round with sweet delight;
Praise with one voice both land and seas,
And now they languish for a breeze;
Dread lest the slack'ning wind should fail,
And welcome every growing gale:
Swift o'er the swelling waves they fly,
And pleasure beams in every eye.

 But, ah! how oft with genial sun,
While the gay course of life we run,
And fancy as we taste the treat,
Our human bliss is now complete:
How oft in that same favour'd hour,
Does the whole sky begin to lour!
The cheering sun-shine's pass'd away,
There comes a dreary doleful day:
Afflictions gather like a cloud;
The swelling tempest roars aloud;

While from yon threat'ning heav'ns so dark,
It thunders round our little bark:
Unskill'd to struggle thro' the breeze,
We toss in new and troubl'd seas,
And life's gay morning all so bright,
Ends in some woeful tale at night.

PART IV.

COME, mournful Muse, and now relate
The awful change in Johnny's fate,
And while the doleful song is sung,
Tell from what cause the ruin sprung.
  Cool'd by the breeze, and half undrest,
The rough gale blust'ring round his breast,
Robb'd of the sun's bright noon-tide ray,
And oft besprinkl'd by the spray,
Forth from yon bottom of the boat
Old Ruffman lugs his sailor's coat,
And while he casts the jacket on,
Leaves roap and rudder all to John.
Ah! now begins the tragic tale,
For now the landsman holds the sail!
He sees around the watery realm,
Yet goes and seizes on the helm;
And seated just in Ruffman's place,
Shews his cock'd hat and tradesman's face:

And

And now, without one sailing art,
E'en simple Nancy bears a part;
Sits playful by her father's side,
And light and gay, and merry-ey'd,
Holds with that hand that held a fan,
Rude ropes, as if she were a man,
While idle Ruffman, freed from care,
Half sleeping, earns his easy fare.
—But hark! from yonder distant shore,
Did you not hear the thunder roar?
See! See! the vivid light'nings play,
And the dark cloud deforms the day:
Now too there comes the whistling breeze,
And sweeps the rudely swelling seas;
Fills with one blast the sail so full,
Wife, mother, daughter, help to pull.
Now sailors, if it seems to blow,
For safety let the canvas go;
But women, not like passive men,
In vengeance always pull again.
Besides, as each her strength apply'd,
Each crouded on the leeward side;
And though a lady's like a feather,
E'en feathers weigh when heap'd together.
   Fierce blows the whirlwind, and of course
The ladies double all their force;
Each pulls and strains, and tugs and strives,
Like people pulling for their lives;
John, honest landsman! simply lets them;
Fear lends them strength, and oversets them.
   Fain would I urge the frighted Muse
To paint the scene which next ensues—

To tell how Ruffman, rous'd from sleep,
Fell headlong down amid the deep;
Then mounting, ey'd the distant shore,
How Nancy sunk to rise no more—
But ah! we'll leave it quite alone,
'Twould break methinks a heart of stone.
—Plung'd in the deep, half lost in death,
Struggling and panting hard for breath;
John thought to struggle now no more,
When his hand lights upon an oar;
His chin uplifted o'er the wave,
He thus escapes a watery grave;
Saves, scarcely saves his wretched life—
Bereft of mother, daughter, wife!
Thus dearly for his fault he pays;
Henceforth a mourner all his days.

    Here ends the tale—My friends arise
And wipe, I pray, your weeping eyes:
My fable—did you think it true?
Was fram'd in fact to picture you;
So next I'll preach to all the nation;
And first, ye Sons of Innovation!

    When Britons, wearied with their lot,
Grow wild to get they know not what,
And quit, through love of Revolution,
Our good old English Constitution;
When Frenchmen lead the mazy dance,
And Britons ape fantastic France;
Methinks, like Johnny once so brave,
They're leaving land to try the wave;
They're quitting ancient house and home,
Mid the wild winds and seas to roam.

                                 When

The Shopkeeper turned Sailor.

When Coblers meet in grand debate,
And little folks feel vastly great;
When each forsooth would quit his station,
And Jack and Will would rule the nation,
Methinks we're then in evil case—
Here's Johnny perch'd in Ruffman's place.

When women too make free to mix,
And try their hand in politics,
Set England right while drinking tea,
And shew how all things ought to be;
Reprove, pass sentence, or acquit,
And talk as grand as Fox or Pitt;
Such ladies never mend my hopes—
Here's Nancy's handling all the ropes.

When Parker rules as grand dictator,
And each Jack Tar's a legislator;
When seamen sit like kings in state,
While lords come down and captains wait:
Again, I say, 'tis just the case
Of Johnny perch'd in Ruffman's place.
Help! Britons, help! we sink, we drown!
They've turn'd our vessel upside down.

When some raw lad, with jockey face,
Has gain'd five thousand at a race,
And flush'd with joy, resolves to stand
For some vile borough, purse in hand;
Rains ribbons round him, half for fun,
At once bids all the barrels run,
Drinks his poor dull opponent down,
And at one onset storms the town;
Then pays with honour half his debts,
And off he flies to mind his bets;

Loses at next Newmarket stand,
Stocks, money, horses, house and land;
With jockey speed runs up to town,
Votes some great question, and runs down;
Grows now a red hot party prater,
And calls himself a legislator.
—Why this, I'd tell him to his face,
Is Johnny perch'd in Ruffman's place.

    When College Youths, well vers'd in vice,
Turn all so reverend in a trice,
From deacon duly rise to priest,
Then run to play, to ball, to feast,
Give their poor flocks no christian light,
While Paine must set our morals right:
Indeed, indeed, it makes me fret,
For then the church is overset;
But should these heads some pulpit grace,
Why then 'tis John in Ruffman's place.

    When hair-brain'd Quacks, without degree,
Presume to take the doctor's fee;
Cure all disorders every day,
In some safe, easy, simple way;
Colds and catarrhs, all aching pain,
Consumption, fever in the brain;
All nervous maladies to boot,
With some soft syrup or new root,
—Oh! dunces, tell them not your case,
'Tis Johnny perch'd in Ruffman's place.

    When men of rank and talents rare,
Make some fine stud their only care,
Though form'd to rule and guide the land,
Love better guiding four in hand,

Pass in the stable half their lives,
Are more with Will than with their wives;
Or when my lady quite descends
And turns her servants into friends,
Of all her equals seems afraid,
And whispers secrets to her maid;
With Betty dwells on this and that,
And dearly loves some kitchen chat.—
—When servants too get much too smart,
And each must act the master's part;
Just like their master when they dine,
Sit long, eat venison, and drink wine;
When footmen get above their place,
And butlers shew their lordly face;
When Betty too disdains her pattens,
And flaunts about in silks and sattins;
Or should she find the fashion varies,
Then follows all the new vagaries,
Adopts at once my lady's taste,
And scarce can bear an inch of waist;
Has ear-rings, just the self-same pair,
Binds the same turban round her hair;
Apes in each part my lady quite,
And trips in muslins just as white;
When such, alas! is all the case,
'Tis Johnny got in Ruffman's place.

Again, when wives have got victorious,
And the poor husband sneaks inglorious,
When John is gentle, Jenny coarse,
And the grey mare's the better horse;
Or when you children have your ways,
And strange to tell, papa obeys!

When

When things are manag'd all so ill
That little Tommy says, "I will;"
Or lastly, let me tell you when—
When men turn women, women men,
Men hate of all things to be rash,
And women, meek'd-eyed women, dash,
Men down their forehead, draw their locks,
And women shew their colour'd clocks,
Discard their shame, forget their sex,
And chuse to open all their necks:
When such again is all the case,
'Tis Johnny got in Ruffman's place.
  Oh! would ye stop the nation's fall
Then every cobler mind your awl;
You labouring lads push home your spade;
Yea trading Johnnies mind your trade;
Ye seamen fight and don't debate;
Watch statesmen well the helm of state;
Ye clergy mind your awful part,
'Tis your's to turn the nation's heart;
Keep parents to the good old way,
And make your children all obey;
Claim not ye wives the chief command,
Keep back ye Nancies of the land,
Let women ne'er be over ready,
You'll trim the boat by sitting steady:
Instructed thus by Johnny's case,
Let ev'ry Briton mind his place.

THE
TRUE HEROES;
OR, THE
NOBLE ARMY OF MARTYRS.

You who love a tale of glory,
    Listen to the song I sing;
Heroes of the Christian story,
    Are the heroes whom I bring.

Warriors of the world, avaunt!
    Other heroes me engage;
'Tis not such as you I want,
    Saints and Martyrs grace my page.

Warriors who the world subdue,
    Were but vain and selfish elves;
While my heroes good and true,
    Greater far, subdu'd themselves.

Fearful

Fearful Christian! hear with wonder,
   Of the Saints of whom I tell;
Some were burnt, some sawn asunder,
   Some by fire or torture fell.

Some to savage beasts were hurl'd,
   Some surviv'd the lion's den;
Was a persecuting world,
   Worthy of these wond'rous men?

Some in fiery furnace thrown,
   Yet escap'd, unsing'd their hair;
There Almighty pow'r was shown,
   For the Son of God was there.

Now we crown with deathless fame,
   Those who scorn'd and hated fell;
Worldlings fear contempt and shame,
   Martyrs fear but sin and hell.

How the shower of stones descended,
   Holy Stephen on thy head!
While thy tongue the truth defended,
   How the glorious Martyr bled!

See his fierce reviler Saul,
   How he rails with impious breath!
Then observe converted Paul,
   Oft in perils, oft in death.

God alone, whose sovereign power,
   Did the lion's fury swage,
Could alone in one short hour,
   Still the persecutor's rage.

Ev'n

The True Heroes.

Ev'n a woman—women hear,
   Read in Maccabees the story!
Conquer'd nature, love, and fear,
   To obtain a crown of glory.

Seven stout sons she saw expire,
   (How the mother's soul was pain'd!)
Some by sword, and some by fire,
   How the Martyr was sustain'd!

Even in death's acutest anguish,
   Each the tyrant still defy'd;
Each she saw in torture languish,
   Last of all the mother dy'd.

Martyrs who were thus arrested,
   In their short but bright career,
By their blood the truth attested,
   Prov'd their faith and love sincere.

Tho' their lot was hard and lowly,
   Tho' they perish'd at the stake;
Now they live with God in glory,
   Since they suffer'd for his sake.

Fierce and unbelieving foes,
   But their bodies could destroy;
Short, tho' bitter were their woes,
   Everlasting is their joy.

                        Z.

A NEW CHRISTMAS HYMN.

O HOW wond'rous is the story
   Of our bleft Redeemer's birth!
See the mighty Lord of Glory
   Leaves his heaven to vifit earth!

Hear with tranfport, every creature,
   Hear the Gofpel's joyful found;
Chrift appears in human nature,
   In our finful world is found;

Comes to pardon our tranfgreffion,
   Like a cloud our fins to blot;
Comes to his own favour'd nation,
   But his own receive him not.

If the angels who attended
   To declare the Saviour's birth,
Who from heaven with fongs defcended
   To proclaim Good will on earth;

If, in pity to our blindnefs,
   They had brought the pardon needed,
Still Jehovah's wond'rous kindnefs
   Had our warmeft hopes exceeded;

A New Christmas Hymn.

If some Prophet had been sent
   With Salvation's joyful news,
Who that heard the blest event
   Could their warmest love refuse?

But 'twas HE to whom in Heaven
   Hallelujah's never cease;
He, the mighty God, was given,
   Given to us a Prince of Peace.

None but he who did create us
   Could redeem from sin and hell;
None but he could re-instate us
   In the rank from which we fell.

Had he come, the glorious stranger,
   Deck'd with all the world calls great,
Had he liv'd in pomp and grandeur,
   Crown'd with more than royal state;

Still our tongues with praise o'erflowing,
   On such boundless love would dwell,
Still our hearts with rapture glowing,
   Speak what words could never tell.

But what wonder should it raise
   Thus our lowest state to borrow!
O the high mysterious ways,
   God's own Son a child of sorrow!

'Twas to bring us endless pleasure,
   He our suffering nature bore,
'Twas to give us heavenly treasure
   He was willing to be poor.

A New Christmas Hymn.

Come ye rich, survey the stable
  Where your infant Saviour lies;
From your full o'erflowing table
  Send the hungry good supplies.

Boast not your ennobled stations,
  Boast not that you're highly fed;
Jesus, hear it all ye nations,
  Had not where to lay his head.

Learn of me, thus cries the Saviour,
  If my kingdom you'd inherit,
Sinner, quit your proud behaviour,
  Learn my meek and lowly spirit.

Come ye servants see your station,
  Freed from all reproach and shame;
He who purchas'd your salvation,
  Bore a servant's humble name.

Come ye poor, some comfort gather,
  Faint not in the race you run,
Hard the lot your gracious father
  Gave his dear, his only Son.

Think, that if your humbler stations,
  Less of worldly good bestow,
You escape those strong temptations
  Which from wealth and grandeur flow.

See your Saviour is ascended!
  See he looks with pity down!
Trust him all will soon be mended,
  Bear his cross you'll share his crown.

A HYMN

A HYMN OF PRAISE

FOR THE

ABUNDANT HARVEST OF 1796,

AFTER A YEAR OF SCARCITY.

GREAT God! when Famine threaten'd late
   To scourge our guilty land,
O did we learn from that dark fate
   To dread thy mighty hand?

X   Did

Did then our sins to mem'ry rise?
  Or own'd we GOD was just?
Or rais'd we penitential cries?
  Or bow'd we in the dust?

Did we forsake one evil path,
  Was any sin abhorr'd?
Or did we deprecate thy wrath,
  And turn us to the Lord?

'Tis true we fail'd not to *repine*,
  But did we too *repent*?
Or own the chastisement divine
  In awful judgment sent?

Tho' the bright chain of Peace is broke,
  And war with ruthless sword
Unpeoples nations at a stroke,
  Yet who regards the Lord?

But GOD, who in his strict decrees
  Remembers mercy still,
Can, in a moment, if he please,
  Our hearts with comfort fill.

He mark'd our angry spirits rise,
  Domestic hate increase;
And for a time withheld supplies,
  To teach us love and peace.

He, when he brings his children low,
  Has blessings still in store;
And when he strikes the heaviest blow,
  He does but love us more.

Now, Frost, and Flood, and Blight no more
   Our golden harvests spoil;
See, what an unexampled store
   Rewards the Reaper's toil!

As when the promis'd harvest fail'd
   In Canaan's fruitful land;
The envious Patriarchs were assail'd
   By famine's pressing hand!

The angry brothers then forgot
   Each fierce and jarring feud;
United by their adverse lot,
   They lov'd as brothers shou'd.

So here, from Heaven's correcting hand,
   Tho' famine fail'd to move;
Let Plenty now throughout the land,
   Rekindle peace and love.

Like the rich fool, let us not say,
   Soul! thou hast goods in store!
But shake the overplus away,
   To feed the aged poor.

Let rich and poor, on whom are now
   Such bounteous crops bestow'd,
Raise many a pure and holy vow
   In gratitude to God!

And while his gracious name we praise
   For bread so kindly given;
Let us beseech him all our days,
   To give the bread of heav'n.

In that blest Prayer our Lord did frame,
   Of all our prayers the guide,
We ask that " hallow'd be *his* name,"
   And then our wants supplied.

For grace he bids us first implore,
   Next, that we may be fed;
We say, " Thy will be done," before
   We ask " our daily bread."

                                      Z.

FINIS.

www.ingramcontent.com/pod-product-compliance
Lightning Source LLC
Chambersburg PA
CBHW080919180426
43192CB00040B/2464